T0301611

Entrepreneurship, Innovation and Regional Development

Entrepreneurship, Innovation and Regional Development

Edited by

David Smallbone

Professor of Small Business and Entrepreneurship, Small Business Research Centre, Kingston University, UK

Markku Virtanen

CEO, Emind Oy, Finland

Arnis Sauka

Stockholm School of Economics in Riga, Latvia

 Edward Elgar
PUBLISHING

Cheltenham, UK • Northampton, MA, USA

Published by
Edward Elgar Publishing Limited
The Lypiatts
15 Lansdown Road
Cheltenham
Glos GL50 2JA
UK

Edward Elgar Publishing, Inc.
William Pratt House
9 Dewey Court
Northampton
Massachusetts 01060
USA

A catalogue record for this book
is available from the British Library

Library of Congress Control Number: 2016931795

This book is available electronically in the **Elgar**online
Business subject collection
DOI 10.4337/9781785365553

ISBN 978 1 78536 554 6 (cased)
ISBN 978 1 78536 555 3 (eBook)

Typeset by Servis Filmsetting Ltd, Stockport, Cheshire

Printed and bound in Great Britain by
TJ International Ltd, Padstow, Cornwall

Contents

PART III   ENTREPRENEURIAL ACTIVITY AND REGIONAL DEVELOPMENT

Contributors

Tyler Chamberlin, Telfer School of Management, University of Ottawa, Canada.

Alexander Chepurenko, Higher School of Economics, Moscow, Russia.

Declan Curran, Dublin City University, Ireland.

Vladimir Elakhovsky, Higher School of Economics, Moscow, Russia.

Mark Freel, Telfer School of Management, University of Ottawa, Canada.

Oleksandra Gumenna, National University of the Kiev Mohyla Academy, Ukraine.

Christos Kalantaridis, De Montfort University, Leicester, UK.

Merle Küttim, Tallinn University of Technology, Estonia.

Tõnis Mets, Queensland University of Technology, Australia.

Colm O'Gorman, Dublin City University, Ireland.

Bogdan Piasecki, University of Social Sciences, Poland.

Ekaterina Popovskaya, Higher School of Economics, Moscow, Russia.

Anita Richter, OECD, South East Europe Division, Paris, France.

Paul Robson, Royal Holloway University of London, UK.

Anna Rogut, University of Social Sciences, Poland.

Stephen Roper, Enterprise Research Centre, Warwick Business School, UK.

Arnis Sauka, Stockholm School of Economics in Riga, Latvia.

Olga Savchenko, National Technical University, Kharkiv Polytechnic Institute, Russia.

Svitlana Slava, Uzhgorod National University, Ukraine.

David Smallbone, Small Business Research Centre, Kingston University, UK.

Urve Venesaar, Tallinn University of Technology, Estonia.

Markku Virtanen, Emind Oy, Finland.

1. Introduction

David Smallbone, Markku Virtanen and Arnis Sauka*

DEFINING KEY CONCEPTS

With its focus on entrepreneurship and innovation, this volume is concerned with the two main drivers of economic development, whether this be considered at a national or a regional level. At the same time, both entrepreneurship and innovation are open to different interpretations based on differences in definition. In each case we propose a broad definition which is generally inclusive whilst recognising circumstances where a narrower definition may be justified.

Entrepreneurship has been defined as:

> the manifest ability and willingness of individuals, on their own, in teams, within and outside existing organizations to perceive and create new economic opportunities (new products, new production methods, new organizational schemes and new product-market combinations), and to introduce their ideas in the market, in the face of uncertainty and other obstacles, by making decisions on location, form and the use of resources and institutions. (Wennekers and Thurik, 1999)

Clearly, this is a relatively narrow definition that refers to what would commonly be described as radical innovation, whereas a narrower definition describes what is sometimes called 'incremental innovation'.

In contrast, some writers define entrepreneurs more broadly as anyone who starts or runs their own business, whether or not the business is growth-oriented. One could argue the rights and wrongs of these alternative definitions, although it is our contention that both broad and narrow definitions may be appropriate depending on the purpose of the study. At the same time, it is important to be clear about the nature of entrepreneurship that is being discussed.

In many ways innovation is a more elusive concept than entrepreneurship. Essentially there are two main definitional issues; the first of which is what should be counted as innovation. Should it include changes which are new to a firm regardless of what other firms in the same market segment are doing? The second definitional issue is the breadth of the definition, for example: products, process, organisational, marketing. In empirical works such as that conducted for the European Innovation Survey, a distinction is sometimes made between products, processes and practices that are simply new to a firm, new to an industry, or new at a global level. The first of these represent incremental innovation and the latter, a more radical form.

The key question really is to what extent should changes that are made at the firm level be included even if the change has been made by many other firms in the sector. The firm is innovating in the sense that it is introducing new ideas, and new processes perhaps, but the innovation is not new in the broader sense. The answer to this question really depends on what the purpose of the application is, because at the individual firm level innovation is important to the competitiveness of a business.

Porter's (1990) definition of innovation as an attempt to create competitive advantage through new and better ways of competing in an industry and bringing them to market is essentially a broad definition, which in practice can mean that much innovation can appear rather mundane and incremental rather than radical from an industry perspective. But if this is the way that firms within a particular sector compete with each other then a broadly based definition that is inclusive would seem to be appropriate.

Many European countries have a regional structure which allows for variation in policy between regions based on need. In Germany, for example, regions are an integral part of the federal system. In such circumstances the combination of policy at the regional and national level is embedded in the system of governance. But alongside this there are other countries which are much more centralised; the United Kingdom (UK) and Romania for example. As a consequence, in Romania the European Union (EU) has found it necessary to create artificial regions, mainly for the purpose of the distribution of EU funds. In the UK, after a period when regional development agencies (RDAs) were actively involved in the promotion of economic development, these agencies have since been scrapped.

The main argument in favour of policies at the regional level is that the priorities for economic development vary considerably between regions. In the context of policies to promote entrepreneurship, the problems faced in the North East of England and Scotland are quite different from those faced in London and the South East. In the former case the rate of business creation needs to be stimulated, whereas in the London and South East region the focus tends to be more on the qualitative characteristics of fledging businesses because high business densities result in high levels

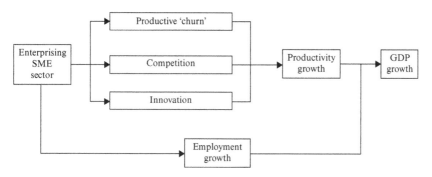

Source: Figure adapted from original presented at a seminar of the Small Business Service (*c.* 2005).

Figure 1.1   Entrepreneurship and economic development

of competition. In addition, it may be argued that it is at a regional level that small business owners typically come into contact with government agencies and government policies, whether these have a positive or negative influence.

THE ROLE OF ENTREPRENEURSHIP AND INNOVATION IN ECONOMIC DEVELOPMENT

The important contribution of entrepreneurship to economic development is summarised in Figure 1.1, where an enterprising small and medium-sized enterprise (SME) sector would seem to be an important source of economic growth.

Figure 1.1 shows that the mechanisms for the transmission of these effects occur through three main channels: (1) competition, although in practice this may be mainly competition from other firms of a similar size rather than from large firms; (2) productive 'churn', where the productivity levels of new businesses are higher than those of firms leaving the market; and (3) innovation, where firms are able to gain competitive advantage over their competitors by developing products that are fundamentally innovative. All three of these processes can contribute to the productivity of individual firms and also of regions. At the same time, the figure probably underestimates the role of innovation in regional competitiveness. This is because of the development of external economies of scale and the emergence of regional innovation systems from regions where the innovative activity is considerable.

An innovation system consists of a production structure and an institutional infrastructure with scope for interaction between the two. The concept of an innovation system is linked to an interactive view of the innovation process. It is also a market-oriented system, with research and development taking place mainly at the individual firm level. This contrasts with the innovation systems operating in Central and East European countries during Soviet times when the main provider of research and development was the state.

Innovation systems are a key element influencing the innovative performance of SMEs in particular, whose size-related characteristics often mean that business owners and managers need to look outside the business from time to time to draw in resources to enable them to innovate. In mature market economies such as the UK, more generally, these innovation systems have evolved over a considerable number of years. The problem for new member states in the European Union and other post-socialist countries is that the innovation systems that existed prior to 1990 were focused mainly on the military effort of the country, and finance was almost entirely from state resources. However, the economic, social and institutional transformation of these countries includes changes to the innovation systems.

INTRODUCING THE CHAPTERS

Following this Introduction there are eight main chapters, which are grouped into the following parts:

- Part I: Innovation (two chapters).
- Part II: Entrepreneurship and SME Policy (three chapters).
- Part III: Entrepreneurial Activity and Regional Development (three chapters).

These chapters are followed by a final chapter, which summarises the main conclusions and draws out some of the implications for policy.

In Chapter 2, Kalantaridis and colleagues are concerned with the role of institutions in influencing the level of innovation in SMEs in Ukraine. Specifically, Kalantaridis et al. point to the role of institutions in influencing the level of innovation in private businesses. It is argued that in post-socialist countries in particular the slow pace of institutional change is a dominant factor. The key research question which the authors of this chapter address is to explore the strategies employed by enterprises operating in post-socialist institutional settings in order to access new knowledge in the process of introducing innovation. More specifically they aim to explain how, and from where, knowledge has been generated.

The second chapter in Part I, Chapter 3, focuses on Eastern Poland and is presented by Rogut and Piasecki. Eastern Poland is a region characterised by rurality and underdevelopment in comparison with the rest of Poland. As a consequence, the region experiences an above-average degree of social exclusion. The authors also explore the notion of intelligent specialisation as a concept rooted in technological progress. Intelligent specialisation represents a mechanism which helps regions and countries to find their place in the global division of labour with respect to innovation. As the Organisation for Economic Co-operation and Development (OECD) and others have noted, rural regions face special challenges from an economic development point of view.

Part II is concerned with entrepreneurship and SME policy and contains three chapters. The first chapter in this section, Chapter 4, deals with entrepreneurship and industrial policy in Ireland and is co-authored by O'Gorman and Curran. Ireland is another country which has experienced rapid industrialisation in recent times. At the same time, industrial policy, which tended to focus initially on the attraction of foreign direct investment, was criticised back in the 1980s for its neglect of domestic enterprises. Encouraging entrepreneurship has been a central tenet in the platform of industrial policy in Ireland as part of a growing emphasis on the encouragement of and support for indigenous economic activity. In this context the authors provide a review of key literature related to entrepreneurship and industrial policy in Ireland, with a particular emphasis on policies affecting entrepreneurship and SME development.

The second chapter in this part, Chapter 5 authored by Roper and Richter, deals with a topic which has been much debated in recent years; namely the advantages and disadvantages of policy transfer. The chapter focuses on the case of the Western Balkans where the desire to join the European Union has resulted in countries following the guidelines contained within the EU's SME Charter. Critics point to the lack of attention paid by the EU to the specific needs of individual countries. The chapter reports on a project which involves the generation of an SME Policy Index for the Western Balkans region. It is this index which provides the main focus for the Roper and Richter chapter. The chapter reports on the implementation of the SME Charter process across seven very diverse Western Balkan countries. Clearly the topic is of wider interest because policy transfer is a dominant theme in much of the economic development consultancy in less-developed countries these days.

Written by Mets, the third and final chapter, Chapter 6, focuses on Estonia and its suitability as a location for born global companies; in other words, on innovative, globalising, hi-tech SMEs. The issue is particularly important because previous research has pointed to the significant contribution of born globals to job creation in Europe. Research commissioned by Eurofound (2012) estimated that about 20 per cent of young enterprises in Europe are born global. Not surprisingly, new member states of the EU are keen to get their share. Mets uses the concept of the entrepreneurial ecosystem which has implications for regional development. The chapter analyses three case study companies in some detail. Overall the chapter raises some important questions by linking the effects of increasing internationalisation on regional development.

Part III, the final part of the book, contains three chapters concerning entrepreneurial activity and regional development. The first of these, Chapter 7 by Chepurenko and colleagues, focuses on entrepreneurship in the Russian population. This chapter is concerned with the factors affecting different levels of early-stage entrepreneurial activity in different regions of Russia, based on survey evidence gathered in 2011. Regional variations in entrepreneurship are found in most countries because of a combination of demand- and supply-side influences. But in post-socialist economies there are additional factors related to the pace of economic reform. Russia as a country emphasised the importance of a spatial dimension to entrepreneurship policy.

The second chapter of this part, Chapter 8 co-authored by Venesaar and Küttim, deals with core–periphery contrasts in the development of entrepreneurial activity, which are illustrated with reference to Estonia. As mentioned above, these regional variations in entrepreneurial activity are a typical feature of economies at different levels of economic development. More specifically they reflect: (1) regional differences in business opportunities; (2) regional and demographic components; and (3) the institutional component, which emphasises attitudes towards self-employment and business ownership as well as more formal institutional factors such as regulation.

The third and final chapter in this part focuses on the capitalisation of new firms and explores the influence of entrepreneurial characteristics on businesses before and after start-up. Chapter 9 by Robson and colleagues is concerned with the effects of the initial capitalisation of new businesses and their survival and growth prospects. The relationship between the survival of new ventures and their initial capitalisation is often rationalised in terms of the effects of capitalisation on the time the entrepreneur has to learn how to run the business and to meet unexpected challenges. In contrast, undercapitalised firms lack this buffer and may be more quickly forced to close because of liquidity problems. The authors infer from this that there are regions where financial capital is relatively abundant and entrepreneurs are better able to use this opportunity to learn as well as to innovate.

NOTE

* The contribution of Arnis Sauka to this volume was supported by National Research Program 5.2. EKOSOC-LV.

REFERENCES

Eurofound (2012), 'Born global: the potential of job creation in new international businesses', Luxembourg: Publications Office of the European Union.

Porter, M. (1990), *The Competitive Advantage of Nations*, New York: Free Press.

Wennekers, S. and R. Thurik (1999), 'Linking entrepreneurship and economic growth', *Small Business Economics*, **13**, 27–55.

PART I

Innovation

2. Innovation processes in adverse institutional settings: connectedness and disconnectedness in three regions of Ukraine

Christos Kalantaridis, Svitlana Slava,
Olga Savchenko and Oleksandra Gumenna

INTRODUCTION

The past 20 years or so have been marked by growing consensus among researchers and policy-makers regarding the importance of innovation and institutions in economic performance. Innovation is viewed increasingly as the engine of sustainable economic growth: seeking advantage in 'putting productive resources to uses hitherto untried in practice, and withdrawing them from the uses they have served so far' (Schumpeter, 1928: 378). The positive contribution of innovation in economic advancement is supported by a growing body of empirical evidence. More specifically, research shows that innovation (measured using various proxies such as levels of research and development – R&D – intensity, patent activity and others) has significant positive effects on growth in real per capita gross domestic product (GDP) (OECD, 2003), multi-factor productivity (Guellec and van Pottelsberghe de la Potterie, 2001) and productivity growth (Khan and Luintel, 2006).

Although the actual and potential benefits of innovation are apparent to researchers and policy-makers alike, investment in innovation (or its effectiveness) may be constrained (OECD, 2007) on account of prevailing institutions (Landes, 1970). The role of institutions in the innovation process is threefold. Firstly, institutions define incentive structures in a society: directing entrepreneurial actors towards either more or less economically productive activities (Baumol, 1990). Secondly, institutions determine, through existing regulations and existing norms, how well (or not) markets operate, and the scope afforded to competitive forces (Barbosa and Faria, 2011). Lastly, and more importantly for the purposes of our research, institutions influence the allocation of resources. Knowledge emerges as the foremost resource for the purposes of our chapter, with institutions acting as channels of communication and uncertainty reduction.

The importance of institutions in facilitating access to external (to the firm) knowledge resources, and thus enabling innovation, acquires particular relevance in the case of post-socialist countries. In the late 1980s and early 1990s they embarked on a process of large-scale change: away from long-established institutions governing planned economies towards the new market ones. Nearly a quarter of a century after the process of post-socialist transformation was initiated, institutions in these countries remain 'different' from those prevailing in advanced market economies (Aidis et al., 2008). Placed within this empirical context, our chapter sets out to explore the strategies developed by enterprises operating in post-socialist institutional settings in order to access and use knowledge in the process of introducing innovation. More specifically, we aim to explore how, and from where (in terms of the geography of the flows) knowledge is accessed.

The nature of our research question is critical in determining the conceptual approach we deploy: open innovation. For our purposes open innovation is defined as 'the use of purposive inflows and outflows of knowledge to accelerate internal innovation, and expand the markets for external use of innovation respectively' (Chesbrough, 2006: 1). Whilst open innovation may be explored at different levels, research to date has tended to focus on the level of the firm with more recent attention directed at teams and projects (West et al., 2014). Our emphasis on both enterprises and the adversity of the institutional setting mean that our chapter will unfold at two levels: the level of the individual firm (where strategies are developed) and of the region (with its institutional and resource base).

Our chapter will focus on the experience of Ukraine, a country that is still confronted with profound challenges in the process of institution building. In doing so we will use the findings of a survey of 120 innovative enterprises that are: (1) broadly representative of the sectoral structure of innovative enterprises in Ukraine; and (2) capture regional diversity in both resource and institutional structures. Thus, we examine three distinct regional settings: the capital Kiev (occupying a central position nationally), the eastern Kharkiv Oblast (which comprises a main urban centre and rural areas and borders Russia), and the western Zakarpattya Oblast (mainly rural, and adjacent to Poland, Slovakia, Hungary and Romania).

Our chapter is organised as follows. The next section revisits open innovation within the institutional setting in post-socialist countries. Then we proceed to discuss the methods used in data collection, key variables used and analytical processes. The main findings of our research are then pre-sented. Finally, we offer some conclusions.

OPEN INNOVATION AND INSTITUTIONS

Open Innovation

The concept of open innovation, originally aimed at a managerial audi-ence, has attracted considerable interest among researchers in the field of innovation studies (as shown in a number of recent reviews: namely Chesbrough and Bogers, 2014; Vanhaverbeke et al., 2014; West et al., 2014). It poses the simple but intellectually attractive notion that innovation takes place within an open system rather than a vertically integrated organisa-tion. Openness is captured through two distinct processes:[1] an inbound one, referring to the internal use of externally generated knowledge; and an outbound one, involving the external exploitation of internally gener-ated knowledge (Huizingh, 2011). Our research in the Ukrainian context focuses squarely on inbound knowledge flows primarily on account of the logic of the empirical problem explored here: that is, how enterprises respond to innovation constraints regarding knowledge use in innovation. Inbound open innovation processes require the focal enterprises to open up their innovation processes to external knowledge (Chesbrough and Bogers, 2014).

The bulk of open innovation research centres on the question of 'how do they do it', that is, how managers make decisions about cooperating with outside parties. Within in this context research focuses invariably on the stages involved in open innovation: ranging from five (Wallin and von Krogh, 2010) to just two (Van de Vrande et al., 2009). The external knowledge may come from customers, suppliers, competitors, research institutions and universities, through formal (licensing, alli-ances or purchasing of services) and informal (network-related) prac-tices. These are brought together by the focal enterprise either in vertical supply chains (with customers, suppliers and subcontractors), or in horizontal relationships with either other businesses in the same sector or institutional actors (such as universities, policy bodies and business support organisations). The profoundly different nature of the relation-ships identified (Tomlinson, 2010) prompted us to use this divide in our empirical study.

Lastly, there is the issue of the type of knowledge involved in inbound open innovation activities. This has two dimensions, which will be exam-ined in our chapter. The first revolves around the transferability of the knowledge: that is, how easily it can be codified and communicated, which in turn depends on the use of a common language or system of meaning (Grant, 1996). In a suggestive contribution, albeit in a different context, Danis and Shipilov (2012) distinguish between technical knowledge, which involves information, processes and tools used in innovation (in our case), and market knowledge, containing information about the supply and demand for specific products and services, and the environmental context of exchange.

They go on to argue that whilst the former is more likely to be transferred via published sources and formal knowledge transfer, the latter is contextual and acquired through social and professional networks. The second dimension involves the existence of a body of knowledge, built in relationships that span considerable periods of time, that facilitate the flow of knowledge that is hard to transfer. This is a kind of underlying tacit knowledge that can facilitate inbound knowledge flows for innovation (Du et al., 2014).

Research that places open innovation within a regional context is still rare. As Beugelsdijk et al. point out, no research field explicitly focuses on 'how the firm's organizational characteristics relate to the firm's fundamental geographical characteristics' (Beugelsdijk et al., 2010, p. 488). In a recent contribution Gassmann et al. (2010) argue that open innovation and the spatial perspective are linked through the increasing globalisation of innovation, where on the one hand, global pipelines and connectivity enable innovation on a global scale, but on the other hand, local nodes are still relevant, as 'being physically close to regional centers of excellence enables a firm to increase its absorptive capacity, therefore promoting access to the knowledge and competencies of the best talents worldwide without having to employ them' (Gassmann et al., 2010: 213). This view is supported empirically by Revilla Diez and Kramer (2011).

Advocates of open innovation view this as a 'new paradigm' (Chesbrough and Bogers, 2014). However, those adopting a more critical perspective argue that companies have always tapped into external sources of knowledge and other resources, thus negating the claim about the emergence of a new paradigm. They claim that closed innovation is a rhetorical straw man that not many companies followed (Trott and Hartmann, 2009). From a different perspective Mowery (2009) argues that the open innovation constitutes a return to a model of innovation that prevailed in the late nineteenth and early twentieth centuries. These critiques helped to shape our approach to open innovation in that they provide the basis for the development of a useful framework for understanding the processes at work rather than marking the dawn of a new era.

Institutions and Post-Socialist Innovation

The term 'institution' has been used increasingly in the literature to represent different aspects of economic, legal, political and social activity, making it difficult to arrive at a single definition. Indeed, three lines of conceptualisation are commonly identified in the literature: old economic institutionalism (Veblen, 1914), new economic institutionalist (North, 1990) and institutional theory (Di Maggio and Powell, 1983). We draw our conceptualisation from the work of New Institutionalists in economics, and particularly Douglass North who defines institutions as 'any form of constraint that human beings devise to shape human interaction' (North, 1994: 3). Within this context, examples of institutions identified include statute law and property rights as well as informal conventions and self-imposed codes of conduct. Thus, North does not confine his definition to formal institutions but explicitly states that institutions 'consist of formal rules, informal constraints (norms of behavior, conventions, and self-imposed codes of conduct)' (North, 1994: 2).

New Institutional economists view the process of institutional change as slow and inherently evolutionary. Post-socialist transformation, nonetheless, was different as it involved radical change to institutions governing economic activity driven by an exogenous (to the institutions affected), and more specifically political and ideological change. There is a voluminous body of literature – its review goes well beyond the confines of our chapter – exploring the outcomes of these processes. Importantly, for our work, researchers in the field (irrespective of their approach) agree that: (1) contemporary institutions in these countries, especially those which remained outside transnational organisations such as the European Union (EU), still impose constraints upon economic actors; and (2) partly as a result of institutional constraints, there is profound resource scarcity, especially in comparison to advanced market economies, in post-socialist countries.

The effect of these on innovation outcomes is well established in the literature: lower incidence of innovation than that reported in advanced market economies (Radosevic and Auriol, 1999; Radosevic, 2004; Krammer, 2009). However, there is precious little research exploring the strategies adopted by the, admittedly, minority of innovative enterprises, particularly regarding the use of knowledge, despite the obvious potential benefits for business practice and policy decision-making. The handful of existing studies focus on multinational corporations (for example Lengyel and Cadil, 2009) and remain detached from the open innovation approach.

Post-socialist institutions form a very different setting for enterprises than that underpinning past open innovation research. More specifically, poorly defined intellectual property rights (IPR) and difficulties in enforcing contracts may have adverse implications upon the incidence of inbound open innovation activities (West et al., 2014). This is because entrepreneurs may be reluctant to engage with external actors, concerned about either the potential of divulging information that is important for market success, or their ability to appropriate returns, opting instead for closed innovation practices. The challenges involved in opening up to external knowledge are particularly profound in instances of vertical, supply-chain relationships, as these invariably necessitate investment in assets specific to the relationship (Williamson, 1985). In contrast, horizontal relationships rely squarely upon trust, reciprocity and a non-hierarchical governance structure (Tomlinson, 2010). The existence of local institutions that support the emergence of relationships governed by trust is thus critical.

METHODOLOGY

Data Collection

Data were drawn through a survey of 120 innovative enterprises in Ukraine. The aim was to achieve representativeness of the population of innovative enterprises in Ukraine, in terms of sector, and ensure the inclusion of relatively diverse settings. In order to attain sectoral representatives we used the bi-annual survey of innovative enterprises produced by the National Statistical Committee of Ukraine. We used the same industrial groupings as included in the official survey. In order to achieve diversity of spatial settings we decided to focus data collection in three diverse regions: the capital Kiev, the eastern Kharkiv Oblast and the western Zakarpattya Oblast. Some 40 interviews were conducted in each of these regions, reflecting the distribution of innovative enterprises. Collectively they are also representative of the industrial distribution of innovative enterprises across Ukraine (Table 2.1).

Enterprises were approached by telephone in order to ensure their eligibility (in terms of innovativeness) for our survey. Once eligibility was established the vast majority of questionnaires were administered by face-to-face interview, whilst telephone interviews were used only in instances where the enterprises requested this. The interviewees were owners and/or managing directors of the enterprises. There were differences in the response rates between the three regions: the highest being in Kharkiv where it reached two-thirds (67 per cent) and the lowest in Zakarpattya (32 per cent). However, even the lowest figure is viewed as satisfactory by national and international standards.

A survey instrument was used for the data collection process.

Table 2.1   *The sectoral composition of enterprises surveyed and population of innovative enterprises in Ukraine*

	Sample	Population
Manufacturing	44	46
Other secondary	5	3
Trade	28	29
Transport	4	9
Business services	19	13
Total	100	100

Source: Survey data and State Statistics Service of Ukraine (2013).

Approximately two-thirds of the questions in the survey instrument were closed, mainly in order to ensure consistency in data collection between: (1) enterprises with very different approaches to innovation; and (2) Ukrainian-speaking (three-quarters) and Russian-speaking respondents. The main issues covered were: the characteristics of enterprise, product/service innovation, process innovation, markets, characteristics of the entrepreneur, linkages with universities, and enterprise performance. This produced a dataset of 131 variables for each case.

Key Variables and Analysis

Innovation, though readily acknowledged as a contributor to enterprise competitiveness and regional and national economic advancement, remains ill-defined and measured. We used entrepreneurial responses captured through six variables, alongside patents, in order to measure product/service and process innovation. The former type of measure was operationalised as follows: a dichotomous response on the incidence of innovation, a variable capturing the entrepreneur's view on the degree of innovativeness (regional, national, international), and the number of innovations introduced since 2009. These were asked separately for product/service and process innovation. The latter measure captured, in one variable, the number of patents granted to the organisation between 2009 and 2011.

  These variables were used in the order to perform a hierarchical cluster analysis. The analysis used the Ward method, a common clustering algorithm, which had also been used effectively in previous studies. This method was selected due to its ability to create compact clusters, which is one of its main advantages (Hair et al., 2006). Indeed, the Ward method merges two clusters, which results in the smallest increase in the overall sum of squared within cluster distances. The sum comprises all distances from each case in the cluster to the centroid of the cluster. The implied distance measure employed by this method is the squared Euclidean distance. The determination of the appropriate number of groups or types is a key but arbitrary decision in hierarchical cluster analysis. In this case, guidance was provided by the increase in within-cluster distances as groups were merged. In the case of Ukraine the four-cluster solution was selected. This is because relatively large increases, that signify the merging of less similar cases (Carlyle, 2001), were apparent from the four- to three-cluster solutions. The outcome also appears to be rather intuitive.

Then we proceeded to explore external knowledge flows by type of innovation. Respondents were asked to focus upon a specific (the one with the highest degree of novelty) innovation introduced by the firm regarding: (1) products/services; and (2) processes, during the three years prior to conducting the survey. Then, for each of these two innovations, they had to respond to questions about the processes at work, particularly the main sources of external knowledge (their type, geography and strength of relationships).

Limitations

There are some limitations that must be taken into account when interpreting our findings. Firstly, the data used are self-reported answers to the questions of the survey, which raises two important considerations: self-reporting bias and self-selection bias. Secondly, the stratification of the sample was based on official statistics: therefore, it may be influenced by the decision of enterprises to report (or not) the incidence of innovative activities. This may be important in the Ukrainian institutional setting, where informality is widespread. Lastly, recording innovation in formal statistics may also be influenced by the definitions used. However, the National Statistical Committee of Ukraine uses a definition that is identical with that used in the EU, capturing a broad range of innovative activities, both radically new, and new to the company in terms of products/services, processes, markets and business organisation.

THE REGIONAL CONTEXTS: KNOWLEDGE RESOURCES, INSTITUTIONS AND INNOVATION PERFORMANCE

Ukraine is a large Eastern European country, with a landmass of some 603 000 square kilometres and a population of some 45.4 million people (including Crimea). It experienced Soviet rule, and a planned economy, for nearly eight decades (considerably longer than many other European transition economies). Its socialist heritage combined with considerable political turbulence meant that the advancement of institutions underpinning a market economy has been protracted. As of 2012, Ukraine was ranked 143rd (out of 148 globally) in property rights development, 133rd in intellectual property rights advancement, and 137th in terms of the burden of government regulation (World Economic Forum, 2014). In contrast, Ukraine appears to possess a relatively strong knowledge infrastructure: ranked tenth in terms of tertiary education enrolment, and 46th in terms of the availability of scientists (World Economic Forum, 2014). However, prevailing institutions impact adversely on the ability of enterprises to exploit this knowledge infrastructure.

The three regions examined here are characterised by considerable disparities in terms of their resource and institutional base (as shown in Table 2.2). Kiev has a population nearly twice that of Kharkiv Oblast, which in turn is more than twice that of Zakarpattya. The region that includes the capital is, not unexpectedly, the most prosperous, in terms of GDP per capita, and thus possesses the largest output market. The size of the regional market stands at 365.4 billion UAH, in comparison to 82 billion for the Eastern oblast, and just 21.4 billion for the westernmost oblast. The size of the regional markets influences in part (alongside geography) the decision of enterprises to sell internationally: this is the highest in Zakarpattya, where two-thirds of production is exported, in comparison to just one-third in Kharkiv. The level of regional demand may also influence the opportunity structure, and the incidence of entrepreneurship. This is particularly high in Kiev, in comparison both to Kharkiv and Zakarpattya.

The institutional base of the three regions involved also differs. Existing research indicates that market institutions (including private property rights, competitive markets and the advancement of banking institutions) in Kiev and western Ukraine (and particularly Zakarpattya) are more developed than in the eastern oblasts (Swain and Mykhnenko, 2007; World Economic Forum, 2008). This, however, should not detract from the fact that even the most advanced oblast, in terms of institution development – that is, Zakarpattya – is at the same level as Azerbaijan and just behind China (World Economic Forum, 2008).

There are also profound disparities in the knowledge base of the three regions examined here. As shown in Table 2.2, the dominance of Kiev is particularly apparent in the knowledge infrastructure, captured here through the number of higher education institutions, the number of scientists per 10 000 inhabitants, and the number of students per 10 000 inhabitants. The contrast with Zakarpattya is particularly profound.

Table 2.2   The characteristics of the regions

	Ukraine	Kyiv oblast and City of Kyiv	Kharkiv	Zakarpattya
Population, average per year, thousands	45 593.3	4550.4	2743.3	1252.6
GDP per capita UAH	32 002	40 483/97 429	29 972	17 088
Unemployment rate	8.1	6.7/6.0	7.2	9.2
Exports as % of production/volume of good	49.3	29.8/48.4	25.7	67.7
Number of enterprises and entrepreneurs per 1000 inhabitants	29	34/103	30	18
Number of higher education institutions	823	139	70	16
Number of scientists (R&D staff) per 10 000 inhabitants (number in thousands)	68.6	70 (31.7)	41 (11.2)	3.2 (0.4)
Number of students per 10 000 inhabitants (number in thousands)	2170.1	1120 (510)	810 (222.3)	207 (25.9)

Source: State Statistics Service of Ukraine (2013).

TYPES AND CHARACTERISTICS OF INNOVATIVE ENTERPRISES IN UKRAINE

Types and Characteristics

The hierarchical cluster analysis helped to identify four types of innovative enterprises. Those falling in the first type are defined as 'radical innovators', because they introduce innovations that are new to either the national or international context regarding both products/services (100 per cent) and processes (86 per cent). They often hold patents, a mean

Table 2.3   Types of innovative enterprises by sector (difference from sample)

	Radical innovators	Incremental innovators	Incremental product/service innovators	Marginal innovators
Manufacturing	53 (+7)	54 (+8)	43 (−3)	39 (−7)
Other secondary	6 (+3)	0 (−3)	5 (+2)	2 (−1)
Transport	15 (+6)	0 (−9)	19 (+10)	5 (−4)
Trade	3 (−26)	33 (+4)	29 (0)	46 (+17)
Business services	24 (+11)	13 (0)	5 (−8)	7 (−6)

Note: $p < 0.01$.

Source: Survey data.

Table 2.4   Types of innovative enterprises by region

	Zakarpattya	Kharkiv	Kyiv
Radical innovators	40	26	34
Incremental innovators	40	20	40
Incremental product/service innovators	60	25	15
Marginal innovators	15	54	32

Note: $p < 0.05$.

Source: Survey data.

of 3.1 per firm, despite the rather poor protection afforded to intellectual property in Ukraine. They are also very active in advancing changes: introducing some 6.8 product/service innovations and 2.9 process innovations during the period 2009–12. Given the centrality of patents in this cluster it is not surprising that they are concentrated primarily in manufacturing (Table 2.3). Business services is another sector where radical innovators are over-represented. In terms of region the largest concentration of radical innovators is recorded in the more rural and peripheral (from the Ukrainian core) but institutionally more advanced Zakarpattya region: some 40 per cent (modestly greater than that for Kiev) (Table 2.4). In terms of size, radical innovators are more commonly reported, in the sample, among large and micro enterprises. Radical innovators adopt a very strong international dimension. As early as 2009 they directed more or less the same percentage of sales to both international and national markets (37 per cent), whilst by 2012 this changed in favour of the former markets (45 per cent and 30 per cent, respectively). A similar trend is apparent in the geography of non-labour inputs, where international sources expanded (from 25 per cent to 33 per cent) at the expense of regional and national ones. Radical innovators account for 29 per cent of respondents in our survey.

The second type may be best described as 'incremental innovators', as they bring forward innovations that are new to the regional setting regarding both products/services (92 per cent) and processes (76 per cent). The nature of the changes combined with poor intellectual property rights mean that patents are virtually non-existent among such firms. However, they are prolific innovators, advancing a mean of 4.5 product/service and 5.0 process innovations during the study period (figures comparable with those for radical innovators). Incremental innovators are more common in manufacturing and trade (see Table 2.3). In terms of geography some 40 per cent of incremental innovators are located in the institutionally more advanced Kiyv, and Zakarpattya. There is a much greater concentration of enterprises of this type among medium-scale firms than any other size band. These enterprises maintain a very strong regional orientation regarding both output (63 per cent) and input (59 per cent) markets. Moreover, this remained virtually unchanged during the period examined here. Some 21 per cent of all innovative enterprises belong in this cluster.

The third type, which bears considerable similarities with the second one, is defined as 'incremental product/service innovators'. This is because all of these enterprises introduce product/service innovations (two-thirds of regional importance, and the remainder of national importance); however, none of them bring forward changes to their processes. Patents are non-existent among these enterprises; however, they report the introduction of a number of product/service innovations, a mean of 3.8 during the period 2009–11. They are over-represented in transport and communication industries (Table 2.3), and are concentrated in very large numbers in Zakarpattya (Table 2.4). In terms of size distribution they possess a very similar profile to their radical counterparts. These enterprises, although primarily focused on regional output (49 per cent) and non-labour inputs (36 per cent), also engage internationally (32 per cent and 25 per cent, respectively). Moreover, the importance of the international market increases by the end of the period examined here. Just 16 per cent of the enterprises surveyed belong in this cluster.

The last, and most populous grouping, includes 'marginal innovators'. All of the enterprises falling in this cluster introduce only process innovations, and in all instances this includes something that is new in the regional context. The incidence of innovations in this type is also very low: just 1.6 across the period 2009–12. Marginal innovators are over-represented in trade (some 46 per cent) and under-represented in all other sectoral settings. Geographically they are concentrated in Kharkiv Oblast (more than half of the total), with relatively weak market institutions and strong knowledge infrastructure. They are also more common among small-scale firms. Marginal innovators report a regional focus regarding both output and non-labour input markets for 2009; an emphasis augmented by 2012. Overall, 34 per cent of Ukrainian innovative enterprises researched here belong in this cluster, making this the largest grouping.

Overview

The evidence presented here shows that the advancement of market institutions in parts of Ukraine combined with geographical proximity to the EU markets (as was the case in Zakarpattya) was linked with the advancement of radical innovation as well as incremental product/service innovation. In contrast, delays in the advancement of market institutions and distance from the EU markets (as is the case in Kharkiv) are linked with the growth of marginal innovation, despite the strong knowledge infrastructure. This diverges with prevailing views in the literature that suggest that innovative enterprises cluster around relatively strong knowledge centres regionally and nationally (Gassmann et al., 2010; Revilla Diez and Kramer, 2011). Sectoral differences were also profound between the four types of innovators identified in the regions of Ukraine examined here, in line with existing research (West et al., 2014). Interestingly, size does not appear to be linked systematically with the incidence of radical innovation.

PROCESSES OF INNOVATION

Knowledge Resources Used in Product/Service Innovation

The differential innovation patterns and enterprise characteristics identified in the previous section are reflected in the processes of product/service innovation. As far as radical innovators are concerned, they appear to rely more on externally generated knowledge in product/service innovation (70 per cent). In more than half of the cases (53 per cent), this comes through horizontal relationships with other enterprises. Vertical relationships (with customers and suppliers) are reported by 44 per cent of

*Table 2.5   The geographical origin of knowledge sources used in product/
service innovation implementation*

	Regional	National	International
Radical innovators	15	53	59
Incremental innovators	32	33	54
Incremental product/service innovators	30	42	45

Source: Survey data.

radical innovators, and horizontal relationships with institutional actors by 30 per cent. The type of knowledge transferred includes the results of R&D (in customer organisations) and technological advances (that is, resembling what is commonly identified in the literature as explicit knowledge). In terms of the geography of externally generated knowledge, in most instances this comes from across the national boundaries.

Indeed, international knowledge flows are reported by nearly nine out of every ten cases regarding idea generation, and some 59 per cent concerning innovation implementation (see Table 2.5). The importance of international customers is not unexpected given the geographical distribution of output markets among radical innovators. They appear to possess the underlying tacit knowledge to manage international knowledge transfer; some 70 per cent of those also direct outputs in these geographical markets (at the beginning of the reporting period). This is reinforced by the durability of the relationships with international knowledge sources, which go back some 11.1 (mean) years.

Externally generated knowledge is used by three-quarters of incremental innovators in product/service innovation. Horizontal relationships are dominant (58 per cent) whilst vertical ones are reported by 44 per cent of enterprises introducing this type of innovation. The flows reported by incremental innovators involve both knowledge about customer characteristics and market demand, and technological advances in the sector. In more than half of the cases the origin of this knowledge is beyond the national boundaries, and it is national and regional in one-third (each) of the cases. The origin of the externally generated knowledge aligns poorly with the geography of output markets. Knowledge generated internationally is the most commonly used, but only 46 per cent of those using knowledge from across boundaries actually sell in these markets. This raises concerns about the tacit knowledge possessed that can be used in the management of relationships. This concern is reinforced by the fact that existing relationships are not as durable as in the case of radical innovators, going back 4.5 years.

Incremental product/service innovators often (in 85 per cent of cases) tap into externally generated knowledge. Vertical relationships are by far the most important means of accessing knowledge for product/service innovation (70 per cent). Interestingly, one in three of such firms also access knowledge through horizontal linkages with institutional actors. Given the importance of customers in this, it is not particularly surprising that the type of knowledge involved centres primarily around customer characteristics and demand. In most instances the sources of knowledge are located internationally. This is reported by all those using knowledge from customers in idea generation, and nearly half of those in product/service innovation implementation (see Table 2.5). This fits well with the increased emphasis placed by incremental product/service innovators in expanding in international markets (as shown in the previous section), as 60 per cent of those using knowledge generated across boundaries direct part of their outputs there. Whilst alignment augers well for the acquisition of knowledge internationally, their accumulated experience is modest as these linkages stretch back just 1.2 years (mean).

Knowledge Resources Used in Process Innovation

A broadly similar pattern regarding the use of externally generated knowledge emerges for process as in product/service innovation in the case of radical innovators. Just over two-thirds of them (69 per cent) use externally generated knowledge. Horizontal relationships are most commonly reported (70 per cent) whilst vertical (48 per cent) are also important. The type of knowledge transferred includes technological constraints and developments, and R&D results. In most instances this knowledge comes from across borders. This is the situation for all cases where external knowledge is used in idea generation. As shown in Table 2.6, in more than two-thirds of cases this knowledge used in process innovation

Table 2.6   The geographical origin of information sources used in process innovation implementation

	Regional	National	International
Radical innovators	24	51	68
Incremental innovators	48	42	63
Marginal innovators	71	51	34

Source: Survey data.

implementation is also international. This compares with just 24 per cent tapping into regional knowledge sources. However, unlike product/service innovation, the alignment between knowledge sources and the geography of non-labour inputs is modest in process innovation implementation: some 44 per cent in the case of international ones. Strong relationships with sources of knowledge used in the implementation of process innovation are of particular importance for radical innovators, reporting a mean duration of some 6.1 years.

Externally generated knowledge is of greater importance for incremental innovators than their radical counterparts. This is the case for 85 per cent of enterprises belonging to the former grouping. Horizontal relationships with enterprises appear to be important means of accessing external knowledge. Knowledge coming through vertical relationships is reported by 55 per cent of cases. Moreover, the knowledge involved includes both customer characteristics and demand, and technological constraints and opportunities. International sources of knowledge are reported by most incremental innovators: all of them regarding idea generation, and more than 60 per cent in process innovation implementation. However, this is linked with poor alignment with the sourcing of non-labour inputs in only 38 per cent of cases, indicating precious little knowledge in managing distant relationships. This is reflected in the development of rather weak relationships, going back just 2.6 years.

Marginal innovators also rely very heavily on externally generated in process innovation. This is the case for 90 per cent of them. This comes from both horizontal linkages with enterprises (85 per cent) and horizontal relationships with institutional actors (30 per cent). However, in both types of relationship the type of knowledge transferred focuses on R&D results. The geography of knowledge sources used differs significantly from all other types of innovative enterprises, as marginal innovators in nearly three-quarters of cases access knowledge from within their regional context. This helps them to overcome problems of alignment with input markets. However, relationships are not particularly durable, standing at just 2.8 years.

Overview

Our study shows that innovative enterprises brave the adverse institutional setting nationally and regionally and tap into external knowledge sources. However, there are significant differences in the strategies adopted. At the one end of the spectrum, radical innovators accessed external knowledge sources through long-established horizontal relationships with partners located outside the national boundaries. This may be influenced by the nature of knowledge sought (primarily explicit), and aligns well with the geography of their markets. Rather surprisingly, marginal innovators also pursue explicit knowledge from sources located in their main markets; although the bulk of their outputs and inputs are regionally oriented. It is interesting that despite the unfavourable institutional setting in Khrakiv Oblast (where more than half of these innovators and source knowledge inputs are located) they use mainly horizontal (often with institutional actors) and not particularly durable relationships.

At the other end of the spectrum, incremental innovators (in particular) adopt a very challenging strategic position in relation to accessing external knowledge for innovation: coming from horizontal relationships that are not particularly durable. This is despite the fact that they use these linkages to access – in the main – tacit knowledge. These relationships often cut across national boundaries, aligning poorly with the geography of their markets.

CONCLUSIONS

Our chapter shows that institutional conditions in Ukraine influence not only the incidence of innovation, a point already recognised in the literature (Radosevic and Auriol, 1999; Radosevic, 2004; Krammer, 2009), but also the types of innovation as well as the processes at work. However, the specifics differ considerably from the accumulated body of literature around open innovation in advanced market economies. It is the advancement of market institutions and not the strength of the regional knowledge infrastructure that appears to encourage radical innovation (as shown in the cases of Zakarpattya on the one hand, and Kharkiv on the other). Proximity to the European core rather than the national ones (Kiev and eastern industrial heartland) also emerges as a positive influence, transforming Zakarpattya into an advantageous location and Kharkiv into a distinctly peripheral one.

From the point of view of enterprises our results show that radical and marginal innovators appear to adopt strategies that are based upon internal competences gained as part of the firms' day-to-day operations. These competences, in turn, are central in enabling these organisations to effectively access and use external knowledge for the purpose of introducing innovation. Thus, our research stresses the importance of embedding open innovation approaches within not only regional but also organisational settings. Indeed, our evidence indicates that ultimately it is enterprise competences that prevail over the constraints imposed by institutions.

Within this context, connectedness and disconnectedness and even the concept of geographical proximity itself may be viewed very differently between (and within) different types of enterprises and regions. This has implications for both horizontal relationships with enterprises (that span global boundaries) as well as the regional innovation system and its development. More specifically, the connectedness of the most radical enterprises in terms of European relationships, and disconnectedness from the region, raises concerns about their ability to act as champions in advancing the development of a strong regional system of innovation. Moreover, positive change in the institutions underpinning the system may impact adversely on the ability of these enterprises to maintain and even advance their position within the relationships.

Our chapter also points towards two areas of future research, linked with the findings from post-socialist Ukraine (and wider implications). The first concerns outbound open innovation practices from elsewhere in the world, the source of the knowledge flows examined in this chapter. More specifically, it concerns how enterprises that work with their Ukrainian counterparts manage within the specificities of the post-socialist institutionalist setting. The second revolves around the implications of the durability of relationships. More specifically, in the medium-term period examined here very strong linkages underpinned the flows of knowledge. Within the same time horizon the absence of a dense network of linkages with proximate actors did not adversely impact upon innovation performance in the case of Zakarpattya Oblast. However, the adoption of a different time perspective, particularly the long term, may have significant implications for how both of these issues are understood.

NOTE

1. This dual perspective has been questioned by those advocating a 'coupled mode' that combines both inbound and outbound flows (Gassman and Enkel, 2004).

REFERENCES

Aidis, R., S. Estrin and T. Mickiewicz (2008), 'Institutions and entrepreneurship development in Russia: a comparative perspective', *Journal of Business Venturing*, **23** (6), 656–72.
Barbosa, N. and A.P. Faria (2011), 'Innovation across Europe: how important are institutional differences?', *Research Policy*, **40** (9), 1157–69.
Baumol, W.J. (1990), 'Entrepreneurship: productive, unproductive and destructive', *Journal of Political Economy*, **98** (5), 893–921.
Beugelsdijk, S., P. McCann and R. Mudambi (2010), 'Introduction: place, space

and organization – economic geography and the multinational enterprise', *Journal of Economic Geography*, **10** (4), 485–93.

Carlyle, A. (2001), 'Developing organized information displays for voluminous works: a study of user clustering behaviour', *Information Processing and Management*, **37** (5), 677–99.

Chesbrough, H. (2006), 'Open innovation: a new paradigm for understanding industrial innovation', in H. Chesbrough, W. Vanhaverbeke and J. West (eds), *Open Innovation: Research a New Paradigm*, Oxford: Oxford University Press, pp. 1–12.

Chesbrough, H. and M. Bogers (2014), 'Explicating open innovation: clarifying an emerging paradigm for understanding innovation', in H. Chebrough, W. Vanhaverbeke and J. West (eds), *New Frontiers in Open Innovation*, Oxford: Oxford University Press, pp. 3–28.

Danis, W.M. and A. Shipilov (2102), 'Knowledge acquisition strategies of small and medium-sized enterprises during institutional transition: evidence from Hungary and Ukraine', *Thunderbird International Business Review*, **54** (3), 327–45.

Di Maggio, P.J. and W.W. Powell (1983), 'The iron cage revisited: institutional isomorphism and collective rationality in organizational fields', *American Sociological Review*, **48** (2), 147–60.

Du, J., B. Leten and W. Vanhaverbeke (2014), 'Managing open innovation projects with science-based and market-based partners', *Research Policy*, **43** (5), 828–40.

Gassmann, O. and E. Enkel (2004), 'Towards a theory of open innovation: three core process archetypes', in *Proceedings of R&D Management Conference*, Lisbon, Portugal.

Gassmann, O., E. Enkel and H. Chesbrough (2010), 'The future of open innovation', *R&D Management*, **40** (3), 213–21.

Grant, R.M. (1996), 'Prospering in dynamically competitive environments: organizational capability as knowledge integration', *Organization Science*, **7**, 375–87.

Guellec, D. and B. van Pottelsberghe de la Potterie (2001), 'R&D and productivity growth: panel data analysis of 16 OECD countries', OECD STI Working Papers, 2001/3, Paris: OECD.

Hair, J.F., Jr, W.C. Black, B.J. Babin, R.E. Anderson and R.L. Tatham (2006), *Multivariate Data Analysis*, 6th edn, Upper Saddle River, NJ: Prentice Hall.

Huizingh, E.K.R.H. (2011), 'Open innovation: state of the art and future perspective', *Technovation*, **31** (1), 2–9.

Khan, M. and K.B. Luintel (2006), 'Sources of knowledge and productivity: how robust is the relationship?', STI Working Paper 2006-6, OECD: Paris.

Krammer, S.M.S. (2009), 'Drivers of national innovation in transition: evidence from a panel of Eastern European economies', *Research Policy*, **38** (5), 845–60.

Landes, D. (1970), *The Unbound Prometheus: Technological Change and Industrial Development in Western Europe from 1750 to the Present*, New York: Cambridge University Press.

Lengyel, B. and V. Cadil (2009), 'Innovation policy challenges in transition countries: foreign business R&D in the Czech Republic and Hungary', *Transition Studies Review*, **16** (1), 174–88.

Mowery, D.C. (2009), 'Plus ca change: industrial R&D in the "third industrial revolution"', *Industrial and Corporate Change*, **18** (1), 1–50.

North, D.C. (1990), *Institution, Institutional Change and Economic Performance*, Cambridge: Cambridge University Press.

North, D.C. (1994), 'Institutional change: a framework of analysis', EconWPA.

OECD (2003), *The Sources of Economic Growth in OECD Countries*, Paris: OECD.

OECD (2007), *Innovation and Growth: Rationale for an Innovation Strategy – A New Perspective*, Paris: OECD.

Radosevic, S. (2004), 'A two-tier or multi-tier Europe? Assessing the innovation capacities of central and east European countries in the enlarged EU', *Journal of Common Market Studies*, **42** (3), 641–66.

Radosevic, S. and L. Auriol (1999), 'Patterns of restructuring in research, development and innovation activities in central and eastern European countries: an analysis based on S&T indicators', *Research Policy*, **28** (4), 351–76.

Revilla Diez, J. and J. Kramer (2011), 'Regions as catalysts of open innovation? The case of SAP in the Regional Innovation System of Baden-Württemberg', available at http://www.krti.ktk.pte.hu/files/tiny_mce/File/Konferencia/2011/Diez.pdf (accessed 9 July 2015).

Schumpeter, J.A. (1928), 'The instability of capitalism', *Economic Journal*, **38**, 361–86.

State Statistics Service of Ukraine (2013), *Statistical Publication Regions of Ukraine*, Kiev.

Swain, A. and V. Mykhnenko (2007), 'The Ukrainian Donbas in "transition"', in A. Swain (ed.), *Reconstructing the Post-Soviet Industrial Region: The Donbas in Transition*, London: Routledge, pp. 7–46.

Tomlinson, P.R. (2010), 'Co-operative ties and innovation: some evidence from UK manufacturing', *Research Policy*, **39** (6), 762–75.

Trott, P. and D. Hartmann (2009), 'Why open innovation is "old wine in new bottles"', *International Journal of Innovation Management*, **13** (4), 715–36.

Van de Vrande, V., J.P.J. de Jong, W. Vanhaverbeke and M. de Rochemont (2009), 'Open innovation in SMEs: trends, motives and management challenges', *Technovation*, **29** (6–7), 423–37.

Vanhaverbeke, W., J. West and H. Chesbrough (2014), 'Surfing the new wave of open innovation research', in H. Chebrough, W. Vanhaverbeke and J. West (eds), *New Frontiers in Open Innovation*, Oxford: Oxford University Press, pp. 281–94.

Veblen, T.B. (1914), *The Instinct of Workmanship, and the State of the Industrial Arts*, New York: Augustus Kelley.

Wallin, M.W. and G. von Krogh (2010), 'Organizing for open innovation: focus on the integration of knowledge', *Organizational Dynamics*, **39** (2), 145–54.

West, J., A. Salter, W. Vanhaverbeke and H. Chesbrough (2014), 'Open innovation: the next decade', *Research Policy*, **43** (5), 805–11.

Williamson, O. (1985), *The Economic Institutions of Capitalism*, New York: Free Press.

World Economic Forum (2008), *The Ukraine Competitiveness Report*, Geneva: WEF.

World Economic Forum (2014), *Global Competitiveness Report*, Geneva: WEF.

3. Smart specialisation as a development opportunity for the peripheral regions of Eastern Poland

Anna Rogut and Bogdan Piasecki

INTRODUCTION

Eastern Poland (Figure 3.1) is a macroregion consisting of five provinces that are among the poorest both in the country and in the European Union (European Union, 2014; GUS, 2013). The Organisation for Economic Co-operation and Development (OECD) defines such regions as non-science and technology (S&T) driven, dominated by the primary sector of the economy, and poorly connected with superregional or global innovation systems (OECD, 2011a). In turn, the European Observation Network for Territorial Development and Cohesion (ESPON)[1] characterises such provinces as areas of imitative innovation with low levels of knowledge, innovation, entrepreneurship and creativity (ESPON, 2012a).

The European cohesion policy has long favoured the view that such regions are in need of assistance (European Commission, 1996; Hjerp et al., 2011; Manzella and Mendez, 2009; Marzinotto, 2012). However, while initially assistance was mostly justified by social considerations (narrowing the gap in economic development levels, alleviation of income inequalities, reduction of the regions' underdevelopment and social exclusion), recently the focus has shifted to economic motives.

Therefore, the objectives of the European cohesion policy for the years 2014–20 prioritise not only a reduction in long-term social exclusion, but primarily the elimination of long-term ineffectiveness (Barca, 2009; European Commission, 2010a, 2012a). Similar goals have been outlined in Polish strategic documents (MAiC, 2012; MRR, 2010; RM, 2012).

In the case of regions such as Eastern Poland, long-term ineffectiveness may be reduced by an increase in absorption capacity (Benneworth and Dassen, 2011; ESPON, 2012a; OECD, 2011b; World Bank, 2008), with the appropriate strategy being one of research and innovation for 'smart

Source: Portal Administracji Publicznej at http://www.gmina.pl/ey/index.php?id=12.

Figure 3.1 Provinces of Eastern Poland

specialisation', an agenda for the transformation of endogenous development potentials (European Commission, 2010b).

'Smart specialisation' is a policy concept incorporated as a key element into the 'EU 2020' innovation plan (Foray et al., 2011). Whilst the concept deserves in itself a more insightful and critical analysis, this chapter is more pragmatically oriented towards characterising the conditions under which smart specialisation may become a development opportunity for Eastern Poland. According to this objective, the chapter begins with a short description of Eastern Poland in the global chain of innovation. Subsequently, potential areas for pursuing smart specialisation in this region are indicated, and the conditions under which smart specialisation may initiate a process of deeper transformation of this macroregion are identified.

THE PLACE OF EASTERN POLAND IN THE GLOBAL CHAIN OF INNOVATION

Smart specialisation is a notion rooted in concepts of technological progress. It involves the choice of a limited number of research and development (R&D) and innovation priorities aimed to stimulate the development of selected types of economic activities. Such activities are important to a given region and already show a certain degree of specialisation. They will be characterised in the future by a competitive advantage on a national or international scale (Foray et al., 2011). Such specialisation helps countries and regions to find their place in the global chain of innovation and makes them focused on either: (1) the development and improvement of so-called general purpose technologies; or (2) the development and improvement of so-called co-invention, or applications allowing for the implementation of general purpose technologies in one or several major areas of regional economy (Dedrick et al., 2011; Giuliani et al., 2005; Hansen and Birkinshaw, 2007; Pietrobelli and Rabellotti, 2011).

R&D and innovation priorities are most often determined by the economic structure, and then corrected for the structure of R&D and technological activity (OECD, 2011c). In turn, a region's place in the chain of innovation is linked to its ability to introduce technological changes with varying degrees of radicalness (Aghiona et al., 2009; Foray et al., 2009), where the degree of radicalness is the development potential of the above-mentioned general purpose technologies. Furthermore, a region's ability to introduce more or less radical technological changes (innovation ability; cf. GFCC, 2012; López-Claros and Mata, 2010; Mahroum et al., 2008; US Department of Commerce, 2012) results from broadly defined territorial capital (Athey et al., 2007; Capello et al., 2009; McCann and Ortega-Argilés, 2011; OECD, 2001), and especially those components which are referred to as technological versus competence competitiveness in some theories (Acemoglu et al., 2006; Ancarani, 2009; Landesmann, 2003; Rodrik, 2003; Vandenbussche et al., 2004) and development versus absorption capacity in others (Cohen and Levinthal, 1990; Fu, 2007; Mahroum et al., 2008; Spithoven et al., 2010; Zahra and George, 2002).

These components always characterise a given region from the point of view of the predominance of either: (1) the potential to create and commercialise new technological knowledge and more radical innovations (technological competitiveness/development capacity); or (2) the potential to acquire and absorb (potential capacity) as well as to transform and use (consumed capacity) existing local and external knowledge for the generation and commercialisation of more incremental innovations (competence competitiveness/innovation absorption capacity). Eastern Poland is a region with a relatively low development capacity, so smart specialisation opens the possibilities for it to pursue and promote co-invention, and thus to make the macroregion's development founded on either an imitative or creative innovation model.

In an imitative innovation model, the (macro)region assumes a passive approach to technological development, focusing on external (mostly foreign) investments as a source of invention, knowledge creation and innovation generation (ESPON, 2012b). However, this development model may carry a relatively high risk linked to foreign direct investments (FDIs). Whilst they generally play a positive role, FDIs do not guarantee growth benefits, especially in situations (which may be the case in Eastern Poland) where the efficiency of the domestic companies in the sector in which FDI is made is typically below that of their foreign competitors (Buigues et al., 1990; European Commission, 2012b; Huwart and Verdier, 2013; Kapil et al., 2013; Manic, 2008). As a consequence, it is recommended that Eastern Poland embrace the creative innovation model based on social networks and pursued by regions capable of joining domestic and international business and innovation networks (ESPON, 2012b). The foundation of the model is 'territorial creativity', or the ability to integrate local knowledge with external knowledge, to identify new needs and to create new solutions based on existing technologies. The substance of the model is co-invention used for the needs of increasing the efficiency of the local economy. This model is akin to the investment-based or catch-up strategies of technological progress that were used for many years, more or less successfully, by a number of emerging economies, such as South Korea, China, Brazil and India (Box 3.1). This similarity is all the more striking in view of the fact that the economic structure of Eastern Poland is dominated by low-tech (and sometimes medium-tech) industries and by low- or medium-knowledge-intensive services, despite the fact that over the past years its economic structure has been slowly evolving towards more technologically advanced sectors (MRR, 2013).

The development of a creative innovation model is all the more important in view of the fact that the low productivity of Eastern Poland results from technological backwardness, and in such a case investments in traditional sectors may bring results comparable to those generated by investments in high-tech sectors (OECD, 2009a, 2009b). This has also been confirmed by OECD experiences, which show that more radical technological innovation stimulates the growth of the most developed regions, while regions lagging behind are not so well stimulated. The development dynamics of the latter depends, to a larger extent, on more incremental

---

BOX 3.1   EXPERIENCES OF SOUTH KOREA, CHINA,
BRAZIL AND INDIA AND THE LESSONS THAT CAN
BE DRAWN FROM THEM: GENERAL
CONCLUSIONS

Although South Korea and China followed somewhat different paths, both countries focused on a combination of support for research and development activity, and assistance for selected sectors (with particular emphasis on stimulating the growth of high-tech industries and on exports). Both countries resisted liberalisation for a long period, taking their time to support companies in selected sectors, to obtain cutting-edge technological knowledge, to increase innovation potential and readiness, and to effectively fight off competition from foreign companies (and/or to become the natural partners of foreign companies). After the opening of the countries to international trade, it has been possible for South Korean and Chinese companies to increase their export expansion significantly, thus achieving additional benefits. In both countries, the process of transformation lasted less than 20 years and led to: (1) a transition from an economy based on agriculture and on traditional labour-intensive industries to an economy based on more technologically advanced industries (which are even more advanced in China than in Korea); and (2) a relatively fast reduction of the development gap.

In contrast, the strategies of Brazil and India were less effective as they were more focused on anti-import practices, and less involved in stimulating the innovativeness of domestic companies and increasing their international competitiveness. Therefore, after opening to international competition at the beginning of the 1990s, it emerged that domestically owned firms were using obsolete technologies and thus were unable to fully benefit from liberalisation. This is not to say that these countries do not have any globally leading sectors. However, their emergence was the result of unplanned events – that is, the Indian information technology (IT) revolution and the Brazilian energy crisis – rather than intentional measures in the form of science and technology policies and innovation policies.

Sources: Based on Dahlman (2009), Chandra et al. (2009) and OECD (2012).

---

technological changes (Chandra et al., 2009; OECD, 2012a), where new ideas are incorporated into existing processes, products and services, and where the focus is on the development of new utility models and designs, as well as marketing and organisational innovations (OECD, 2011d).

POTENTIAL DIRECTIONS OF SMART SPECIALISATION OF EASTERN POLAND

The identification of smart specialisation areas is an entrepreneurial discovery process involving all regional stakeholders and based on the self-assessment of:

1. resources and potential of the economy;
2. science, knowledge and the creativity sector;
3. the (self-)governing sector;
4. the quality of the regional development and innovation policy (European Commission, 2012c; Joanneum Research Graz, 2012).

Specialisation indicators of economic structure, R&D activity and technological activity (OECD, 2011c) can also guide stakeholders. This process of self-assessment and identification of smart specialisation areas has been initiated in all Eastern Poland provinces, leading to a short list of economic activity areas with solid grounding in Eastern Poland, which already exhibit, or may exhibit in the future, some competitive advantages on a domestic and/or international scale. These areas include primarily: petroleum and natural gas extraction; rock, sand and clay mining; manufacturing of computers, and electronic and optical products; the chemical industry; the pharmaceutical industry; boat and yacht production; electrical appliance manufacturing; waste collection, processing and treatment, as well as recycling; production and distribution of electrical energy, gas, steam, hot water and air for heating, ventilation and air conditioning (HVAC) systems; telecommunications; IT and information services; and health care (Boguszewski, 2012; Szlachta and Zalewski, 2012; Urząd Marszałkowski Województwa Lubelskiego, 2013; Urząd Marszałkowski Województwa Podlaskiego, 2013; Zalewski et al., 2012; Zarząd Województwa Podkarpackiego, 2011; Zarząd Województwa Warmińsko-Mazurskiego, 2013).

The reports of the Polish Information and Foreign Investment Agency expand the above list to include the aviation industry, renewable energy production, tourism, logistics, non-metallic product manufacturing, the machine industry, the textile and clothing industry, and the construction industry (PAIiI, 2010a, 2010b, 2010c, 2010d, 2010e, 2010f, 2010g, 2010h).

Most of these areas of economic activity are of supraregional nature, common to at least two provinces. Three provinces may work on developing zones functionally conducive to the development of the following smart specialisations: bioeconomy, eco-business and the medical industry.

The bioeconomy may be defined as the sustainable production and conversion of renewable biomass into products and energy (European Commission, 2012d). According to the OECD, the bioeconomy includes primarily such sectors as: plant and livestock production, the agri-food industries, feed production, the pharmaceutical and chemical industries (and so on), the environmental industries and services, renewable sources of energy (biorefineries, biofuels), and public health (OECD, 2009c). In turn, eco-business consists of production and service activity aimed at:

1. measurement, prevention, reduction, minimisation and removal of environmental damage in the domains of water, air, earth, waste, noise and ecosystems;
2. the development of cleaner manufacturing technologies and products;
3. the development of services containing environmental hazards, reducing pollution and preventing the depletion of natural resources.

From the sectoral point of view, eco-business involves waste disposal and recycling, liquid waste treatment, air pollution monitoring, environmental management, land and groundwater remediation, noise monitoring, environmental R&D services, monitoring of the environment and laboratory analytics, water supply, renewable energy production, product regeneration, environmental protection, and environmentally friendly buildings (Ecorys, 2009; European Commission, 2006). The medical industry involves activities linked to disease prevention and treatment, patient rehabilitation and palliative care. From the sectoral point of view, it includes broadly defined health care[2] and the related life sciences, the manufacture of medical equipment and the associated services, and pharmaceutical production.

The bioeconomy and eco-business include some of the fastest-growing global markets (Ecorys, 2009; ETPs and EUFETEC, 2011; European Commission, 2012e; OECD 2009c), and the technologies they use are characterised by considerable diversity, going beyond the borders of particular sectors. Moreover, the development of environmental technologies has been evolving from the previous efforts focused on 'end pipe' treatment to process integration and system redefinition, and to future systemic and functional innovations offering new configurations of technological, organisational and institutional changes implemented at the level of both individual companies and the entire society (Weber, 2005).

Fast-growing markets also include the medical industry, whose dynamic development is attributable to both civilisational and demographic changes and the breakthrough in the health care system observed in the past couple of decades. This breakthrough involves, amongst others, telecare, telemedicine, e-health, pharmacogenomics, gene diagnostics and therapy, stem cells, bioinformatics, minimally invasive surgery, nanotechnological applications, tissue engineering, artificial and bio-artificial organs, regenerative medicine, xenotransplantation, and so on (Braun, 2008; Nordmann, 2004). Other elements of the health care breakthrough are the service-like nature of medicine (healthy lifestyles: the use of spas, food, exercise, and so on, in disease prevention and treatment), the growing personalisation and individualisation of health care, and the empowerment of patients.

An additional functional area conducive to the development of smart specialisation in Eastern Poland is aviation, one of the few high-tech industries

---

BOX 3.2   EXAMPLES OF REGIONAL SCIENTIFIC SPECIALISATIONS OF EASTERN POLAND

Analysis of the grants awarded to scientists working at universities in Lublin reveals a specialisation in agricultural sciences (crop science, soil science, veterinary and livestock science, agricultural engineering) and environmental protection (management and protection of the natural environment, environmental protection engineering), which is due to the presence of specialised research institutions in Lublin and Puławy.

In addition, the social sciences (philosophy, theology, pedagogy and psychology) and health sciences (paediatrics and non-surgical clinical sciences) are characterised by a relatively large research potential. Bibliometric analysis has revealed high specialisation in veterinary sciences (almost every third Polish paper in this field, indexed with the Web of Science, was written in Lublin Province, of which 55 per cent were in Lublin and 44 per cent in Puławy). Other major areas include: (1) pharmacology and pharmaceutical sciences; (2) public health, environmental health and occupational medicine; (3) environmental sciences and ecology; (4) agriculture; and (5) food and nutrition sciences. Paper citations indicate high specialisation in materials sciences, agriculture, neurological sciences, botany, oncology and biophysics.

The specialisation of Podlaskie Province in medical sciences is linked to the R&D and academic units of the Medical University of Białystok and the University of Białystok. At the former, of particular importance are the Centre for Experimental Medicine and the Centre for Innovative Research (which has the status of a leading national research centre); and at the latter, of special note is the BioNanoTechno Centre for Synthesis and Analysis.

In turn, Warmińsko-Mazurskie Province can boast a gross value added per person in the agricultural sector that is almost twice the national average, largely thanks to the agricultural and biological research potential of the University of Warmia and Mazury and the Institute of Animal Reproduction and Food Research, Polish Academy of Sciences.

Sources: Based on Olechnicka and Płoszaj (2012) and Zarząd Województwa Warmińsko-Mazurskiego (2013).

---

that thrive there: 90 per cent of the Polish aviation industry is located in that region. This industry is also one of the most modern sectors of the world's economy, characterised by high market potential (PAIiI, 2010a). All of these functional areas are well grounded in the scientific competence of the academic and R&D institutions of Eastern Poland (Box 3.2).

All regional specialisation areas are backed by relatively good educational infrastructure, although Eastern Poland is affected by an increasing rate of out-migration, particularly concerning people with higher education and especially those aged 25 to 34 years. This, in combination with the processes of depopulation and population ageing, decreases the innovative potential of this region and makes it necessary to mobilise the whole labour force, including people aged 50+ and 60+, through life-long learning strategies (Celińska-Janowicz et al., 2010; Mazurkiewicz, 2012; Szlachta and Zalewski, 2012; Urząd Marszałkowski Województwa Podlaskiego, 2013; Zarząd Województwa Warmińsko-Mazurskiego, 2013; Zarząd Województwa Podkarpackiego, 2011).

CONDITIONS UNDER WHICH SMART SPECIALISATION MAY BECOME A DEVELOPMENT OPPORTUNITY FOR THE PERIPHERAL REGIONS OF EASTERN POLAND

The above-mentioned functional areas of Eastern Poland may be transformed into actual smart specialisation areas, leading to the development of a creative innovation model. This is as long as the barriers that have been blocking the developmental potential of the region since time immemorial are quickly overcome. These barriers include:

1. Low demand for innovation:

   - a low entrepreneurship level (including technological entrepreneurship) as measured by the number of companies per 10000 inhabitants;
   - low innovation potential as measured by the value of outlays on innovation activity in companies;
   - low innovation activity of companies as measured by the intensity of spending on innovation activity per worker;
   - a low level of innovation commercialisation as measured by the share of innovation products in the net sales of products.

2. Low supply of innovation:

   - a relatively poorly developed science sector with a lower ratio of workers employed in the science sector to total workers than the average for Poland;
   - low research potential of academic institutions (as estimated on the basis of the position of the region's universities in national university rankings and on the basis of domestic and international research cooperation);
   - low level of participation of the region's research units in national and international research programmes and cooperation networks.

3. An inefficient research and innovation system combined with an inef-
    fective knowledge and technology transfer system:

    ● relatively low qualifications of business support organisations'
       personnel;
    ● little contribution of R&D units to the process of innovation
       creation and innovation diffusion to the business sector;
    ● low interest of companies in cooperation with the local R&D
       infrastructure and business support organisations;
    ● a predominance of external, foreign sources of innovation,
       mostly transferred through machine and apparatus purchases;
    ● relatively poor development of the financial markets, and espe-
       cially venture capital;
    ● relatively low competences of the personnel of those units (too
       low in the context of providing pro-innovation services).

These barriers are of great importance in the context of SWOT (strengths,
weaknesses, opportunities, threats) analysis of the current economic,
innovative, research, technological and institutional potential of Eastern
Poland (Table 3.1).

It is imperative to quickly create conditions conducive to overcoming
barriers in Eastern Poland, to strengthen the development potential of
the region, and to implement a creative innovation model. Such conducive
conditions include primarily:

1. Development of demand for innovation through expanding the exist-
    ing tools available under research, technological and innovation
    policies to also include some demand instruments (such as innovation-
    oriented public procurement) and regulatory instruments, such as
    standards.
2. Development and strengthening of the absorption capacity of the
    economy, especially in the early stages of technological development;
    the extent and type of support for regional development capacity
    (research) should be aligned with the needs of the economy.
3. A flexible approach to deploying public interventions based on a
    lower number of more comprehensive (stimulating both supply and
    demand) and often experimental actions with a certain degree of
    freedom to modify them depending on the changing conditions or
    needs.
4. Shifting the focus from financing new R&D infrastructure and busi-
    ness support organisation to increasing the effectiveness of the existing
    assets (the fundamental objectives being integration, consolidation

Table 3.1 SWOT analysis of today's economic, innovative, research, technological, and institutional potential of Eastern Poland

Strengths	Weaknesses
Human capital (number and education of business and research personnel)	Maladjustment of manpower in terms of competence and qualifications and a low level of lifelong learning
Higher education institutions	Outflow of educated manpower
	Insufficient readiness of primary and secondary schools to educate personnel for the knowledge-based economy
	Low mobility and entrepreneurship of the research personnel
Potential for building cooperation systems (clusters, cooperation networks, research networks, etc.)	Low level of actual cooperation: (1) among entrepreneurs; (2) between entrepreneurs and research units; (3) with foreign partners
Research potential	
Good infrastructure for research and innovations, including business support organisations	Low level of commercialisation of R&D results
	Poor financial standing of the R&D sector
	Low level of R&D internationalisation
	Low national and international standing of R&D units and scientific units
	Concentration of business support organisations in large cities
	Low availability of specialised services and institutions
	Low effectiveness of technology transfer centres and low potential of science and technology parks
	Low activity of business support organisations and low effectiveness of applications for structural and European Union (EU) funds

Table 3.1 (continued)

Strengths	Weaknesses
Innovative potential	Low level of innovativeness of the economy
	Low demand on innovation, including: (1) low tendency to innovate; (2) relatively low outlays on innovative activity; (3) the structure of innovative activity is dominated by machine and apparatus purchases at the cost of implementation of new products and processes, especially innovative ones, on a national or global scale; (4) low patent activity
	Insufficient R&D infrastructure in companies
	Low entrepreneurship level
	Inadequately developed system for financing high-risk ventures
	Social capital: low level of social trust, attachment to stereotypes, resistance to change
	The regional and local authorities have very limited possibilities of financing innovative policy with their own money, which implies a large degree of dependence on the structural funds
	Relatively low coordination of pro-innovation initiatives and activities

Opportunities	Threats
Eastern Partnership	Population aging and increasing emigration, especially of young and well-educated people
Prioritising of Eastern Poland in national strategies and prioritising regions like Eastern Poland in EU strategies	Strong competition from Polish provinces outside Eastern Poland and from foreign regions

Availability of structural funds for targeted
   development goals
Good prospects for further increasing the
   transportation accessibility of the macroregion
   as a result of completion of infrastructural
   investments under the 2007–13 and 2014–20
   financing perspectives
Influx of external investors that undertake
   innovative activity in the macroregion
Inclusion of Eastern Poland in local, national and
   international research cooperation networks

Eastern Poland faces a widening development gap and its
   image as a peripheral region persists
An incoherent and unstable legal system
Lack of a stable governmental policy towards
   entrepreneurship and SMEs
Excessive fiscalism
Governmental policy excessively focused on short-term economic calculus,
   which deters large outlays on innovative activity with long-term returns

Sources: Based on Gaczek et al. (2011), Mazurkiewicz (2012), Szlachta and Zalewski (2012), Urząd Marszałkowski Województwa Podlaskiego (2013), Zarząd Województwa Podkarpackiego (2011) and Zarząd Województwa Warmińsko-Mazurskiego (2013).

and achieving a critical mass) and attaining a real increase in innovative capacity.

5. Integration of measures supporting R&D activity with those supporting the improvement of competitiveness of small and medium-sized enterprises (SMEs) and the real sector, especially in terms of entrepreneurship and internationalisation; and creating in this way more comprehensive investment streams directed at the development of smart specialisation in Eastern Poland.

6. Development of stable pro-innovative market mechanisms (various forms of returnable financial support) that would facilitate the adaptation of innovation policy to the conditions of reduced aid from the structural funds.

7. Defining complementary measures, especially in terms of: (a) increased availability, use and quality of information and communication technology (ICT); (b) supporting the transition to a low-emissions economy in all sectors; (c) environmental protection and more effective use of resources; (d) supporting worker employment and mobility; and (e) investment in education, skills and lifelong learning.

These postulates are justified by the fact that innovation development is determined both by innovation supply (research) and by innovation demand (the economy). In Eastern Poland there is a well-developed supply side, lacking a similarly strong demand side (cf., e.g., Mazurkiewicz, 2012; Plawgo et al., 2013).

Demand-side innovation instruments include:

1. systemic policies (creation and development of clusters around the value added chain);
2. innovation-oriented public procurement (direct, cooperative, catalysing and pre-competitive);
3. regulatory instruments (standardisation and certification, technological platforms created for the coordination of technological development, including legal regulations).

In turn, supply-side innovation instruments consist of:

1. grants to R&D units for financing infrastructure and R&D activity, and grants to companies for financing R&D activity as well as for training, education, supplementary education and mobility;
2. capital support and returnable instruments;
3. services (information and brokerage and network creation and development).

An increased proportion of demand instruments in the overall pool of public assistance leads to a chain reaction, initiated by a better diagnosis of innovative needs and leading to gradual improvement in productivity and economic growth dynamics. According to European experiences, certain demand-side instruments have become part of the practice of regional innovation strategies. These are primarily systemic policies and funds stimulating private demand for innovation. Systemic policies are very useful in the development of lead markets. Traditional instruments which stimulate private demand greatly enhance the diffusion of existing innovations, and thus are more suitable for catch-up strategies, especially in terms of the application of general purpose technologies.

In contrast, public procurement has rarely been used at the regional level despite the fact that it has a considerable potential for generating demand for innovation, especially at later stages, due to the large scale of public funds at the regions' disposal. The same is true for standardisation. Both instruments may be included in existing demand-oriented policies, which may be of special relevance for smaller regions, as long as the competences of the local or regional authorities are improved.

Growth in innovation demand must be accompanied by strengthening of the absorption capacity of the economy, especially at the early stages of technology development, as those stages are decisive in terms of implementation of new and/or improved products and/or processes (innovation). However, these development stages are under threat as a result of competition for other priorities within the firms and decreased public support. This gives rise to a financing gap, often referred to as the 'death valley', which implies a simultaneous loss of access to public funds and significant difficulties in acquiring private investment (Auerswald and Branscomb, 2003; European Commission, 2009).

Support at the early stages of technology development is additionally justified by the fact that existing Polish public investments favour late stages of innovation (Kapil et al., 2013), which carry a smaller risk of market failure (56 per cent invested funds). This is in contrast to the early stages, where that risk is much higher (30 per cent of investment money is spent on research and concept development, and 7 per cent on the early stage of technology development). This structure of outlays delays the transition from completed research to its application in innovation. As a result, the growth of innovation capacity slows down.

Greater integration of measures supporting R&D activity with measures aimed at the improvement of SME competitiveness follows from the role of so-called technological entrepreneurship in technological development, and especially in: (1) converting scientific knowledge into basic technologies and/or directly into applied technologies; and (2) adjusting basic technologies to specific needs and tasks, and enabling flexible specialisation. The first of these areas is the domain of companies based on scientific knowledge, while the second is the domain of engineering companies (Almor and Sperling, 2008; Carnabuci and Bruggeman, 2009; Moray and Clarysse, 2005). The emergence of young innovative companies is also an element of a more fundamental rearrangement of the economic structure, with an increasingly important role played by the high- and medium-tech sector and knowledge-intensive services. Furthermore, many studies indicate an interrelationship between innovation and internationalisation. It is often suggested that internationalisation and innovation policies should be integrated, and especially that in recent years different forms of trade in technologies have become some of the most dynamic areas of internationalisation. According to some forecasts, revenues from technology trade may, in the future, exceed those from the sales of goods and services. The integration of innovation, entrepreneurship and internationalisation may lead to the emergence of so-called 'born globals' or 'international new ventures' (Chaplin, 2009; De Maeseneire and Claeys, 2007; EIM, 2010; Evers, 2010; Onodera, 2008).

Actually, the coming years offer an opportunity for these conditions to come true, as by 2020 Eastern Poland will have access to considerable structural funds allocated to R&D and innovation activity, implemented not only at the regional level, but also at the macroregional and national levels. At the regional level, each province will run its own regional operational programme (ROP). In turn, the Eastern Poland Operational Programme (EP OP) will be implemented at the macroregional level.

At the national level, Eastern Poland (similarly to other regions) will have access to other operational programmes and, in particular, to the Smart Growth Operational Programme (SG OP), oriented towards growth of innovation and research and promoting links between them and the business sphere. Nevertheless, one needs to draw a rational demarcation line between measures financed at different levels to prevent duplication of the implemented initiatives.

In the case of the SG OP and the EP OP, investment directions may delineate this demarcation line: the SG OP would mainly focus on R&D investments, while the EP OP would concentrate on innovation investments (Box 3.3), and especially on the commercialisation of R&D results.

In the case of the relationship between ROPs and the EP OP, the demarcation line may be defined by the geographic range of investments; those implemented under the EP OP would be aimed at supporting supra-regional undertakings (carried out by entities from at least two different provinces) and supraregional activities consolidating and integrating the existing R&D and innovation infrastructure, such as incubators, technological parks and other business support organisations.

BOX 3.3   SCOPE OF SPENDING ON INNOVATION ACTIVITY

1. Purchasing knowledge from external sources in the form of patents, non-patented inventions (solutions), designs, utility models and industrial designs, licences, know-how disclosures, trademarks, and technical services linked to product and process innovation implementation.
2. Purchasing of software necessary for the implementation of product and process innovations.
3. Purchasing and installation of machines and technical apparatus; purchasing of vehicles, tools, implements, movables and equipment; outlays on the construction, extension and modernisation of buildings with a view to the implementation of product and process innovations.
4. Personnel training (purchasing external training services and/or internal training) linked to innovative activity from the design stage to the marketing stage.
5. Marketing of new or significantly improved products; outlays on preliminary market research, market tests, and advertising of the launched new, or significantly improved, products.
6. R&D work linked to the development of new, or significantly improved, products (product innovations) and processes (process innovations) conducted by a firm's own R&D unit or acquired from other units.
7. Other steps necessary for the implementation of product or process innovations including activities not falling under R&D, such as feasibility studies, testing and assessment of new or significantly improved products and processes (excluding testing falling under R&D, for example prototyping), standard software development and improvement, equipment, preparatory and engineering work.

Source: GUS (2012).

This demarcation is motivated by the intention to transform Eastern Poland into a knowledge-based region. This transformation may be directed at developing a region that would be:

1. technologically advanced: that is, a region in which the economic structure is dominated by high-tech or knowledge-based industries/services;
2. science-based: that is, a region leading in terms of R&D and academic services, which is home to large and internationally recognised research units;
3. based on a knowledge network: that is, a region having a high 'cognitive capability', meaning the ability to acquire and transform information and inventions in innovation and increased productivity through cooperation and market mechanisms.

The above directions may be either complementary or substitutive (ESPON, 2012a). Currently, Eastern Poland is not a technologically advanced or science-based region and will not become one by 2020. However, it has all that it takes to develop a strong knowledge network so long as it surmounts three fundamental barriers to innovation capacity:

1. Fragmentation and relatively low effectiveness (in terms of the intensiveness of services for business and the number of research programmes) of the existing scientific and research infrastructure. In view of the low demand for innovations this makes it impossible to achieve a critical scale of activity.
2. Fragmentation and relatively low effectiveness (in terms of the match between the offered solutions and the needs of the economy, the number of new high- and medium-tech companies, the intensiveness of technology transfer and commercialisation, and so on) of the existing business support organisations, including science and technology parks.
3. Deficit in relations and/or connections within innovation systems (the so-called x-effectiveness of innovation systems; cf. Nioso, 2002).

Therefore, support under the EP OP may not replace measures undertaken at the level of regional research and innovation strategies in the various Eastern Poland provinces; it should rather be a tool for overcoming the above-mentioned barriers.

CONCLUSIONS

In the theory of regional development, there are three different paradigms providing a framework for managing strategic development:

1. A nihilist paradigm, according to which regions are not the subjects of their future but are merely fragments of the global scene.
2. A voluntarist paradigm, in which regions are treated as autonomous subjects of their future, with the will of the authorities and society being the decisive force shaping their future.
3. A realist paradigm, in which regions are autonomous subjects of their future, but they must reckon with the external circumstances limiting their autonomy.

Depending on the adopted paradigm, a region may be the scene of: (1) the *'longue durée'* (long term) in economic, social and cultural terms; (2) 'turning points'; or (3) path-dependence (Jakubowska et al., 2008). The phenomenon of the *longue durée* involves certain mental, consciousness, perception and behavioural structures. Generally speaking, the *longue durée* consists of the region's resources, which in most cases are resources for the future, but may also represent a 'negative heritage', which transmits development barriers to future generations and gives rise to 'jamming' of the region's development mechanisms.

'Turning points' are deep and rapid transformation of the structures and driving forces of development processes, where a region can: (1) be a recipient of turning points that arise due to the large-scale processes and entities of the global, European and national scenes (an adaptive region); (2) be an initiator of turning points (a creative region); or (3) remain beyond major change processes (a passive region). Under path-dependence, changes result from progress occurring through the accumulation of previous outcomes (continuity of development processes).

The main challenge for Eastern Poland is to overcome the syndrome of a relatively low development level. This syndrome has a natural tendency to self-replicate (it is often considered a symptom of *longue durée*), so it is difficult to eradicate. However, smart specialisation may provide a stimulus for the development of this macroregion with a view to embracing the realistic development paradigm, combining the perspective of turning points with the creation of a new development path, and thus actually initiating the formation of this path. This is corroborated by some theories of socio-economic development, according to which path-dependence and *longue durée* are themselves symptoms of more fundamental evolutionary mechanisms, such as adaptation and the processes of technological and non-technological learning (David, 2000; Garud and Karnøe, 2001; Martin, 2009; Maskell and Malmberg, 2007). To increase the likelihood of the emergence of this development scenario in Eastern Poland, over the next several years the focus should be on the following developments.

The Development of Markets for Innovation

The development of innovation is determined by both innovation supply (research) and innovation demand (the economy). In Eastern Poland there is a well-developed supply side, lacking a similarly strong demand side, which is confirmed by SWOT analysis of the support area under Objective 1, showing a low level of innovativeness of Eastern Poland's economy and an insufficient demand for innovations. Other weaknesses include a low tendency to innovate; a relatively low level of outlays on innovation activity; the predominance of machine and apparatus purchasing at the cost of implementation of new products and processes, especially innovative ones, on the national or global scale; and low patenting activity.

Effective instruments of demand development include innovation-oriented public procurement (direct, cooperative, catalysing and pre-competitive) and regulatory instruments, such as standardisation and certification. Even though these instruments have been rarely used at the regional level, they have a considerable potential for generating demand for innovation due to the large scale of public funds at the regions' disposal.

Development of Supraregional Centres for Growth and Innovation

The measures that have been implemented so far in Poland have led to a dramatic increase in the research potential of regional academic research units and R&D units, and to high saturation with business support organisations (BSOs). On the other hand: (1) the existing BSOs are concentrated in a few leading cities of the macroregion (mostly those with universities) and are thus poorly accessible to businesses located outside those cities; and (2) their personnel are inadequately prepared, without practical experience in supporting and developing innovative entrepreneurship. Moreover, the activity of the existing academic research units and R&D units is not well adjusted to the needs of the economy, as a result of which entrepreneurs are not very interested in working with them, while the macroregion's potential for creating new technology parks and technology transfer parks is almost exhausted. Furthermore, the existing organisations may fall short of their statutory activity and turn into ordinary business centres. As a result, the current state of BSO infrastructure, and in particular its fragmentation and relatively low effectiveness, as well as the poor coordination of pro-innovation initiatives and measures, are some of the major barriers to improving Eastern Poland's innovation and competitiveness levels. The integration and enhanced effectiveness of the existing business support organisations, including incubators, science and technology parks, and so on, and the fine-tuning of the existing science and research infrastructure to the needs of business innovation activity, would enable the creation of new competitive advantages linked to smart specialisation.

Development of Technological Entrepreneurship

Technological entrepreneurship plays a major role in the process of technology commercialisation and transfer, and especially in: (1) converting scientific knowledge into basic technologies and/or directly into applied technologies; and (2) adjusting basic technologies to specific needs and tasks, as well as promoting flexible specialisation. Many technological entrepreneurs are companies known as 'born globals' or 'international new ventures'. The emergence of dynamic innovative enterprises is also an element of deeper rearrangement of the economic structure involving the growing importance of the high- and medium-technology sectors and knowledge-intensive services. However, Eastern Poland is characterised by a low level of entrepreneurship as measured by the number of newly opened firms, especially technological ones, and a low level of mobility and entrepreneurship of the research personnel. Thus, the development of technological entrepreneurship, and an increase in the number of companies in high- and medium-technology sectors and in knowledge-intensive services, would enhance the effectiveness of technology commercialisation and transfer, and accelerate the transformation of the macroregion's economic structure.

The Development of Financial Engineering for Innovation

The process of technology commercialisation occurs in the early stages of technology development. This carries a risk due to competing demands for funding within the businesses together with a decrease in public support. This risk is a major barrier to the growth of demand for innovations. Eastern Poland lacks a well-developed system of financing high-risk ventures. This problem is additionally compounded by the fact that the local authorities are hardly able to finance innovation policy using their own money and, in this respect, they are dependent on the Structural Funds. The development of stable, pro-innovation market mechanisms would not only overcome one of the major barriers to innovation development, but also initiate mechanisms of adapting innovation policy to the conditions of decreased support from the Structural Funds.

NOTES

1. A research programme initiated in 2002 with a view to analysing trends in the territorial development of Europe and the influence of the implemented policies on European regions.
2. Including: (i) the activity of general and specialised hospitals, sanatoria, preventoria, rehabilitation centres, and other medical institutions providing accommodation and meals to the patients; (ii) medical doctors' and dentists' practices, as well as practices run by middle medical personnel; (iii) physiotherapeutic and emergency medical activity; and (iv) other health care activity.

REFERENCES

Acemoglu, D., P. Aghion and F. Zilibotti (2006), 'Distance to frontier, selection, and economic growth', *Journal of the European Economic Association*, **4** (1), 37–74.

Aghiona, P., P.A. David and D. Foray (2009), 'Science, technology and innovation for economic growth: linking policy research and practice in "STIG Systems"', *Research Policy*, **38**, 681–93.

Almor, T. and G. Sperling (2008), 'Israeli, born global, knowledge-intensive firms: an empirical inquiry', in L.-P. Dana, M. Han, V. Ratten and I.M. Welpe (eds), *Handbook of Research on European Business and Entrepreneurship: Towards a Theory of Internationalization*, Cheltenham, UK and Northampton, MA, USA: Edward Elgar, pp. 316–36.

Ancarani, V. (2009), 'Policies at the technological frontier. Europe and us: the follower's trap or divergent trajectories?', available at www.allacademic.com/one/isa/isa09/index.php?cmd=isa09_search&offset=0&limit=5&multi_search_search_mode=publication&multi_search_publication_fulltext_mod=full text&textfield_submit=true&search_module=multi_search&search=Search&search_field=title_idx&fulltext_search=Policies+at+the+Technological+Frontier+in+Europe+-+Trap+of+the+Follower+or+Divergent+Trajectories.

Athey, G., M. Nathan and C. Webber (2007), 'What role do cities play in innovation, and to what extent do we need city-based innovation policies and approaches?', NESTA Working Paper 01/June 2007.

Auerswald, P.E. and L.M. Branscomb (2003), 'Valleys of death and Darwinian seas: financing the invention to innovation transition in the United States', *Journal of Technology Transfer*, **28**, 227–39.

Barca, F. (2009), 'An agenda for a reformed cohesion policy: a place-based approach to meeting European Union challenges and expectations', available at ec.europa.eu/regional_policy/archive/policy/future/pdf/report_barca_v0306.pdf.

Benneworth, P. and A. Dassen (2011), 'Strengthening global-local connectivity in regional innovation strategies: implications for regional innovation policy', OECD Regional Development Working Papers, 2011/01, OECD Publishing, available at http://dx.doi.org/10.1787/5kgc6d80nns4-en.

Boguszewski R. (2012), 'Wnioski z diagnozy do określenia inteligentnych obszarów specjalizacji', available at http://www.rsi.lubelskie.pl/images/zalaczniki/materialy/wnioski%20z%20diagnozy%20do_okreslenia%20inteligentnych%20obszarow%20specjalizacjir._boguszewski%20pdf.pdf.

Braun, A. (2008), 'Healthcare: key technologies for Europe', available at ftp.cordis.europa.eu/pub/foresight/docs/kte_healthcare.pdf.

Buigues, P., F. Ilzkovitz and J. Lebrun (1990), 'The impact of the single market by industrial sector: the challenge for member states', *European Economy*, Special Edition, Brussels.

Capello, R., A. Caragliu and P. Nijkamp (2009), 'Territorial capital and regional growth: increasing returns in cognitive knowledge use', available at www.tinbergen.nl/discussionpapers/09059.pdf.

Carnabuci J. and J. Bruggeman (2009), 'Knowledge specialization, knowledge brokerage and the uneven growth of technology domains', *Social Forces*, **88** (2), 607–41.

Celińska-Janowicz, D., A. Miszczuk, A. Płoszaj and M. Smętkowski (2010), 'Aktualne problemy demograficzne regionu Polski wschodniej', Warsaw: Raporty i analizy EUROREG.

Chandra, V., I. Osorio-Rodarte and C.A. Primo Braga (2009), 'Korea and the BICs: catching-up experiences', in V. Chandra, D. Eröcal, P.C. Padoan and C.A. Primo Braga (eds), *Innovation and Growth, Chasing a Moving Frontier*, Paris:

OECD and International Bank for Reconstruction and Development/World Bank, pp. 25–66.

Chaplin, H. (2009), 'An investigation of the barriers to internationalisation faced by young technology intensive firms', available at www.ukti.gov.uk/uktihome/item/108510.html.

Cohen, W.M. and D.A. Levinthal (1990), 'Absorptive capacity: a new perspective on learning and innovation', *Administrative Science Quarterly*, **35** (1), 128–52.

Dahlman, C. (2009), 'Different innovation strategies, different results: Brazil, Russia, India, China and Korea (the BRICKs)', in V. Chandra, D. Eröcal, P.C. Padoan and C.A. Primo Braga (eds), *Innovation and Growth, Chasing a Moving Frontier*, Paris: OECD and International Bank for Reconstruction and Development/World Bank, pp. 131–68.

David, P.A. (2000), 'Path dependence, its critics and the quest for "historical economics"', available at www-siepr.stanford.edu/workp/swp00011.pdf.

De Maeseneire, W. and T. Claeys (2007), SMEs, FDI and financial constraints, available at www.vlerick.com/en/6551/version/default/part/AttachmentData/data.

Dedrick, J., K.L. Kraemer and G. Linden (2011), 'The distribution of value in the mobile phone supply chain', *Telecommunications Policy*, **35**, 505–21.

Ecorys (2009), 'Study on the competitiveness of the EU eco-industry. Within the Framework Contract of Sectoral Competitiveness Studies – ENTR/06/054. Final report Part I and II', available at http://ec.europa.eu/enterprise/newsroom/cf/_getdocument.cfm?doc_id=5416.

EIM (2010), 'Internationalisation of European SMEs. Final Report, Brussels', European Commission.

ESPON (2012a), 'KIT. Knowledge, Innovation, Territory', Luxembourg: ESPON and Politecnico di Milano.

ESPON (2012b), 'KIT. Knowledge, Innovation, Territory. Applied Research 2013/1/13. Final Scientific Report, vol. I', available at http://www.espon.eu/export/sites/default/Documents/Projects/AppliedResearch/KIT/FinalReport/KIT_Final-Scientific-Report_Volume-1.pdf.

ETPs and EUFETEC (2011), 'The European bioeconomy in 2030. Delivering sustainable growth by addressing the grand societal challenges', available at www.fz-juelich.de/SharedDocs/Downloads/IBG/IBG-2/EN/White_Paper_Bioeconomy-2010-2030.pdf;jsessionid=8EC1171B933BEF5828FE59C4F329019A?__blob=publicationFile.

European Commission (1996), 'Firs report on economic and social cohesion', Luxembourg: Office for Official Publications of the European Commission.

European Commission (2006), 'Eco-industry, its size, employment, perspectives and barriers to growth in an enlarged EU', Final Report, available at http://ec.europa.eu/environment/enveco/eco_industry/pdf/ecoindustry2006.pdf.

European Commission (2009), 'Bridging the valley of death: public support for commercialisation of eco-innovation', Final Report, available at http://ec.europa.eu/environment/enveco/innovation_technology/pdf/bridging_valley_report.pdf.

European Commission (2010a), 'Europe 2020. A strategy for smart, sustainable and inclusive growth', COM(2010) 2020.

European Commission (2010b), 'Europe 2020 Flagship Initiative. Innovation Union', COM(2010) 546 final.

European Commission (2012a), 'Commission Staff Working Document. Elements for a Common Strategic Framework 2014 to 2020 the European Regional

Development Fund the European Social Fund, the Cohesion Fund, the European Agricultural Fund for Rural Development and the European Maritime and Fisheries Fund', SWD(2012) 61 final, Part I and II.

European Commission (2012b), *Global Europe 2050*, Luxembourg: Publications Office of the European Union.

European Commission (2012c), 'Guide to research and innovation strategies for smart specialisation (RIS3)', available at http://s3platform.jrc.ec.europa.eu/en/c/document_library/get_file?uuid=e50397e3-f2b1-4086-8608-7b86e69e8553&groupId=10157.

European Commission (2012d), 'Innovating for sustainable growth: a bioeconomy for Europe. Communication from the Commission to the European Parliament, the Council, the European Economic and Social Committee and the Committee of the Regions', COM(2012) 60 final.

European Commission (2012e), 'Commission staff working document. Accompanying the document Communication on innovating for sustainable growth: a bioeconomy for Europe', available at http://ec.europa.eu/research/bioeconomy/pdf/201202_commision_staff_working.pdf.

European Union (2014), 'Regional Innovation Scoreboard 2014', available at http://ec.europa.eu/news/pdf/2014_regional_union_scoreboard_en.pdf.

Evers, N. (2010), 'Factors influencing the internationalization of new ventures in the Irish aquaculture industry: an exploratory study', *Journal of International Entrepreneurship*, **8**, 392–416.

Foray, D., P.A. David and B. Hall (2009), 'Smart specialisation – the concept', Knowledge Economists Policy Brief 9.

Foray, D., P.A. David and B.H. Hall (2011), 'Smart specialization. From academic idea to political instrument, the surprising career of a concept and the difficulties involved in its implementation', MTEI Working Paper 2011-001.

Fu, X. (2007), 'Foreign direct investment, absorptive capacity and regional innovation capabilities: evidence from China', available at www.oecd.org/dataoecd/44/23/40306798.pdf.

Gaczek, W.M., M. Matusiak, A. Mrozińska and H. Ziółkowska (2011), 'Innowacyjność gospodarek województw Polski Wschodniej – ocena, znaczenie, perspektywy', available at http://www.mrr.gov.pl/rozwoj_regionalny/Polityka_regionalna/Strategia_rozwoju_polski_wschodniej_do_2020/Dokumenty/Documents/Innowacyjnosc_gospodarek.pdf.

Garud, R. and P. Karnøe (eds) (2001), 'Path dependence and creation, Mahwah', Lawrence Erlbaum Associates.

GFCC (2012), 'Innovation capacity: best practices in competitiveness strategy', Washington: Global Federation of Competitiveness Councils.

Giuliani, E., C. Pietrobelli and R. Rabellotti (2005), 'Upgrading in global value chains: lessons from Latin American clusters', *World Development*, **33** (4), 549–73.

GUS (2012), 'Nauka i technika w 2011r.', Warsaw: Główny Urząd Statystyczny.

GUS (2013), 'Regiony Polski', Warsaw: Główny Urząd Statystyczny.

Hansen, M.T. and J. Birkinshaw (2007), 'The innovation value chain', *Harvard Business Review*, **85** (6), 121–30.

Hjerp, P., K. Medarova-Bergstrom, F. Cachia, D. Evers, D. Grubbe, P. Hausemer, P. Kalinka, M. Kettunen, J. Medhurst, G. Peterlongo, I. Skinner and ten P. Brink (2011), 'Cohesion policy and sustainable development', report for DG Regio, available at http://ec.europa.eu/regional_policy/sources/docgener/studies/pdf/sustainable_development/sd_final_report.pdf.

Huwart, J.Y. and L. Verdier (2013), 'Economic globalisation: origins and consequences', OECD Insights, OECD Publishing, available at http://dx.doi.org/10.1787/9789264111899-en.

Jakubowska, P., A. Kukliński and P. Żuber (eds) (2008), 'Problematyka przyszłości regionów. W poszukiwaniu nowego paradygmatu', Warsaw: Ministerstwo Rozwoju Regionalnego.

Joanneum Research Graz (2012), 'S3 – Smart specialization strategies. Getting started with the RIS3 key', available at www.era.gv.at/attach/ris33.7.-eweb.pdf.

Kapil, N., M. Piątkowski, I. Radwan and J.J. Gutierrez (2013), 'Poland enterprise innovation support review: from catching up to moving ahead', World Bank.

Landesmann, M.A. (2003), 'Structural features of economic integration in an Enlarged Europe: patterns of catching-up and industrial specialization', European Economy, Economic Papers 181, Brussels: European Communities.

López-Claros, A. and Y.N. Mata (2010), 'Policies and institutions underpinning country innovation: results from the Innovation Capacity Index', in A. López-Claros (ed.), *Innovation for Development Report 2010–2011. Innovation as a Driver of Productivity and Economic Growth*, Basingstoke, UK and New York, USA: Palgrave Macmillan, pp. 3–63.

Mahroum, S., R. Huggins, R. Clayton, R. Pain and P. Taylor (2008), 'Innovation by adoption: measuring and mapping absorptive capacity in UK nations and regions', London: NESTA.

MAiC (2012), 'Polska 2030. Trzecia fala nowoczesności, Ministerstwo Administracji i Cyfryzacji', available at https://mac.gov.pl/wp-content/uploads/2011/12/Polska2030_final_november2012.pdf.

Manic, S. (2008), 'Is technological leadership decisive for competitiveness?', *Analele Stiintifice ale Universitatii "Alexandru Ioan Cuza" din Iasi*, **55**, 190–97.

Manzella, G.P. and C. Mendez (2009), 'The turning points of EU Cohesion policy', available at http://ec.europa.eu/regional_policy/archive/policy/future/pdf/8_manzella_final-formatted.pdf.

Martin, R. (2009), 'Rethinking regional path dependence', *Beyond lock-in to evolution, Papers in Evolutionary Economic Geography # 09.10*, available at econ.geo.uu.nl/peeg/peeg.html (10 April 2010).

Marzinotto, B. (2012), 'The growth effects of EU cohesion policy: a meta-analysis', Bruegel Working Paper 2012/14.

Maskell, P. and A. Malmberg (2007), 'Myopia, knowledge development and cluster evolution', *Journal of Economic Geography*, **7**, 603–18.

Mazurkiewicz, D. (2012), 'Diagnoza lubelskiego rynku innowacji – synteza ekspertyz na potrzeby RSI 2020', available at www.rsi.lubelskie.pl/images/DIAGNOZA/Diagnoza%20do%20RSI.pdf.

McCann, P. and R. Ortega-Argilés (2011), 'Smart specialization, regional growth and applications to EU cohesion policy', available at http://ipts.jrc.ec.europa.eu/docs/s3_mccann_ortega.pdf.

Moray, N. and B. Clarysse (2005), 'Institutional change and resource endowments to science-based entrepreneurial firms', *Research Policy*, **34**, 1010–27.

MRR (2010), 'Krajowa Strategia Rozwoju Regionalnego 2010–2012. regiony, miasta, obszary wiejskie', available at http://www.mrr.gov.pl/aktualnosci/polityka_rozwoju/Documents/KSRR_13_07_2010.pdf.

MRR (2013), 'Projekt zaktualizowanej Strategii rozwoju społeczno-gospodarczego Polski Wschodniej do roku 2020', available at http://www.mrr.gov.pl/

rozwoj_regionalny/Polityka_regionalna/Strategia_rozwoju_polski_wschodniej_do_2020/Dokumenty/Documents/SPW_www_9_04_13.pdf.
Nioso, J. (2002), 'National systems of innovations are "x-efficient" (and x-effective). Why some are slow learners', *Research Policy*, **31**, 291–302.
Nordmann, A. (2004), 'Converging technologies – shaping the future of European societies. High Level Expert Group "Foresighting the New Technology Wave"', available at ec.europa.eu/research/conferences/2004/ntw/pdf/final_report_en.pdf.
OECD (2001), 'Territorial outlook. Territorial economy', Paris: OECD Publishing.
OECD (2009a), 'How regions grow: trends and analysis', available at www.sourceoecd.org/9789264039452.
OECD (2009b), 'The OECD Innovation Strategy: getting a head start on tomorrow', Paris: OECD Publishing.
OECD (2009c), 'The bioeconomy to 2030: designing a policy agenda', Paris: OECD Publishing.
OECD (2011a), 'Regions and innovation policy', OECD Reviews of Regional Innovation, OECD Publishing, available at http://dx.doi.org/10.1787/9789264097803-en.
OECD (2011b), 'OECD Regional Outlook 2011: building resilient regions for stronger economies', OECD Publishing, available at http://dx.doi.org/10.1787/9789264120983-en.
OECD (2011c), 'Project proposal for the TIP work on smart specialisation in global value chains: designing and assessing smart specialisation strategies', Working Party on Innovation and Technology Policy. Revised Proposal for TIP Work on Smart Specialisation, DSTI/STP/TIP(2011)5.
OECD (2011d), 'Business innovation policies: selected country comparisons', OECD Publishing, available at http://dx.doi.org/10.1787/9789264115668-en.
OECD (2012), 'Promoting growth in all regions', Paris: OECD Publishing, available at http://dx.doi.org/10.1787/9789264174634-en.
Olechnicka, A. and A. Płoszaj (2012), 'Potencjał placówek naukowo-badawczych województwa lubelskiego', available at https://depot.ceon.pl/bitstream/handle/123456789/1301/potencja_placwek_naukowo-badawczych_wojewdztwa_lubelskiego_fin.pdf?sequence=1.
Onodera, O. (2008), 'Trade and Innovation project: a synthesis paper', OECD Trade Policy Working Papers 72, OECD Publishing. doi: 10.1787/240602178318.
PAIiI (2010a), 'Sektor lotniczy w Polsce Wschodniej, Polska Agencja Informacji i Inwestycji Zagranicznych', available at http://whyeasternpoland.eu/upload/files/7c0fcc27099c2779fb7a520d82e052d2.pdf.
PAIiI (2010b), 'Sektor odnawialnych źródeł energii w Polsce Wschodniej, Polska Agencja Informacji i Inwestycji Zagranicznych', available at http://whyeasternpoland.eu/upload/files/53da5d969a77abad74fba027fb097410.pdf.
PAIiI (2010c), 'Sektor turystyki biznesowej w Polsce Wschodniej, Polska Agencja Informacji i Inwestycji Zagranicznych', available at http://whyeasternpoland.eu/upload/files/8fc19b4f35b3bd64452ecfd1a02ccf59.pdf.
PAIiI (2010d), 'Sektor logistyczny w Polsce Wschodniej, Polska Agencja Informacji i Inwestycji Zagranicznych', available at http://whyeasternpoland.eu/upload/files/febe5f8cfed2d651d8cc6d0063c71951.pdf.
PAIiI (2010e), 'Sektor wyrobów z surowców niemetalicznych w Polsce Wschodniej, Polska Agencja Informacji i Inwestycji Zagranicznych', available at http://whyeasternpoland.eu/upload/files/432dd8925489d1dca1dfbdb47fe4dd7f.pdf.

PAIiI (2010f), 'Sektor maszynowy w Polsce Wschodniej, Polska Agencja Informacji i Inwestycji Zagranicznych', available at http://whyeasternpoland.eu/upload/files /55a0c13ff5383620f02280d5a44153c5.pdf.

PAIiI (2010g), 'Sektor odzieżowy w Polsce Wschodniej, Polska Agencja Informacji i Inwestycji Zagranicznych', available at http://whyeasternpoland.eu/upload/files /3bcd73f988493632a0270fab3f3ec355.pdf.

PAIiI (2010h), 'Sektor budowlany w Polsce Wschodniej, Polska Agencja Informacji i Inwestycji Zagranicznych', available at http://whyeasternpoland.eu/upload/ files/c2a70818cbd35931344ee36ccb18c3f6.pdf.

Pietrobelli, C. and R. Rabellotti (2011), 'Global value chains meet innovation systems: are there learning opportunities for developing countries?', *World Development*, **39** (7), 1261–9.

Plawgo, B., T. Klimczak, P. Czyż, R. Boguszewski and A. Kowalczyk (2013), 'Regionalne systemy innowacji w Polsce. Raport z badań', Warsaw: Polska Agencja Rozwoju Przedsiębiorczości.

RM (2012), 'Strategia Rozwoju Kraju 2020. Aktywne społeczeństwo, konkurencyjna gospodarka, sprawne państwo', *Monitor Polski*, 27.04.2012, poz. 252.

Rodrik, D. (2003), 'Growth strategies', Working Paper 0317, available at www. econ.jku.at/papers/2003/wp0317.pdf.

Spithoven, A., B. Clarysse and M. Knockaert (2010), 'Building absorptive capacity to organize inbound open innovation in traditional industries', *Technoinnovation*, **30**, 130–41.

Szlachta, J. and J. Zalewski (eds) (2012), 'Aktualizacja Strategii Rozwoju Województwa Świętokrzyskiego do roku 2020. Projekt', Wrocław: Wrocławska Agencja Rozwoju Regionalnego.

Urząd Marszałkowski Województwa Lubelskiego (2013), 'Regionalna Strategia Innowacji Województwa Lubelskiego do 2020 roku. Wersja robocza', manuscript.

Urząd Marszałkowski Województwa Podlaskiego (2013), 'Strategia Rozwoju Województwa Podlaskiego do roku 2020, Załącznik nr 1 do Uchwały nr 150/2157/2013 Zarządu Województwa Podlaskiego z dnia 19 marca 2013 r', Białystok: Urząd Marszałkowski Województwa Lubelskiego.

US Department of Commerce (2012), 'The competitiveness and innovative capacity of the United States', available at http://www.commerce.gov/sites/default/ files/documents/2012/january/competes_010511_0.pdf.

Vandenbussche, J., P. Aghion and C. Meghir (2004), 'Distance to technological frontier and composition of human capital', available at www.merit.unimaas.nl/ workshop/aghion.pdf.

Weber, K.M. (2005), 'Environmental technologies. Background paper for the European Commission's High Level Group on "Key Technologies"', available at ftp.cordis.europa.eu/pub/foresight/docs/kte_environmental.pdf.

World Bank (2008), 'Global economic prospects: technology diffusion in the developing world', Washington, DC: International Bank for Reconstruction and Development/World Bank.

Zahra, S.A. and G. George (2002), 'Absorptive capacity: a review, reconceptualization, and extension', *Academy of Management Review*, **27** (2), 185–203.

Zalewski, J., Z. Mogiła, T. Korf, M. Wysocka and M. Zaleska (2012), 'Aneks do aktualizacji Strategii Rozwoju Województwa Świętokrzyskiego do roku 2020. Diagnoza społeczno-gospodarcza (wersja robocza)', Wrocław: Wrocławska Agencja Rozwoju Regionalnego.

Zarząd Województwa Podkarpackiego (2011), 'Aktualizacja Regionalnej Strategii

Innowacji Województwa Podkarpackiego na lata 2005–2013', available at http://rsi.podkarpackie.pl/Aktualnosci/Strony/Aktualizacja-RSI-2005-2013.aspx.

Zarząd Województwa Warmińsko-Mazurskiego (2013), 'Strategia rozwoju społeczno-gospodarczego województwa warmińsko-mazurskiego do roku 2025', available at http://strategia2025.warmia.mazury.pl/artykuly/8/projekt-strategii.html.

PART II

Entrepreneurship and SME Policy

4. Entrepreneurship and industrial policy in Ireland

Colm O'Gorman and Declan Curran

INTRODUCTION[1]

In this chapter we review entrepreneurship policy in Ireland. We investigate how Irish policy-makers have sought to influence the extent and nature of entrepreneurship in Ireland. Ireland represents an interesting case for exploring entrepreneurship policy and industrial development in the context of the challenges facing policy-makers in the 'new' Europe, because the Irish government has pursued an active and interventionist industrial development strategy, with entrepreneurship policy embedded within this wider industrial development strategy. Furthermore, Ireland is a relatively young state that has experienced rapid industrialisation in the past 50 years. However, critiques of Irish industrial policy have suggested that Ireland has experienced long periods of low levels of industrialisation and that Ireland's industrial development policy has been overly reliant on inward foreign direct investment.

Encouraging entrepreneurship is a central component of industrial policy in many countries. Broadly speaking, industrial policy might influence the extent and nature of entrepreneurship by:

1. creating a supportive institutional context (for example, taxes and laws);
2. fostering technological progress by supporting the development of innovations and the adoption of technology from overseas;
3. redistributing resources in favour of specific industries or regions (Lee et al., 2012).

More specifically, entrepreneurship policy can be framed as addressing factors that influence the supply of entrepreneurs (for example, cultural attitudes, regulations impacting upon start-ups) and the opportunities for entrepreneurs (for example, demand conditions).

This chapter is structured as follows. First we discuss explanations of national levels of entrepreneurship. We then describe Ireland's industrial policy and Ireland's entrepreneurship policy, focusing on the period since 1958. We then review critiques of Irish policy. This is followed by a discussion of evidence of entrepreneurship policy, in terms of outcomes in recent years, using data from the Global Entrepreneurship Monitor (GEM). We conclude with a discussion of how the Irish policy experience might inform policy-makers in the 'new' Europe.

LITERATURE: THE DETERMINANTS OF LEVELS OF ENTREPRENEURSHIP

The economic performance and development of nation-states suggests that stimulating productive economic activity is neither an easy process nor a 'natural' outcome in a democratic free market economy (North, 1990). In his study of the determinants of growth in productivity, Baumol (1990, 1993) argues that an important determinant of growth is the supply of productive entrepreneurship. In his seminal work, Kilby (1971) argues that an understanding of the supply of entrepreneurial services is critical to any explanation of economic growth. Kilby also argues that the shortage of entrepreneurial talent is associated with low levels of economic development in developing economies.

However, while policy choices give rise to the evolution of differing institutional arrangements between countries, providing direct and indisputable evidence of the relationship between any given institutional arrangements and entrepreneurial activity is difficult (Davidsson and Henrekson, 2002). As such, there is ambiguity about which aspects of context explain variation in entrepreneurial activity generally, and 'productive' entrepreneurship in particular (Storey, 2000). Not all national economic systems are equally good at supporting entrepreneurship, as evidenced by variations in the levels of entrepreneurial activity across national contexts (Audretsch et al., 2002), within national contexts (Johnson, 2004) and over time (Carree et al., 2002). Furthermore, state institutions can 'amplify or compromise governments' policies and firms' innovation strategies' (Spencer et al., 2005: 321).

There is an extensive literature within the entrepreneurship domain that focuses on identifying and explaining variations in levels of entrepreneurial activity. For example, Lundström and Stevenson (2005) identify a list of more than 40 variables that have been used to explain entrepreneurial activity. These include factors such as: entrepreneurial characteristics and preferences, aspects of national culture, the extent and nature of demand, tax rates, and the time and costs of business registration. In the eclectic theory of entrepreneurship, Verheul et al. (2002: 37) integrate demand- and supply-side determinants of entrepreneurship, arguing that 'demand and supply factors create conditions for the entrepreneurial decision at the individual level'. In their 'eclectic theory', the determinants of entrepreneurship are aggregate conditions (level of economic development, technology, demography, culture and institutions) that create the demand for, and supply of, entrepreneurs. Demand for entrepreneurs reflects the opportunities available to entrepreneurs. The supply of entrepreneurs reflects the capabilities and preferences of individuals. The interaction of these factors allows individuals to make assessments about their personal risks and rewards associated with starting a given business, and as such determines the overall level of entrepreneurship in a national context.

The determinants of entrepreneurship may vary over both the short term and the long term. Reynolds (1999) argues that in the US the short-term determinants of levels of creative destruction are greater personal wealth, population growth, the absence of unemployed or economically desperate individuals, and economic diversity. He argues that there is little direct evidence that lower costs, direct government support or a 'positive business climate' have a consistent effect in promoting births or growth of new firms. Overall, the relationship between institutional structure (pay-offs) and the extent of entrepreneurial activity is unclear. Entrepreneurship research cannot predict 'when and where in social or economic space, new organisations will arise in large numbers' (Romanelli and Schoonhoven, 2001: 40). Furthermore, it is not obvious when entrepreneurial activity will represent productive economic activity. Even if the appropriate set of conditions could be identified, it is unclear how the institutional environment can be adapted to achieve the aim of an increased supply of entrepreneurs, as North (1990) has argued that institutional change is both incremental and path-dependent. Informed by these ideas, we review industrial policy and entrepreneurship policy in Ireland. We investigate how Irish policy-makers have sought to influence the extent and nature of entrepreneurship in Ireland.

IRISH INDUSTRIAL POLICY AND PERFORMANCE

Industrial Development in Ireland

In the period since the 1920s, Ireland's gross domestic product (GDP) per capita (in fixed prices) has increased elevenfold (Bielenberg and Ryan, 2013). However, it took 44 years (1922 to 1966) for GDP per capita to double, while in the subsequent 42 years (1966 to 2008) there was a five

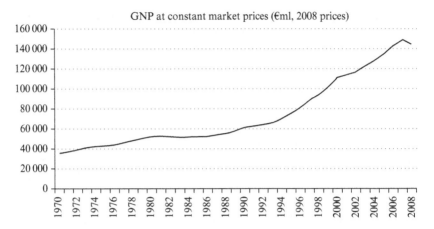

GNP at constant market prices (€ml, 2008 prices)

Notes:
1. The Central Statistics Office Ireland (CSO) has been unable to make estimates of Financial Intermediation Services Indirectly Measured (FISIM) for 1970–1995, so the 1970–1995 historical gross national product (GNP) series is not directly comparable to the latest GNP data for the years 1995 to 2008, which include FISIM. Both series are joined here for illustrative purposes only.
2. GNP is used, rather than GDP, as it excludes repatriated profits of multinational enterprises, which have been substantial in the Irish case.

Source: Data from Central Statistics Office Ireland, Statbank database (www.cso.ie).

Figure 4.1   Growth of the Irish economy

and a half times increase. For the period 1958 to 2008 there was a seven times increase, as GDP had only grown one and a half times by 1958. More recently, the Irish economy has grown by 300 per cent over the period 1971 to 2008, or 3.8 per cent p.a. (Figure 4.1). Over this time the composition of GDP has changed, with a decline in the relative importance of agriculture and an increase in services outputs.

Irish Industrial and Entrepreneurship Policy

Since the founding of the Irish state in 1921, the Irish government has pursued an active policy of supporting industrialisation (Burke, 1995). Since 1958 successive Irish governments have pursued a policy of opening the Irish economy. Over a relatively short period (1958 to 1973) Ireland was transformed from an agricultural-orientated economy to an industrial economy.

Since 1958 Ireland's industrial development policy has involved two components: (1) the attraction of export-orientated, foreign-owned firms into Ireland; and (2) the development of export-orientated, Irish-owned firms in both traditional sectors such as the manufacturing of food and beverages, and newer sectors such as information and communication technology (ICT). Within this, Irish entrepreneurship policy has selectively focused on export-orientated new ventures.

The following characteristics of Ireland's industrial development are notable. First, Ireland has pursued an active policy of supporting industrialisation. Since the foundation of the state, 'government policy has taken an active role in encouraging enterprise' (Burke, 1995: 4). This has manifested itself in many ways, including:

1. direct engagement in industry through the creation of semi-state businesses;
2. the policies of creating barriers to trade (the era of protectionist tariffs in the 1930s to 1950s) and the opening of the Irish economy to free trade (since the late 1950s);
3. the development of sector development strategies;
4. state-funded investment banks;
5. direct and indirect support for export-orientated new and existing firms engaged in manufacturing and internationally traded services firms (since the 1950s);
6. support for local new business creation through the City and County Enterprise Boards (in the 1990s).

Second, there has been a strong focus on the attraction of export-orientated, inward foreign direct investment into Ireland. A consequence of Ireland's industrial development policy of attracting inward foreign direct investment is that there are more than 1000 foreign-owned subsidiaries located in Ireland. The success of Ireland at attracting foreign firms has been attributed to a number of factors, including: the emergence of new clusters of firms, such as ICT firms; the extension of Ireland's incentives to service-based firms; and Ireland's reputation as a foreign direct investment (FDI)-friendly location (Murphy and Ruane, 2004).

Ireland's policy of attracting foreign direct investment has evolved over time. The change in policy emphasis can be seen in the changing sectoral composition of firms located in Ireland. In the 1970s foreign firms located in Ireland operated primarily in low-tech sectors. However, by the 1990s more than half of foreign firms operating in Ireland were in new high-technology sectors (Naveretti and Venables, 2004).

Third, Ireland has not had a defined 'small business' or 'entrepreneurship policy'. Entrepreneurship policy is embedded within the broader industrial development policies and within sector policies (for example, tourism) and government policies more generally, particularly with regard to education and taxation. Successive governments have stated that their role is to create an environment supportive of entrepreneurs.

Fourth, entrepreneurship support from government has been highly selective. A number of government programmes illustrate the selective nature of entrepreneurship support in Ireland. The Enterprise Development Programme, started in 1978, supported mainly professionals such as engineers and experienced managers in starting export-orientated or import substitution businesses. This programme supported more than 350 businesses between 1978 and 1998 (Acs et al., 2007). The Linkages Programme supported both existing and new businesses that sought to become sub-suppliers to multinational firms that had located in Ireland. These programmes were replaced by the High Potential Start-Up Programme. Typically these 'high-potential start-ups' are in newer sectors of the economy such as ICT and biotechnology, although they include firms in traditional sectors such as food. A 'high-potential start-up' is defined as an Irish business (that is less than five years old) that:

1. introduces a new or innovative product or service to international markets, in manufacturing or internationally traded services sectors;
2. is capable of creating ten jobs in Ireland and realising €1 million in sales within three to four years of starting up; and
3. is led by an experienced management team.

The commercialisation of state-funded university research was also targeted as a potential source of new businesses. Following a significant investment in research capacity in science and engineering at institutes of higher education in 2003, development agencies focused on increasing the capacity of universities to commercialise this research. This involved specific grant aid to researchers to commercialise research, as well as more general investment in incubation facilities.

Notwithstanding the performance of the Irish economy as a whole since the 1950s, reviews of Ireland's industrial policy have argued that the relative industrial performance of indigenous firms has been poor. These reviews have highlighted an entrepreneurial deficit in Ireland, Ireland's reliance on inward foreign direct investment, and the relatively poor performance of Irish-owned industry. Reflecting on the economic performance of Ireland for the period from the 1920s to the 1980s, the Irish historian Joe Lee (1989: 521) argued that 'it is difficult to avoid the conclusion that Irish economic performance has been the least impressive in Western Europe, perhaps all of Europe, in the twentieth century'.

The weakness in Irish industrial performance was highlighted in a government-funded review of industrial development strategy in the early 1980s. The Telesis Report (National Economic and Social Council, 1982) highlighted the poor performance of Irish-owned firms in terms of low levels of profitability, being overdependent on the domestic and United Kingdom (UK) markets, and characterised by commodity products the demand for which was highly price sensitive. The relative poor performance of Irish-owned firms compared to foreign-owned firms persisted into the 1990s. For example, Barry et al. (1999) found performance differences in terms of levels of innovation, extent and destination of exports, productivity and sector composition. Irish-owned firms were characterised by low levels of innovation, low levels of exporting, and much lower levels of productivity. Furthermore, they tended to be concentrated in traditional rather than modern sectors.

In 1992 and again in 2004, the effectiveness of Irish industrial policy was again questioned in state-funded reviews of industrial policy. The Culliton Report suggested that 'the competitive edge of Irish industry has been distracted from serving the market and achieving high productivity, into maximising the grant or tax benefit' (Industrial Policy Review Group, 1992: 22). In 2004 the O'Driscoll Report, which again highlighted the perceived poor performance of Irish-owned firms, argued that: 'Ireland's economic success over the past decade was driven largely by the performance of the internationally-traded goods and services sectors, and in particular by the growth of foreign direct investment' (Enterprise Strategy Group, 2004: 4).

ENTREPRENEURSHIP IN IRELAND

Ireland's Entrepreneurial Deficit?

Part of Lee's explanation for the poor performance of the Irish state from the 1920s to the 1980s was that there has been a historical deficiency in the supply of entrepreneurs (Lee, 1989). Lee argued that 'native businessmen of the necessary quality simply were not, for whatever reason, available', suggesting that a 'native entrepreneurial cadre of the requisite quality had failed to emerge' (ibid.: 536). In a similar vein, Fogarty (1973) argued that from the perspective of the entrepreneurs he studied in the early 1970s, the difficulties in Ireland were: 'that too many people still fail to acquire in their families, in the schools and colleges, in the Church or in work itself the qualities needed for initiative and enterprise' (ibid.: 28–9).

Keating and Desmond (1993: 190) argued that the Irish are poor entrepreneurs not because of objective factors such as 'absence of means and opportunities', but because of subjective, cultural factors. An alternative explanation for Ireland's poor industrial performance (in terms of indigenous Irish firms) focuses on opportunity conditions, including spin-off processes. O'Farrell (1986: 202) argued that 'the size distribution *and* industry mix of the national economy, and as a corollary, regional and sub-regional economies will greatly influence the number and type of new firms being established'. O'Farrell (1986) noted that about half of all entrepreneurs remained within the same industry group. An issue in Ireland was that in the period from the 1950s to the 1980s many traditional industries were in decline due to increased competition from overseas. Barrett (1995) suggested that profit opportunities in Ireland were skewed in favour of rent-seeking behaviour.

Entrepreneurship Forum Report

In 2007 Ireland was experiencing a period of rapid growth: the so-called 'Celtic Tiger'. A report commissioned by the state highlighted Ireland's strengths with regard to entrepreneurship as follows:

> The current environment in Ireland is shown to be highly conducive to entrepreneurial activity at present. The demographic profile of the population is very strong, as is the personal context of individuals, many of whom have confidence in their ability to successfully start and run a business. The culture is also highly supportive of entrepreneurs and their activity. The economy remains strong, with buoyant consumer demand. There is generally agreement that Ireland is characterised by a pro-business policy, which has been in place for many years and is supported by all the main political parties. (Forfas, 2007: 5)

However, the economic and financial crisis of 2008, and the decline in Ireland's economic performance, resulted in a renewed focus on the role that entrepreneurship could play in Ireland's recovery, with the establishment by the government in 2013 of the Entrepreneurship Forum. The report of the Entrepreneurship Forum (2014: 5) identified six 'pillars of an effective start-up ecosystem':

1. An innovative 'can-do' culture that encourages entrepreneurship.
2. Increased mentorship and peer learning, though the state's role should be in facilitating rather than the provision of such services.
3. The encouragement of entrepreneurial 'hot spots'.
4. Facilitating new firms to access workforce.
5. Improve access to finance.
6. An integrated approach by government in terms of policies that impact on start-ups.

Table 4.1 Entrepreneurship in Ireland, 2003 to 2012 (%)

Year	Aspiring entrepreneurs	New business owners	Owner-managers of established businesses	Entrepreneurs discontinuing businesses
2012	8.0	2.3	8.3	1.2
2011	8.5	3.1	8.0	2.8
2010	8.4	2.5	8.6	1.2
2009	–	–	–	–
2008	10.0	4.3	9.0	1.8
2007	11.2	4.2	9.0	1.9
2006	9.8	2.9	7.8	1.8
2005	12.6	4.7	8.1	2.3
2004	11.0	3.6	6.5	1.3
2003	11.3	3.8	6.7	2.5

Source: Fitzsimons and O'Gorman (2013).

Rates of Entrepreneurship in Ireland

The Global Entrepreneurship Monitor (GEM) provides data on levels of entrepreneurship in Ireland. Table 4.1 summarises rates of entrepreneurial activity in Ireland for the period 2003 to 2012 (Fitzsimons and O'Gorman, 2013). These data suggest that for the period referred to as the 'Celtic Tiger', Ireland experienced higher rates of entrepreneurial activity across a range of measures, including the number of individuals involved in starting new businesses and the number of individuals aspiring to start a new business. For the period since the onset of the economic crises of 2008, Ireland has been characterised by lower rates of entrepreneurial activity.

The 2012 GEM report for Ireland highlighted the following (Fitzsimons and O'Gorman, 2013). First, the rate at which people in Ireland were setting up new businesses[2] in the period 2003 to 2008 averaged 3.9 per cent, compared to 2.6 per cent for the period 2010 to 2012. During this period, rates in Ireland were higher than in many other Western European countries. Second, the numbers aspiring to start businesses[3] were higher in the period 2003 to 2008, an average of 11 per cent, than they were for the period 2010 to 2012, an average of 8.3 per cent. Third, the motives of entrepreneurs changed over time. Responding to a perceived opportunity remained the dominant motivational factor cited by early-stage entrepreneurs throughout the ten-year period. The rate at which necessity was cited as the principal motivator, however, increased steadily from 6 per cent in 2007 to 19 per cent in 2008 and 32 per cent in 2010. It has declined slightly from this peak more recently, but necessity motives are still at levels not seen in the earlier part of the ten-year period. However, some aspects of entrepreneurial activity did not decline. The GEM 2012 report highlights the following: the rate of owner-managers of established business[4] in Ireland in the most recent period was, on average, 8.3 per cent, while for the earlier period the rate was, on average, 7.8 per cent; the rate at which entrepreneurs were exiting and closing businesses[5] reached a peak in 2011, but in general the rates in the earlier period (1.9 per cent average) were broadly similar to the rates in the later period (1.7 per cent average).

Rates of Entrepreneurship in the New Europe

By way of comparison, Table 4.2 presents rates of entrepreneurship in Ireland and in selected Eastern European countries for 2013 using data from the GEM project. As a measure of culture, the GEM measures the perceptions of the adult population of successful entrepreneurs. In Ireland, in 2013, 81 per cent of adults considered that successful entrepreneurs had a high status. The average for ten Eastern European countries is 61 per cent, with a range of 43 per cent in Croatia to 74 per cent in Hungary.

Of those who are planning to start or have recently started a new business (the 'Total Early-Stage Entrepreneurial Activity' or TEA measure in the GEM), 44 per cent of entrepreneurs in Ireland report that they are opportunity driven. The average in the ten Eastern European countries is 41 per cent, with four countries (the Czech Republic, Estonia, Lithuania and Slovenia) reporting rates higher than Ireland. Six Eastern European countries have data for 2013. The average for 2013 for these six countries is 38 per cent.

As a measure of opportunities for entrepreneurship, 28 per cent of Irish adults believe that there are opportunities to start businesses in their local area. The average for the ten Eastern European countries is slightly lower, 25 per cent, though three countries report rates higher than Ireland (Estonia, Lithuania and Macedonia). Four Eastern European countries report data for 2013. For these, the average perception of opportunity is 20 per cent for 2013.

With respect to intention to start a new business, the rate in Ireland (13 per cent) in 2013 was lower than the average for the ten Eastern European countries (19 per cent). In 2013, nine of the ten Eastern European countries were characterised by higher rates of intention (the exception was Slovenia). In terms of the rate of new business owners in the adult population (that is, those who have started a business in the past three and a half years) the average rate in the ten Eastern European countries and Ireland is similar: 4 per cent and 3.8 per cent, respectively. The rate of established

Table 4.2 Entrepreneurial attitudes, motives, aspirations and activity in Ireland and selected Eastern European countries (2013)

Country	Status of entrepreneurs % of adult population	Motives: opportunity driven % of TEA	Opportunities for entrepreneurship % of adult population	Aspiring entrepreneurs % of adult population	New business owners % of adult population	Owner-managers of established businesses % of adult population
Bosnia and Herzegovina[1]	72	22	23	22	4.6	4.5
Croatia	43	30	18	20	2.0	3.3
Czech Republic[2]	48	60	23	14	2.7	5.3
Estonia	59	50	46	19	4.5	5.0
Hungary[3]	74	39	19	14	3.7	7.2
Lithuania	57	55	29	22	6.4	8.3
Macedonia	68	23	37	29	3.5	7.3
Poland[4]	60	33	26	17	4.3	6.5
Slovak Republic	59	40	16	16	3.6	5.4
Slovenia	68	53	16	12	2.9	5.7
Average (10)	61	41	25	19	4.0	6.0
Ireland	81	44	28	13	3.8	7.5

Notes:
[1] 2008 is average figure for 2008 and 2009.
[2] 2008 not available, 2006 data reported.
[3] 2003 not available, 2004 data reported.
[4] 2003 not available, 2004 data reported.

Source: Global Entrepreneurship Monitor data.

business owners in the adult population in the ten Eastern European countries is lower at 6.0 per cent compared to 7.5 per cent in Ireland.

In summary, there is some evidence that when compared to Eastern European countries, the higher rates of entrepreneurship (new business owners) previously observed in Ireland were not observed in 2013. This suggests a possible 'catch-up' in rates of entrepreneurship in Eastern European countries. However, in terms of entrepreneurial intentions, the GEM data indicate that intentions are higher in the selected Eastern European countries. In contrast, the rate of established owner-managers is higher in Ireland. Ireland is also characterised by a more positive culture, with the status of successful entrepreneurship higher in Ireland. However, in terms of motives for entrepreneurship and the perception of entrepreneurial opportunity, there is a much smaller difference between Ireland and the Eastern European countries.

IMPLICATIONS FOR COUNTRIES FROM THE 'NEW' EUROPE

While understanding what determines the supply of productive entrepreneurship is core to the study of entrepreneurship (Baumol, 1993), providing direct and indisputable evidence of the relationship between any given institutional arrangements and entrepreneurial activity is difficult (Davidsson and Henrekson, 2002). Baumol (1993: 23) argues that 'there is no way that one can hope to rank the influence' of the factors that determine the supply of entrepreneurship. Notwithstanding this, we identify a number of lessons from our description of Ireland's recent industrial development experience for countries in the 'new' Europe.

First, policy-makers should not pursue stand-alone entrepreneurship policies. Entrepreneurship policies on their own cannot address the challenges of industrial development. Where countries develop specific entrepreneurship policies, these need to be designed as part of a broader industrial development policy. Ireland's entrepreneurship support is part of a broader industrial development policy. A core focus of Ireland's industrial development policy for the period since 1960 has been on opening the Irish economy. At a broad level this policy has been effective, as Ireland experienced a period of rapid industrialisation and economic convergence with more developed European countries. There is evidence that some Irish-owned firms, with the assistance of direct state support, have exploited the opportunities offered by increased European economic integration, as evidenced by increased levels of internationalisation in large Irish-owned firms and the emergence of new large firms that are active in international markets (O'Gorman and Curran, 2014). For Irish firms interested in exporting, the state has provided a range of direct support such as supporting access to international markets, and supporting investment in research and development (R&D). For firms in smaller countries, access to larger markets through institutions such as the European Union may provide selective opportunities for growth.

Second, policy-makers should measure the success of entrepreneurship policies in terms of the impact of entrepreneurship, rather than in terms of increases in the rate of entrepreneurship. Policies that focus on increasing the rate of entrepreneurship may not deliver the required economic benefits, as higher rates of entrepreneurship may result from increased levels of self-employment activity in the context of expanding domestic market conditions. For example, the high rates of entrepreneurship reported in Ireland during the past decade appear to overlap with the period of rapid growth in the economy; the so-called 'Celtic Tiger'. This suggests, as is evident from other research, that higher rates of entrepreneurship occur in the context of market growth. Interestingly, the high rates of entrepreneurship observed in Ireland occurred at a time when Ireland did not have a general entrepreneurship or small- and medium-sized enterprise policy. This may mean that in terms of promoting entrepreneurship, macro-level and demand-led policies may be most effective at encouraging higher rates of entrepreneurship.

Third, policy-makers must target entrepreneurship policies. Support for entrepreneurs and new businesses should be targeted at the individuals and businesses that have the potential to make the most economic impact. This may involve a focus not just on new technology-based industries but also on entrepreneurs innovating in other industries that have a strong domestic base. Most of Ireland's support for entrepreneurs has been highly selective and has, in general, been targeted at supporting the creation of new enterprises, rather than supporting existing small- and medium-sized enterprises. Since the 1980s, this has involved intensive selective policy support directed at the internationalisation of firms and the development of firms in newer sectors, such as ICT, that have the potential to internationalise. Such support has included firm-level support (for example, direct grants and investments, support for attending trade shows) and selective sector policies (for example, support for the development of venture capital funds). In this regard, Ireland's development policy has differed from the focus in some countries, where small- and medium-sized enterprises more generally have been the target of policy support. In addition, in Ireland, the policy and support framework has focused, for selective firms, on the direct provision of assistance.

Entrepreneurship policies can also be targeted in terms of supporting or exploiting other policies. For example, the policy of stimulating industrial development through inward foreign direct investment may, in some industry contexts, lead to entrepreneurship, provided that policy-makers pursue targeted policies to support entrepreneurs in related sectors. In Ireland, the policy of attracting export-orientated inward foreign direct investment may have had a positive impact on the development of Irish firms in some sectors such as ICT. While Ireland's success in this regard is often attributed to a low tax rate, the policy has evolved significantly over the past four decades, with a significant change in the composition of foreign-owned firms in Ireland. In the past two decades, inward foreign direct investment has been concentrated in high-technology sectors. While levels of embeddedness of foreign-owned firms has been criticised, there is some evidence that the policy of attracting inward foreign direct investment has positively affected the development of Irish industry. This includes managerial up-skilling and an increase in demand in sectors such as software (O'Malley et al., 1997). More generally, successive Irish governments have developed a regulatory and tax policy that is supportive of businesses located in Ireland.

Fourth, policy-makers need to be patient. Entrepreneurship policies require time to produce the desired impact. In Ireland, policy interventions directed at industrial development took time to develop and it took time for the benefits to be realised. The entrepreneurship supports provided in Ireland have emerged over a period of more than 50 years. However, despite persistent efforts at improving the export performance of Irish-owned firms, many reviews of the industrial policy suggest that Irish-owned firms have been characterised by relative poor performance. The outcomes of entrepreneurship policy may require time to have an impact, as it takes time for new firms and new industries to emerge and grow. Policy-makers need to recognise that there may be no immediate or quick 'fixes' in terms of entrepreneurship policies. What is evident in Ireland is that support has consistently focused on developing export-orientated manufacturing and service business.

NOTES

1. This chapter draws on a forthcoming publication, C. O'Gorman, 'The study of entrepreneurship in Ireland', *Irish Journal of Management*; and a conference paper, C. O'Gorman and D. Curran, 'The supply of "productive entrepreneurship" in Ireland: 1960 to 2010: an analysis of established business owners in Ireland', 5th GEM (Global Entrepreneurship Monitor) Research Conference, Cartagena de las Indias, Columbia, 6–8 October 2011.
2. New business owners are entrepreneurs who at least part own and manage a new business that is between four and 42 months old and have not paid salaries for longer than this period. These new ventures are in the first 42 months after the new venture has been set up. The rate is for those in the adult population aged 18–64 years inclusive.

3. Aspiring entrepreneurs are those who expect to start a business in the next three years. The rate is for those in the adult population aged 18–64 years inclusive.
4. In addition to those people who are currently involved in the early stages of a business, there are also many people who have set up businesses that they have continued to own and manage. These people are included in the established business owner index which captures the percentage of people in the population who have set up businesses that they have continued to own and manage and which have paid wages or salaries for more than 42 months. The rate is for those in the adult population aged 18–64 years inclusive.
5. Closed a business in the previous 12 months and the business was discontinued.

REFERENCES

Acs, Z., C. O'Gorman, L. Szerb and S. Terjesen (2007), 'Could the Irish miracle be repeated in Hungary?', *Small Business Economics*, **28** (2–3), 123–42.

Audretsch, D., M. Carree, A. van Stel and R. Thurik (2002), 'Impeded industrial restructuring: the growth penalty', *Kyklos*, **55** (1), 81–98.

Barrett, S. (1995), 'Rent-seeking opportunities', in Andrew Burke (ed.), *Enterprise and the Irish Economy*, Dublin: Oak Tree Press, pp. 271–88.

Barry, F., J. Bradley and E. O'Malley (1999), 'Indigenous and foreign industry: characteristics and performance', in Frank Barry (ed.), *Understanding Ireland's Economic Growth*, London: Macmillan Press, pp. 45–74.

Baumol, W. (1990), 'Entrepreneurship: productive, unproductive, and destructive', *Journal of Political Economy*, **98** (5), 893–921.

Baumol, W. (1993), *Entrepreneurship, Management, and the Structure of Payoffs*, Cambridge, MA: MIT Press.

Bielenberg, A. and R. Ryan (2013), *An Economic History of Ireland Since Independence*, London: Routledge.

Burke, A. (1995), 'The re-emergence of entrepreneurial analyses', in Andrew Burke (ed.), *Enterprise and the Irish Economy*, Dublin: Oak Tree Press, pp. 3–20.

Carree, M., A. van Stel, R. Thurk and S. Wennekers (2002), 'Economic development and business ownership: an analysis using data of 23 OECD countries in the period of 1976–1996', *Small Business Economics*, **19** (3), 271–90.

Davidsson, P. and M. Henrekson (2002), 'Determinants of the prevalence of start-ups and high growth firms', *Small Business Economics*, **19** (2), 81–94.

Enterprise Strategy Group (2004), *Ahead of the Curve – Ireland's Place in the Global Economy*, Dublin: Government Publications.

Entrepreneurship Forum (2014), *Entrepreneurship in Ireland – Strengthening the Start-up Community*, Dublin: Government Publications.

Fitzsimons, P. and C. O'Gorman (2013), *Entrepreneurship in Ireland in 2012: Global Entrepreneurship Monitor, The Irish Annual Report*, Dublin: Dublin City University.

Fogarty, M. (1973), 'Irish entrepreneurs speak for themselves', Research Series, Number BS08, November, Dublin: Economic and Social Research Institute.

Forfas (2007), *Towards Developing an Entrepreneurship Policy for Ireland*, Dublin: Government Publications.

Industrial Policy Review Group (1992), *A Time for Change: Industrial Policy in the 1990s*, Dublin: Government Publications.

Johnson, P. (2004), 'Differences in regional firm formation rates: a decomposition analysis', *Entrepreneurship Theory and Practice*, **28** (5), 431–45.

Keating, P. and D. Desmond (1993), *Culture and Capitalism in Contemporary Ireland*, Aldershot: Avebury.
Kilby, P. (1971), *Entrepreneurship and Economic Development*, New York: Free Press.
Lee, J. (1989), *Ireland, 1912–1985: Politics and Society*, Cambridge: Cambridge University Press.
Lee, J., I. Clacher and K. Keasey (2012), 'Industrial policy as an engine of economic growth: a framework for analysis and evidence from South Korea (1960–96)', *Business History*, **54** (5), 713–40.
Lundström, A. and L. Stevenson (2005), *Entrepreneurship Policy – Theory and Practice*, New York: Springer.
Murphy, A. and F. Ruane (2004), 'Foreign direct investment in Ireland: an updated assessment', in Central Bank and Financial Services Authority, *Annual Report 2003*, Dublin, pp. 127–45.
Naveretti, G. and A. Venables (2004), 'FDI and the host economy: a case study of Ireland', in J. Haaland and A. Venables (eds), *Multinational Firms in the World Economy*, Princeton, NJ: Princeton University Press, pp. 187–216.
National Economic and Social Council (1982), *Review of Industrial Policy: A Report Prepared by the Telesis Consultancy Group*, Report No. 64, Dublin: Government Publications.
North, D. (1990), *Institutions, Institutional Change and Economic Performance*, Cambridge: Cambridge University Press.
O'Farrell, P. (1986), *Entrepreneurs and Industrial Change: the Process of Change in Irish Manufacturing*, Dublin: Irish Management Institute.
O'Gorman, C. and D. Curran (2014), 'Strategic transformations in large Irish-owned businesses', unpublished working paper, Dublin City University.
O'Malley, E., C. O'Gorman and J. Mooney (1997), 'The indigenous software industry: an application of Porter's cluster analysis', Research Paper Series, No. 3, Dublin: National Economic & Social Council.
Romanelli, E. and C. Schoonhoven (2001), 'The local origins of new firms', in C. Schoonhoven and E. Romanelli (eds), *The Entrepreneurship Dynamic: Origins of Entrepreneurship and the Evolution of Industries*, Stanford, CA: Stanford University Press, pp. 40–67.
Reynolds, P. (1999), 'Creative destruction: source or symptom of economic growth', in Z. Acs, B. Carlsson and C. Carlsson (eds), *Entrepreneurship, Small and Medium-Sized Enterprises and the Macroeconomy*, Cambridge: Cambridge University Press, pp. 97–136.
Spencer, J., T. Murtha and S. Lenway (2005), 'How governments matter to new industry creation', *Academy of Management Review*, **30** (2), 321–37.
Storey, D. (2000), 'Six steps to heaven: evaluating the impact of public policies to support small businesses in developed economics', in D. Sexton and H. Landström (eds), *Blackwell Handbook of Entrepreneurship*, Oxford: Blackwell, pp. 176–93.
Verheul, I., S. Wennekers, D. Audretsch and R. Thurik (2002), 'An eclectic theory of entrepreneurship: policies, institutions and culture', in D. Audretsch, R. Thurik, I. Verheul and S. Wennekers (eds), *Entrepreneurship: Determinants and Policy in a European–US Comparison*, Boston, MA, USA and Dordrecht, Netherlands: Springer, pp. 11–81.

5. Towards Europe: the Small Business Charter and SME policy upgrading in the Western Balkans

Stephen Roper and Anita Richter

INTRODUCTION

Since 2003 the seven countries comprising the Western Balkans have been involved in a process of small business policy development following their adoption of the European Charter for SMEs (hereafter referred as the Charter).[1] The implementation of the Charter process has been monitored through an Organisation for Economic Co-operation and Development (OECD)-led process called the SME Policy Index. The SME Policy Index has involved three major policy benchmarking exercises in 2007, 2009 and 2012 and a more continuous series of capacity-building workshops and policy networking events.[2] The main aim of the SME Policy Index – as stated in 2007 – was 'to rank countries' performance and to identify regional and thematic trends in Charter implementation' (OECD, 2007: 14). This should have enabled the Western Balkans countries (WBCs) to 'Learn from each other's experience; identify good practices in policy elaboration and implementation; identify strengths and weaknesses at national and regional levels; improve policy planning; and, contribute to the definition of policy priorities and targets' (OECD, 2007: 14).

The implementation of the SME Charter process across the seven very diverse WBCs provides an interesting natural experiment in policy transfer. Essentially the same development process or set of opportunities has been applied in each country. Has this led to policy upgrading and convergence? Which countries have proved most receptive? Or, at least, which have benefited most from the type of policy development opportunities offered by the SME Charter process? Was it those WBCs – Croatia, Serbia – which already enjoyed relatively well-resourced and developed policy institutions? Or economies such as Bosnia and Herzgovina or Kosovo, with less well-developed and resourced policy frameworks?

The remainder of this chapter is organised as follows. First it provides an overview of the WBCs since 2007, the time of the first SME Policy Index. This emphasises the diversity of the seven WBCs. The following section examines the Charter Process through the lens of the literature on policy transfer and emphasises the determinants of effective transfer mechanisms. Here, our approach reflects that adopted by Xheneti and Kitching (2011) in their discussion of Albania. The chapter then profiles the SME Charter Process with a focus on the benchmarks implicit in the SME Policy Index, before examining the impact of the Charter process – at least as it is reflected in the SME Policy Index benchmarks. The final section concludes with an overview of the effectiveness of the Charter process and Policy Index and evaluates its transferability to other geographic contexts.

STUDY REGION: THE WESTERN BALKAN COUNTRIES

The focuses of our analysis are the seven countries of the Western Balkans: Croatia, Serbia, Macedonia, Albania, Kosovo, Montenegro, and Bosnia and Herzegovina. Aside from Albania, which experienced a destabilising financial crisis in 1997, the recent history of the other WBCs has been marked by conflict during the 1990s, and a subsequent and difficult period of economic, social and political transition. In more recent years the aspiration of the WBCs to join the European Union (EU) – formally recognised by the EU itself in the Thessaloniki Summit of 2003 – has been a significant influence on policy development.[3] However, despite significant aid and assistance, and continued external support for policy and institutional development, social and economic development across the region has been uneven. Croatia joined the EU in 2013. Montenegro, Serbia and Macedonia are candidate countries, with Albania, Bosnia and Herzegovina and Kosovo remaining 'potential candidates'.[4]

More generally, the WBCs continue to undergo a process of transition to a market economy with the steady privatisation of state-owned companies and unbalanced business demography. In Serbia, for example, while some larger firms have made a successful transition from the public to private sectors their medium-sized suppliers have often fared less well. This has led to an industrial structure dominated by small (often micro) firms with relatively few medium-sized and larger companies.[5] Despite the difficulties of the transition process the WBCs experienced rapid growth prior to the 2008 economic crisis due primarily to growth in telecommunications, wholesale and retail trades, construction and finance. This economic growth was accompanied by rapid structural change, with significant inward investment in banking, finance and other consumer-related services. Fundamental macroeconomic issues remain across the region, however, including significant unemployment, persistent trade deficits and a continuing dependence on agricultural exports (Table 5.1).

Structural changes have been accompanied by important developments in small and medium-sized enterprise (SME) policy since 2003. Targeted primarily at combating unemployment and stimulating growth in more peripheral areas, these developments have focused on education and training for entrepreneurship, skills availability, information provision for small firms and strengthening the technological capacity of existing SMEs. In Serbia, for example, the government's 2008 Strategy for Developing Competitive and Innovative SMEs and related 2009 Action Plan identified five key pillars where policy development was necessary: incubators as an aid to business start-up, skills and human resources, finance and taxation including the development of equity financing, clusters and business networks, and the regulatory environment. Promotion of a culture of enterprise has also been seen as important across the region. In Serbia again, for example, the Serbian Agency for the Development of SMEs and Entrepreneurship has organised the annual International Trade Fair of Entrepreneurship 'Business Base', regional and local enterprise events, and the regular publication of the widely distributed *SME News*.[6] Donor organisations also organise enterprise promotion activities among high-school and university students across the WBCs.

Although SME policy has developed rapidly in recent years across the WBCs there has until recently been little progress in the development of public support for innovation, a key focus of the EU Small Business Act[7] (SBA). Such policy initiatives as there have been have tended to be small scale and focused on raising the profile of innovation. More fundamental issues such as low levels of research and development (R&D) investment and the particularly low proportion of R&D undertaken in the corporate sector remain largely unaddressed.

POLICY TRANSFER AND THE EVIDENCE BASE

International best practice in policy development has emphasised the role of evidence-based policy formulation, that is:

> evidence-informed policy is about decisions based on careful use of the most up-to-date evidence. There has been relatively little prior discussion of the nature of policy transfer in SME or entrepreneurship policy (Xheneti and Kitching, 2011). Making policies and decisions in this way increases the success of policies, their value for money and their impact by basing decisions on what we know.[8]

Table 5.1   Region data for the WBCs, 2007, 2009 and 2012

	Croatia			Albania			Serbia		
	2007	2009	2012	2007	2009	2012	2007	2009	2012
Demography									
Population (total, million)	4.44	4.43	4.27	3.17	3.15	3.16	7.38	7.32	7.22
Life expectancy at birth, total (years)	75.7	76.2	76.9	76.5	76.8	77.4	73.4	73.7	75.2
Population growth (annual %)	−0.09	−0.11	−0.30	−0.42	−0.17	0.26	−0.41	−0.40	−0.48
Economy									
GDP per capita (constant 2005 USD)	11.1	10.6	10.5	2.9	3.3	3.5	3.7	3.8	3.9
GDP growth (annual %)	5.1	−6.9	−2.0	5.9	3.3	1.6	5.4	−3.5	−1.7
Agriculture, value added (% of GDP)	4.9	5.1	5.0	20.5	19.2	18.3	10.3	9.6	–
Industry, value added (% of GDP)	27.5	27.5	26.3	18.8	18.2	15.6	28.3	27.9	–
Services, etc., value added (% of GDP)	67.6	67.4	68.8	60.7	62.6	66.1	61.4	62.4	–
Inflation, GDP deflator (annual %)	4.1	2.9	2.0	2.0	2.4	3.0	10.1	5.9	5.5
Labour force participation rate (% population)	53.1	52.7	51.3	56.7	55.2	55.1	54.9	53.0	52.3
Unemployment, total (% labour force)	9.6	9.1	15.8	13.5	13.8	14.7	18.1	16.6	19.6
Trade and investment									
Gross capital formation (% of GDP)	29.4	24.9	19.4	29.8	28.9	24.7	29.0	22.9	–
Imports of goods/ services (% of GDP)	49.5	40.1	42.7	55.0	53.5	49.1	54.7	46.9	–
Exports of goods/ services (% of GDP)	42.3	39.7	43.4	28.8	32.4	31.3	30.5	36.2	–

Source: Data from the World Development Indicators Database (World Bank, n.d.).

At best, this type of policy formulation requires a well-developed analytical capability within government – and/or the national academic community – and a consistent approach to the use of evidence in policy-making. This contrasts with the situation in the WBCs as Bartlett (2013: 456–7) suggests: 'In most WBCs there is no permanent civil service that could carry policy lessons from one administration to the next . . . Poor pay and conditions have also contributed to high turnover among civil servants,

Macedonia			Montenegro			Bosnia and Herzegovina			Kosovo		
2007	2009	2012	2007	2009	2012	2007	2009	2012	2007	2009	2012
2.10	2.10	2.11	0.62	0.62	0.62	3.87	3.85	3.83	1.73	1.76	1.81
74.3	74.6	75.0	73.9	74.3	74.6	75.4	75.7	76.1	69.2	69.6	70.5
0.13	0.09	0.08	0.15	0.12	0.07	−0.17	−0.20	−0.14	0.80	0.80	0.90
3.2	3.3	3.5	4.4	4.4	4.6	3.2	3.3	3.4	2.4	2.6	2.8
6.1	−0.9	−0.3	10.7	−5.7	−0.5	6.8	−2.9	−0.7	8.3	3.0	2.7
10.6	11.2	11.5	9.1	10.0	10.1	8.8	7.8	8.4	12.0	12.0	14.0
31.0	27.5	26.0	20.9	20.1	20.1	28.6	28.3	24.8	20.0	20.0	19.5
58.5	61.4	62.6	70.0	69.9	69.8	62.6	63.9	66.8	68.0	68.0	66.5
7.4	0.7	0.0	12.7	2.4	1.9	5.7	0.1	0.6	2.4	−0.3	2.4
54.5	55.4	55.1	52.1	51.7	50.0	44.2	44.6	45.3	–	–	–
34.9	32.2	31.0	19.4	19.1	19.6	29.7	24.1	28.2	–	–	–
24.6	26.2	28.6	33.8	27.1	17.9	31.0	21.0	22.1	25.8	28.8	29.6
70.8	61.0	75.5	86.0	65.4	66.1	79.9	54.4	55.1	51.7	52.3	52.8
52.4	46.6	53.2	43.7	34.7	42.4	43.3	35.5	31.2	15.8	20.3	18.4

discouraging project implementation and reducing the effectiveness of the public administration'. Political influence on policy-making may also be disruptive, with Bartlett (2013: 458) again commenting: 'the countries of the Western Balkans appear to have especially weak public administrations with high degrees of discretionary behaviour and political interference'.

For new countries, or those lacking a domestic policy analysis and evaluation capability, international policy transfer drawing on experience elsewhere may provide an alternative means of policy development to evidence-based policy-making. Policy transfer has been defined as the process by which 'knowledge about how policies, administrative arrangements, institutions and administrative arrangements, institutions and ideas in one political setting is used in the development of policies, administrative arrangements, institutions and ideas in another political setting' (Dolowitz and Marsh, 2000: 5). International policy transfer may enable economies to leap-frog or at least accelerate some of the development stages which have characterised free market economies. Williamson (2000), for example, suggests that establishing appropriate institutions and organisations for economic development might involve a 10–100-year time horizon in free market economies shaped primarily by endogenous development processes (Williamson, 2000: 597, Fig. 1). Policy transfer – through mechanisms such as the SME Charter Process – may help to speed up this development and avoid policy mistakes.

Modalities or mechanisms for policy transfer vary widely, however, with Stone (2012) identifying five alternative modalities involving: the transfer of broad policy goals or ideas; institutions; regulatory or judicial tools; ideas and ideologies; and, finally, people. The SME Charter has focused primarily on the first two of these modalities involving: (1) the transfer of policy goals and ideas relating to SME support and development; and (2) the transfer of specific institutional forms such as incubators, science and technology parks and so on which have been reflected in specific indicators in the SME Policy Index.

Issues also arise in the effectiveness of alternative policy transfer mechanisms. Bartlett (2013) identifies four specific issues. The first relates to whether policy transfer is coercive or voluntary, with Unalan (2009: 439) arguing that 'one of the key factors we need to understand is what drives actors to engage in the process, as these reasons can influence the whole process'. Purely voluntary policy transfers include mechanisms such as OECD Territorial Reviews which are conducted by invitation of the host national or regional government as a means of identifying international best practice of relevance to local policy development. On the other hand, the structural adjustment programmes of the World Bank and International Monetary Fund (IMF) might be considered 'coercive' (Stone, 2012). In the EU enlargement process – of which the SME Charter Process is part – coercion is not direct, but may instead be seen as indirect, with the WBCs required to Europeanise SME policy as part of the EU candidacy process. In the context of policy transfer from the EU to Turkey (interestingly, a participant in the 2012 SME Policy Index) Unalan develops the idea of 'obligation-based policy transfer' reflecting the 'extent to which the EU's policy's obligations are incorporated, or as the degree to which domestic institutions are changed in order to comply with the relevant policy requirements' (Unalan, 2009: 444).

The question of the extent of compulsion or obligation in any policy transfer activity is important as it may influence outcomes. As Bartlett (2013: 460) comments, the question is 'how far the appearance of voluntary transfer based upon the mechanisms of participation, ownership and consultation in fact disguise[s] more or less effectively the practice of coercive policy transfer'. The difficulty is that coercive policy transfer, whether any coercion is direct or indirect, and participation therefore not voluntary, may result in a nominal or minimal compliance with the expectations of the policy transfer agencies while achieving otherwise ineffectual outcomes (Dimitrova, 2002; Noutcheva, 2009).[9]

A second aspect of effectiveness is whether policy transfer processes such as the SME Charter Process, which are embedded within wider agendas like the EU enlargement process, lead to policy convergence and an inappropriate 'one size fits all' pattern of policy development. Or whether the structure of the SME Charter process is flexible or broad enough to allow for policy divergence, reflecting specific national priorities, requirements and resources. A third, and related, issue concerns the potential for policy transfer to result in policy failure due to the implementation of measures which are poorly aligned with local needs or context, where conflicts exist between policy transfer organisations. Xheneti and Kitching (2011) emphasise the lack of consistency between policy transfer activities in Albania and the needs of the local economy, a point which it could be argued is relevant to a number of the WBCs. A further barrier to the effectiveness of policy transfer activity is where stand-alone policy initiatives are poorly coordinated with, for example, a lack of consistency and coordination between the activities of different international donors.

Finally, there is the question of whether policy transfer processes such as the SME Charter complement local development processes or displace them, reducing local policy learning. For example, key aspects of policy learning are monitoring and evaluation, and the feedback of evaluation results. How effective has the Charter been in enhancing the potential for policy learning in the different WBCs? Or has the Charter process itself crowded out or discouraged more local evaluation activity? It has been argued that, in the context of the WBCs where local administrations may be 'especially weak', the 'policy making process is [particularly] vulnerable to the imposition of policy advice from external advisors and donor agencies and weakens the ability of the domestic civil servants to engage in long-term policy learning process' (Bartlett, 2013: 457). In the context of the SME Policy Index, however, the experience of the authors has been rather different, suggesting that external policy support has largely complemented or reinforced existing policy-making activity. The self-assessment element of the Policy Index, in particular, has provided a framework within which governments are required to reflect on their existing policy measures, itself a learning process (see also the more in-depth discussion of the Albanian experience in Xheneti and Kitching, 2011).

THE SME CHARTER PROCESS

The SME Charter Process is a predominantly political process led by the European Commission to which EU Member States and EU Enlargement countries have committed to improve the business environment for SMEs. To monitor the implementation of the Charter the European Commission mandated the OECD and partners to develop a methodology and indicators: the SME Policy Index. This has comprised two main strands: a periodic policy benchmarking exercise, and a more ongoing process of policy advice, development and knowledge sharing.

In each of the WBCs, National Charter Co-ordinators – typically government officials – have played a key role in contributing to the development of the Charter process, coordinating national inputs to the SME Policy Index benchmarking exercises and ensuring the engagement in the Charter process of SME policy stakeholders. In the 2009 policy benchmarking exercise the role of the Charter Coordinators was complemented by independent national assessments primarily by consultants located in each country, an approach also adopted in 2012.[10] For the 2012 assessment the structure of the SME Policy Index was also changed and extended to reflect the provisions of the Small Business Act (SBA) for Europe[11] and incorporating new policy areas such as women's entrepreneurship, bankruptcy procedures, public procurement and green growth for the first time (OECD, 2012: 19).[12]

The SME Policy Index

The policy approach underpinning the SBA assessment is that SME policy consists of a mix of horizontal and targeted policies. Horizontal policies are defined as policies intended to improve the operational environment for all enterprises, such as regulatory simplification and improvement in the regulatory framework for access to finance. Targeted measures aim at specific segments of the enterprise population, such as innovative enterprises, start-ups or export-oriented enterprises (OECD, 2012: 19).

Policy benchmarking through the SME Policy Index works by mapping the extent of policy implementation in a particular area on a five-point scale. The 2007 SME Policy Index included 56 indicators on which each country was ranked on a five-point scale. The policy areas covered in the 2007 and 2009 Policy Indices were:

1. Education and training for entrepreneurship.
2. Cheaper and faster start-up.
3. Better legislation and regulation.
4. Availability of skills.
5. Improving on-line access.
6. Getting more out of the single market.
7. Taxation and financial matters.
8. Strengthening the technological capacity of small enterprises.
9. Successful e-business models and top-class business support.
10. Developing stronger, more effective representation of small enterprises' interests.

In 2009 the number of individual indicators was increased, and by 2012 had reached 108 individual indicators. In 2012 the SME Policy Index was also restructured to match the ten Principles of the EU Small Business Act. For the first time this meant that the Policy Index included material on women's enterprise, public procurement and green innovation.

Changes to the indicators used between the three benchmark assessments mean that only a subset of 37 indicators remain unchanged between the 2007, 2009 and 2012 Policy Indices, and the values of these on the five-point scale are reported in Tables 5.1 and 5.2. For example, one area of policy development which appears in each of the Charter reports relates to the development of business incubators.[13] The different levels of this indicator are as follows:

- Level 1 – No incubators in place and no plans to establish them.
- Level 2 – Strategy on incubators under discussion or local initiatives in preparation.
- Level 3 – Strategy on incubators approved: detailed proposals and budget allocations either at local or national level. Pilot incubators in operation. Focus on job creation, no exit strategies.
- Level 4 – Level 3 plus several incubators in operation, out of the experimental phase. Provisions of basic services, some incubators used to foster innovation. Partial implementation of OECD guidelines on business incubators.
- Level 5 – Level 4 plus network of incubators throughout the economy. Focus on innovation, provision of high-quality services and existence of exit strategies. OECD guidelines widely implemented.

It is perhaps useful to consider the implicit assumptions reflected in these levels. First, the inclusion of this area of policy development within the SME Policy Index, and the implementation profile implied by the levels implicitly suggests that incubators are a significant and necessary element of SME policy. While incubators certainly are widespread across the OECD, robust evidence of the extent of additionality from incubators is actually rather limited (Schwartz, 2013). Moreover, the notion of an 'incubator' itself varies widely, from serviced office or factory space to supportive virtual networks. The levels also imply that the value of incubators can be assessed in a stand-alone sense. However, the evidence suggests that incubators' success is strongly conditional on the wider institutional setting; working best, for example, when they are linked to venture capital provision (Avnimelech et al., 2007). Despite these potential concerns the indicator suggests that significant progress has taken place across the WBCs in terms of incubator development (Table 5.2). Croatia was placed at Level 3.5 in the 2007 assessment, with subsequent extensions of the incubator network leading Croatia to reach Level 4 in 2009 and 2012. Albania on other hand started at Level 1 in 2007, with no incubators or incubator strategy. By 2012, significant progress had been made in Albania in terms of the development of pilot incubators, placing the country at Level 3.5 (Table 5.2).

Another indicator, relating to a rather different aspect of SME policy development which also appears in each of the three SME Policy Indices (that is, 2007, 2009 and 2012), relates to the creation and operation of an SME policy implementation agency. Here the five levels are defined as follows:

- Level 1 – No SME policy implementation agency with an executive role exists.
- Level 2 – Government considering the establishment of an SME policy implementation agency.
- Level 3 – SME implementation agency established. Staff, structure and budget in place. Range of output to be covered by agency being drafted.
- Level 4 – SME implementation agency fully operational and covers a range of activities with measurable outcomes. Staffing is complete and the required expertise is in place. Solid implementation record of SME strategy based on achievements of time-bound targets as detailed in action plan.
- Level 5 – SME implementation entity is the main body for implementation of the SME strategy, operating with full political support. The entity has a clear reporting system in place and a recognised

Table 5.2   Scores in SME Policy Index for the WBCs, 2007, 2009 and 2012

	Croatia			Albania			Montenegro			Kosovo			Serbia			Macedonia			Bosnia and Herzegovina		
	2007	2009	2012	2007	2009	2012	2007	2009	2012	2007	2009	2012	2007	2009	2012	2007	2009	2012	2007	2009	2012
I Institutional and regulatory framework																					
1 SME development strategy	4	4	4	2	2.5	3.5	4	3.5	3	3.5	2	2	2.5	3.5	4	3.5	3	3.5	2	2	2.5
2 SME policy implementation agency	3.5	3.5	4	3	4	4.5	4.5	3.5	3.5	3.5	2	2	4	4.5	4.5	3.5	3.5	3.5	2	2	2
3 Intergovernmental coordination in policy elaboration	4	4	4	4	3	4	4	4	4	4	2	2	3	4	4	4	4	4	2	2	2
4 Use of regulatory impact analysis	4	4.5	4.5	1.5	4.5	4.5	5	1.5	3	4.5	1.5	1.5	4.5	4.5	5	1.5	3	4.5	1.5	1.5	1.5
5 Business simplification	3	4	3.5	3	2	3	4.5	1	4	4	2	3	2	3	4.5	1	4	4	2	3	3
6 Silence-is-consent principle	1	1.5	1	2	2	2.5	5	1	2.5	5	1	1	2	2.5	5	1	2.5	5	1	1	1
7 Public–private consultation frequency	3.5	4	4	3	2	4	4	3	3	3.5	2	2	2	4	4	3	3	3.5	2	2	2
8 Public–private consultation representation	4	4	4	3	2	3	3	3	3	3.5	3	2	2	3	3	3	3	3.5	3	2	2
Average	3.38	3.69	3.63	2.69	2.75	3.63	4.25	2.56	3.25	3.94	1.94	1.94	2.75	3.63	4.25	2.56	3.25	3.94	1.94	1.94	2.00

Table 5.2 (continued)

		Croatia			Albania			Montenegro			Kosovo			Serbia			Macedonia			Bosnia and Herzgovina		
		2007	2009	2012	2007	2009	2012	2007	2009	2012	2007	2009	2012	2007	2009	2012	2007	2009	2012	2007	2009	2012
II	*Business registration*																					
9	Number of days: company registration	3.5	3.5	4	2.5	4	4	4	4	5	5	3	3	4	4	4	4	5	5	3	3	3
10	Number of administrative steps: company registration	5	5	5	3	4	4	4	5	5	5	3	3	5	4	4	5	5	5	3	3	3
11	Official costs: company registration	1	1	1	3	3	3	4	3	3	4	1	1.5	3	3	4	3	3	4	1	1.5	1
12	Admin. identification numbers in dealing with public admin.	4	4	5	5	4	4	2	3	4	5	3	3	3	4	2	3	4	5	3	3	3
13	Number of days: overall registration process	1	1	3	1	2	2	3	2	3	4	1	1	2	2	3	2	3	4	1	1	1
14	Costs of registration: overall registration period	1	1	2	1	1	2	2	2	3	4	1	1	1	2	2	2	3	4	1	1	1
15	Minimal capital requirements: overall registration	2	3	3	2	4	4	4	1	5	5	1	2	4	4	4	1	5	5	1	2	2
16	Online registration	3	4	4	3	3	3.5	4	1.5	2.5	2.5	1.5	1.5	1.5	3.5	2.5	1.5	2.5	2.5	1.5	1.5	1.5
	Average	2.56	2.81	3.38	2.31	3.13	3.31	3.19	2.69	3.81	4.31	1.81	2.00	3.13	3.31	3.19	2.69	3.81	4.31	1.81	2.00	1.94

III SME support services

#	Item												Average
17	Tax returns online	4	4	4	1	3	3	4	3	3	2.5	1.5	4
18	Online information for SMEs	4	4.5	4.5	2	3	3	4	3	3	3	2	2.5
19	Electronic signatures	4	4	4	1	3	3.5	4	3	3	3.5	2	2
20	Range of business services	5	5	5	2	2	2.5	3.5	3	2.5	3.5	3	3
21	Availability and accessibility of information	4	4	4.5	2	3	4	4	3	3	4	2	2.5
22	Business incubators	3.5	4	4	1	3	3.5	3.5	3	3	3.5	3.5	3.5
	Average	4.08	4.25	4.33	1.50	2.50	3.08	3.83	3.00	2.92	3.17	2.25	2.92

IV Access to finance (sources and framework)

#	Item												Average
23	Credit guarantee schemes	3.5	3	3.5	2.5	3	3	3	3.5	5	2	2	3.5
24	Leasing	4	4	4.5	3	5	4	4	4	4	3.5	2	3
25	Availability of risk capital	4	4	3.5	2	3	3	3	4	4	3.5	3.5	1
26	Cadastre	4.5	4.5	4.5	3	3	3	3.5	3	3	3	3	4
27	Collateral requirements	3.5	4	3.5	2	3	4	3	3	3	1.5	2.5	3
28	Law on bankruptcy	4	4	4	3	3	4	4	4	3	3.5	3.5	4
	Average	3.92	3.92	3.92	2.58	3.33	3.50	3.42	3.58	3.67	3.08	2.58	3.08

V Enterprise skills and training

29	Training needs analysis	2	2.5	3	2	1	2.5	3	1.5	1.5	3	1.5	2

Table 5.2 (continued)

	Croatia			Albania			Montenegro			Kosovo			Serbia			Macedonia			Bosnia and Herzegovina		
	2007	2009	2012	2007	2009	2012	2007	2009	2012	2007	2009	2012	2007	2009	2012	2007	2009	2012	2007	2009	2012
30 Enterprise/start-up training	3	2.5	2	1	2	3	2	1	2	2	2	1	2	3	2	1	2	2	2	1	2
31 Quality assurance	2	3.5	3.5	1	3	3	3.5	1	2.5	4	2	2	1	3	3.5	1	2.5	4	2	2	3
32 Access to training	4	4	4	2	3	3	3	3	3	4.5	2	2.5	3	3	3	3	3	4.5	2	2.5	3
33 Entrepreneurial learning (non-formal)	3.5	4.5	4	2	2	1.5	4	2	1.5	4	3.5	1.5	2	1.5	4	2	1.5	4	3.5	1.5	1
Average	2.90	3.40	3.30	1.60	1.80	2.60	3.10	1.60	2.10	3.50	2.20	1.70	1.80	2.60	3.10	1.60	2.10	3.50	2.20	1.70	2.20
VI Technology and innovation																					
34 Interfirm clusters and networks	4	4	3.5	2	3	4	2.5	4	3	1.5	2	3	3	4	2.5	4	3	1.5	2	3	2
35 Science parks/clusters	4	4	4	2	3	4	3	4	3	1	2	3	3	4	3	4	3	1	2	3	3.5
36 Intellectual property rights	3.5	4.5	4.5	3.5	3.5	4	4	3.5	4	4	3	3	3.5	4	4	3.5	4	4	3	3	3
Average	3.83	4.17	4.00	2.50	3.17	4.00	3.17	3.83	3.33	2.17	2.33	3.00	3.17	4.00	3.17	3.83	3.33	2.17	2.33	3.00	2.83
VII Internationalisation of SMEs																					
37 Export promotion programmes	4.00	4.00	4.00	2.50	3.00	4.50	4.50	3.00	3.50	4.00	2.00	2.00	3.00	4.50	4.50	3.00	3.50	4.00	2.00	2.00	2.50

Sources: OECD (2007, 2009, 2012).

advocacy and policy advice role. The entity is well funded, wide-reaching and its activities have proven to be effective in supporting SME development with measurable outcomes.

As of 2012, none of the WBCs were recorded as reaching Level 5 on this indicator (Table 5.2). Serbia has reached the highest level of convergence in this direction, being classified as Level 4.5 in 2012, up from Level 4 in 2007. At the other extreme, Bosnia and Herzegovina has made little progress in this aspect of SME policy development, ranked on Level 2 in both the 2007 and 2012 assessments (Table 5.2). Two points are perhaps worth making here. First, as in the case of the incubator indicator, there is a clear presumption in the levels that having a specialist SME policy implementation agency is valuable. This may indeed be the case – although countries such as Germany and the United Kingdom (UK) have no such agency – but there is no very clear evidence base upon which this presumption is based. Second, the very different nature of the SME agency and incubator indicators highlight a broader issue in the SME Policy Index, with some indicators relating to very specific legislative or regulatory issues (for example, cost of registering a company, recognition of electronic signatures) and others relating to broad areas of policy-making or development (for example, availability of risk capital, export promotion programmes).

Knowledge Transfer

Policy transfer may include a sharing of both policy ideas and knowledge exchange, with the latter primarily a face-to-face process. Reflecting the earlier comments by Bartlett (2013) on the weakness of the capabilities of civil services in some WBCs, the SME Charter Process has also included an explicit objective to develop SME policy design and implementation capability. This has been undertaken through engagement between local policy-makers and staff from the implementation bodies – primarily the OECD and European Training Foundation (ETF) and European Commission (EC) – the involvement of international experts, and networking and policy learning between the WBCs. For example, as part of each of the three Charter assessments, bilateral meetings have been held between the implementation bodies and local government representatives to prioritise policy developments (OECD, 2007: 30). In the 2009 and 2012 reports additional thematic analyses (on policy for fast growth and local economic development) were also conducted alongside the main SME Policy Index analysis with the support of subject specialists. The group of Charter Coordinators, and their colleagues, have also met every few months since the inception of the Charter process in a number of thematic (for example, enterprise, investment, tax, education, innovation policy) and sector-specific working groups (for example, automotive, agribusiness, tourism) to exchange experiences across the region. In addition, they have participated in capacity-building activities to enhance skills in designing, implementing and monitoring policies and instruments in support of small business development. The common experience of the Charter process, and the engagement with thematic and sector working groups, has led to the development of strong network relationships among the Charter Coordinators.

Strengths and Limitations of the SME Policy Index

Perhaps the key strength of the Policy Index assessment process is that it actively engages policy-makers through self-evaluation and policy dialogue at national and regional levels. Further, it enables comparison among the WBCs and benchmarking against international best practices. The regional assessment conducted every two to three years also permits the measurement of progress over time, the identification of gaps and the proposal of reforms to overcome challenges. The obverse of the uniformity of the Policy Index and the application of the same framework in each country is that it does not necessarily reflect the needs of any individual economy (Xheneti and Kitching, 2011).

It is important to recognise, however, that the focus of the SME Policy Index has been on institution-building and policy processes rather than the effectiveness of policies and their impact on SMEs. No conclusions related to the actual performance of policies can be drawn even where countries have reached a solid level of institutional set-up and policy implementation. The Index has also relied strongly on qualitative information and has not fully integrated national business statistics, policy data and company-level data in the assessment to measure the performance of policies on the ground.

As the data situation in the WBC has improved over the last decade, and the need to deepen the assessment has emerged, the original methodology has been revised for the 2015 SBA assessment cycle. The five-level indicator grid has been replaced by a detailed questionnaire, consisting of closed (binary and multi-choice) and open questions to collect both qualitative and quantitative data in the 2015 SBA assessment cycle. Hence, with the revision, greater emphasis will be placed on the quality of policies and their accordance with good practices. Business demographics, policy data and firm perceptions data will also provide context and a broader overview of the policy performance.

SME POLICY DEVELOPMENTS AND THE CHARTER

Assessing the impact of the SME Charter Process is difficult due primarily to the difficulty of constructing a realistic counterfactual and ensuring that any policy change which is observed can be attributed to the Charter Process. Even if an effective counterfactual could be developed – and issues of attribution resolved – however, any realistic estimate of the cost-effectiveness of the Charter initiative is likely to be elusive due to the difficulty of estimating the costs involved in countries' implementation of the Charter and SME Policy Index, and the benefits which have been (and will be) derived from related policy developments. Any consideration of the impact of the Charter process must therefore remain tentative.[14]

Here we consider two potential indicators of impact derived from the SME Policy Index itself. We first consider progress on the 37 indicators which are common to all three Policy Index assessments (Tables 5.1 and 5.2). For some key aspects of SME policy these provide a relatively fine-grained indication of policy development over the 2007 to 2012 period. Second, we derive from these 37 individual indicators a simple (unweighted) average benchmark for each country for 2007, 2009 and 2012. Comparing these across countries provides an indication of the extent to which SME policy implementation across the WBCs has either converged or diverged over the 2007 to 2012 period (Bartlett, 2013).

Progress in Individual Policy Areas

Since the endorsement of the SME Charter process the WBCs have made consistent and significant progress in strengthening the institutional and regulatory framework for SME policy-making, in simplifying business registration procedures, and enhancing skills and training structures for small firms. On the other hand, more unequal progress is evident in the development of business support services, improving access to finance, and supporting technological transfer and innovation in SMEs. To some extent this divergence can be explained by the nature of the implied reforms and the costs involved. Light-touch and cost-effective reforms can be implemented in the short to mid-term; complex and resource-intensive changes require more time and coordination. For example, the number of days, administrative steps and costs involved in business registration can be reduced quickly without requiring significant resources. Over the 2007 to 2012 period, for example, Macedonia reduced the number of administrative steps necessary to start a business from ten to three, while Albania reduced the number of days it takes to start a business from 39 to

5.5. These simplifications in the business registration process resulted in a progression by two levels for Albania (from 2.3 to 3.3) and 1.6 levels for Macedonia (from 2.7 to 4.3).[15]

On the other hand, underwriting credit guarantee schemes or establishing science parks are more complex and costly policy instruments, which place a higher financial burden on governments and involve more stakeholders. With regards to a credit guarantee facility, for example, typically three parties are involved: a government agency (as regulator, guarantor), banks (as credit providers) and SMEs (as credit receivers). This risk-sharing mechanism is particularly valuable in those economies with a vulnerable financial market and transitioning market economy. While the WBCs enhanced their overall performance in the access to finance dimension between 2007 and 2009 (from 3.0 to 3.3), it deteriorated between 2009 and 2012 (from 3.3 to 3.1). This deterioration can be explained primarily by the financial crisis, which impacted severely on SMEs in the region, restricted bank lending and eroded international capital inflows.

Progress in Overall SME Policy Development

Averaging the 37 indicators in Tables 5.1 and 5.2 into a single number policy index provides an indication of the overall development of SME policy in each of the WBCs over the 2007 to 2012 period. It also provides a ranking for countries on the basis of each of the SME Policy Indices (Table 5.3). In each case, as for the individual indicators in the Policy Index, the single number indices range from values 1 to 5 with higher values representing better-developed SME policy regimes. Overall, all countries have converged closer to EU SME policy practices and standards between 2007 and 2012 but the pace of convergence and progress have been uneven across the region. In 2007 Croatia was the only country with sound frameworks and institutions in place and providing a number of services to the SME population (combined score 3.4). The other six WB countries were in the institution-building phase, with Montenegro, Macedonia and Serbia being more advanced (c.2.8) than Albania, Bosnia and Herzegovina, and Kosovo, being in an early stage of SME development (c.2.2). In contrast, by 2012 five countries achieved good levels of policy convergence (average 3.5). Only Kosovo and Bosnia and Herzegovina were still lagging behind (c.2.4). In these five years the biggest progress was achieved by Albania (+1.1), followed by Serbia and Macedonia (+0.7).

Looking at the single number indices, four other observations stand out. First, as might have been anticipated given the individual indices discussed earlier, Croatia tops the rankings, as having consistently the best-developed SME policy regime. Kosovo and Bosnia and Herzegovina hold

Table 5.3 Single number SME policy indices by country, 2007, 2009 and 2012

	2007			2009			2012		Change in ranking
	Index value	Rank		Index value	Rank		Index value	Rank	
Croatia	3.40	1	Croatia	3.64	1	Croatia	3.73	1	+0
Montenegro	2.88	2	Serbia	3.36	2	Serbia	3.57	2	+2
Macedonia	2.82	3	Macedonia	3.23	3	Macedonia	3.53	3	+0
Serbia	2.79	4	Albania	2.95	4	Albania	3.37	4	+1
Albania	2.23	5	Montenegro	2.93	5	Montenegro	3.21	5	−2
Kosovo	2.17	6	B & H	2.36	6	Kosovo	2.46	6	0
B & H	2.14	7	Kosovo	2.35	7	B & H	2.43	7	0
Average	2.63		Average	2.97		Average	3.19		

Note: Indices are based on the measures included in Table 5.2.

Sources: OECD (2007, 2009, 2012).

up the table in each of the three assessments. Second, across each of the countries and each of the periods between assessments (that is, 2007–10, 2009–12) the single number indices increase, suggesting improvements in the development of the SME policy regime.[16] More interesting perhaps are the contrasts between the progress made by individual economies: those gaining in terms of the ranking are Serbia and Albania, with Montenegro losing some ground during both the 2007–09 and 2009–12 periods. Finally it is interesting to note that in 2012 the single number indices for Kosovo and Bosnia and Herzegovina (BiH) take broadly the same numerical values as those of Serbia and Albania in 2007. One interpretation is that SME policy development in Kosovo and BiH lagged that in Serbia and Albania by around five years. A similar comparison would suggest that SME policy development in Albania as of 2012 was broadly similar to that of Croatia in 2007.

One other question suggested by the literature on policy transfer is whether mechanisms such as the SME Policy Charter lead to convergence or divergence of policy (Bartlett, 2013). In terms of the single number indices, convergence would be reflected in increasing similarity of index numbers as the SME Policy Charter matures. In fact we see little such evidence, with the coefficient of variation between the 2007 indices at 0.55 almost exactly the same as that in 2012 (Table 5.3). The implication is that although the WBCs have clearly converged more closely to EU SME policy since 2007, the progress has been rather uneven with an increase between the leading and lagging economies.[17] BiH and Kosovo are somewhat particular cases, however. BiH is caught in the Dayton Agreement. Much is happening at entity level, particularly in Republika Srpska, but the SME Policy Index looks at national policies and entity developments and only scores national progress. In the case of Kosovo, de facto it only started with its institution and policy-building since its independence in 2008. As most institutional frameworks are now in place and are in the implementation phase, more rapid progress might be anticipated in the future.

CONCLUSIONS AND DISCUSSION

International policy transfer has attracted significant attention in recent years as nations seek to improve their competitiveness and economic performance by accelerating the process of institutional development (Williamson, 2000). Policy transfer also plays a significant strategic role, as an element of the process by which countries seek to meet the criteria for membership of supranational organisations such as the EU or World Trade Organization (WTO). Here, we consider the impact of the SME

Charter Process in the WBCs, part of a broader 'Europeanisation' of policy across the Balkans (Xheneti and Kitching, 2011).

Assessing the broad impact of the SME Charter Process is difficult, due to the breadth of the initiative – covering skills, legislation and targeted policy initiatives and actions – but also because of the lack of any very clear or measurable objectives. Assessed in terms of the SME Policy Index metrics, however, the Charter Process does seem to have achieved its broad objective of stimulating and upgrading SME policy development: each of the WBCs improved its overall SME policy 'score' between 2007 and 2012 (Table 5.3).

The Charter Process has perhaps been less effective in terms of its objectives to help countries identify and remedy policy weaknesses (OECD, 2007: 14). Success here would have involved the spread of leading practice across the region, and a levelling-up of the quality of policy frameworks. Instead, as our analysis shows, progress remains uneven, with significant thematic and geographic disparities in policy development. In thematic terms, progress has been most rapid in areas such as simplifying business registration procedures and enhancing skills and training structures for small firms. Both represent relatively simple and low-cost initiatives. Progress has been less consistent where more institutional coordination or investment is needed, in business support services, improving access to finance, and supporting technological transfer and innovation in SMEs (Roper, 2010). Our analysis suggests that a better connection between the SME Policy Index monitoring and the existing EU programmes and financial instruments for candidate or potential candidate countries (for example, the Instrument for Pre-Accession Assistance) will help to accelerate the policy transfer process.

In geographic terms, and despite the general progress towards EU policy norms, we observe little convergence between the Policy Index Scores of the WBCs over the 2007 to 2012 period, suggesting little evidence of any levelling-up of policy development across countries (Table 5.3). The rank order of the seven WBCs also remains largely unchanged over the period, with Kosovo and BiH consistently at the bottom of the table. The relative lack of development of the SME policy framework in these two countries suggests the difficulty of international policy transfer in situations where either resource constraints (Kosovo) or administrative structures (BiH) make it difficult to achieve progress. This highlights the targeted nature of the SME Charter, and emphasises the importance of broader social and economic conditions – framework conditions – on the success of international policy transfer.

Assessing the value of the SME Policy Index, the benchmarking element of the Charter Process, is perhaps easier. Here, the main aim of the SME Policy Index – as stated in 2007 – was 'to rank countries' performance and to identify regional and thematic trends in Charter implementation' (OECD, 2007: 14). The three benchmark reports published to date are effective in this sense, and the 2012 report in particular provides a detailed perspective on the WBCs' adoption of the ten principles of the EU Small Business Act. One important limitation of this comparison, however, is that it currently relates only to the WBCs (and in 2012, Turkey) and broader comparisons may be helpful as the WBCs steadily improve their policy frameworks. It is also evident that the WBCs have largely failed to reach Level 5 in almost any policy areas. Typically this involves monitoring and evaluation, which remains a weakness across the region, reflecting some of the personnel and capability issues discussed in Bartlett (2013).

These limitations suggest some potential developments if the SME Charter process – and more specifically, the SME Policy Index – is to remain of value to the WBCs. In conceptual terms there is perhaps value in the development of an overall logic model for the Charter, highlighting policy need, modalities, outputs and outcomes (Jordan, 2010). This model might also usefully highlight implementation issues and contingent factors. This would help to clarify process objectives and success. In addition, the inclusion of a wider range of countries within the Charter process would help to identify more challenging benchmarks, particularly for the more advanced WBCs.

NOTES

1. The Western Balkans includes Albania and six countries which were formerly part of Yugoslavia: Bosnia and Herzegovina, Croatia, Kosovo, the former Yugoslav Republic of Macedonia, Montenegro and Serbia. The term 'Western Balkans' was coined by the EU in 1999 as part of the establishment of the Stabilisation and Association Process prior to the Thessaloniki Summit of June 2003 (Batt, 2007).
2. Development of the SME Policy Index was led by the OECD with support from the EU DG Enterprise, the European Training Foundation (ETF) and the European Bank for Reconstruction and Development (EBRD).
3. Slovenia – also formerly part of Yugoslavia – which joined the EU in May 2004 (Batt, 2007).
4. See http://europa.eu/about-eu/countries/index_en.htm (accessed 5 May 2014).
5. In 2007, for example, there were only 598 large firms in Serbia, 2752 medium-sized enterprises and 283 640 micro firms (including sole proprietors) (Ministry of Economy and Regional Development, 2007: p. 24, Table 19).
6. See, for example, the discussion of various enterprise and business plan competitions in the Serbian Agency for the Development of SMEs and Entrepreneurship, Annual Report 2007.
7. The Small Business Act for Europe was adopted in 2008, replacing the EU Charter for SMEs.

8. Quote attributed to the UK Department for International Development as quoted in Bartlett (2013).
9. For example, prior to the 2009 Policy Assessment the authors came across a number of SME policy initiatives (sometimes described as pilot projects) which complied with the literal requirements of the Policy Index but were poorly funded – cases of nominal compliance.
10. Expert assessments for the human capital dimensions of the SME Policy Index in 2009 and 2012 were made not by local consultants but by consultants from the ETF (OECD, 2009: 33).
11. See http://ec.europa.eu/enterprise/policies/sme/small-business-act/index_en.htm (accessed 13 June 2014).
12. Turkey also took part in the 2012 Policy Index for the first time and one area – taxation – included in the 2012 Policy Index was dropped.
13. Typically 'the role of business incubators is to provide a supportive environment, where new entrepreneurs receive training and assistance in business management and marketing, various other business services, and access to seed capital' (Avnimelech et al., 2007: 1185).
14. The same would be true of any assessment of the 'success' of the Charter Process due to a lack of clear and measurable objectives and timelines. The lack of clear and measurable objectives is somewhat ironic in an initiative which aims to promote best practice in SME policy-making.
15. These types of policy improvements have implications well beyond their practical benefits and compliance with the SME Policy Index, however. As the business registration process is part of the World Bank's 'Doing Business' Index, improvements in registration processes have significant international reputational gains.
16. There is only one exception: the single number index for Kosovo falls marginally between 2009 and 2012.
17. Looking at Table 5.3 we see that in 2007 only Croatia was above Level 3, a critical point, indicating that institutions or framework are in place. The other six countries were below this level. By 2012, five out of the seven WBCs had surpassed Level 3 and the regional average had moved beyond Level 3 as well.

REFERENCES

Avnimelech, G., D. Schwartz and R. Bar-El (2007), 'Entrepreneurial high-tech cluster development: Israel's experience with venture capital and technological incubators', *European Planning Studies*, **15** (9), 1181–98.

Bartlett, W. (2013), 'Obstacles to evidence-based policy-making in the EU enlargement countries: the case of skills policies', *Social Policy and Administration*, **47** (4), 451–67.

Batt, J. (2007), 'The Western Balkans', in S. White, J. Batt and P.G. Lewis (eds), *Developments in Central and Eastern European Politics 4*, Basingstoke: Palgrave-Macmillan, pp. 72–89.

Dimitrova, A. (2002), 'Enlargement, institution building and the EU's administrative capacity requirement', *West European Politics*, **25** (4), 171–90.

Dolowitz, D. and D. Marsh (2000), 'Learning from abroad: the role of policy transfer in contemporary policy making', *Governance*, **13** (1), 5–24.

Jordan, G.B. (2010), 'A theory-based logic model for innovation policy and evaluation', *Research Evaluation*, **19** (4), 263–73.

Ministry of Economy and Regional Development (2007), 'Report on small and medium-sized enterprises 2007', Belgrade.

Noutcheva, G. (2009), 'Fake, partial and imposed compliance: the limits of the EU's normative power in the Western Balkans', *Journal of European Public Policy*, **16** (7), 1065–84.

OECD (2007), 'Report on the implementation of the European Charter for Small Enterprises in the Western Balkans – SME policy index 2007', Paris: OECD.

OECD (2009), 'Progress in the implementation of the European Charter for Small Enterprises in the Western Balkans', Paris: OECD/European Commission/ European Training Foundation/European Bank for Reconstruction and Development.

OECD (2012), *SME Policy Index – Western Balkans and Turkey 2012 – Progress in the Implementation of the Small Business Act for Europe*, Paris: OECD.

Roper, S. (2010), 'Moving on: from enterprise policy to innovation policy in the Western Balkans', *South-Eastern Europe*, **34** (2), 170–92.

Schwartz, M. (2013), 'A control group study of incubators' impact to promote firm survival', *Journal of Technology Transfer*, **38** (3), 302–31.

Stone, D. (2012), 'Transfer and translation of policy', *Policy Studies*, **33** (6), 483–99.

Unalan, D. (2009), 'An analytical framework for policy transfer in the EU context', *Politics and Society*, **37** (3), 439–52.

Williamson, O.E. (2000), 'The new institutional economics: taking stock, looking ahead', *Journal of Economic Literature*, **38** (3), 595–613.

World Bank (n.d.), 'World Development Indicators Database', available at http://web.worldbank.org (accessed 10 May 2014).

Xheneti, M. and J. Kitching (2011), 'From discourse to implementation: enterprise policy development in postcommunist Albania', *Environment and Planning C-Government and Policy*, **29** (6), 1018–36.

6. Is Estonia becoming a better home for 'born globals'?

Tõnis Mets*

INTRODUCTION

The importance of innovative globalising high-tech small and medium-sized enterprises (HSMEs) in the economy has grown particularly for small emerging countries because of the need for balanced development of their innovation system, knowledge-based economy and society generally. It does not mean discrimination against low-tech or traditional industry, but rather high-, middle- and low-tech industry in symbiotic partnership should be seen (Varblane et al., 2007). New jobs in the field of technology innovation induce more jobs in other sectors. The multiplying effect can reach even five times that of any other sector (Moretti, 2012). However, technology-based start-ups cannot usually remain entirely on the local market, especially in small countries whose periphery regions are far from large markets of European capital areas, but rather they must go international or even global.

Early internationalisation is often seen as a way to cover research and development (R&D) expenses ('push' factor), because of the tiny domestic market and the attractiveness of foreign markets ('pull' factor) (Luostarinen and Gabrielsson, 2004). This is influencing companies and countries' innovation systems, and not only in such a small open-economy country as Finland, positioned 41st in the world in 2012 (UN, 2014). It may seem surprising that even the sixth-largest economy in the world, the United Kingdom, 'is too small to provide an adequate market' for some high-technology companies, and that this market in the UK does not even exist (Kudina et al., 2008: 40). In these cases internationalisation is essential to business survival, although the extent to which this is true varies between different technologies and also the extent of the market niche.

Although the definition of 'hi-tech' is defined differently by many authors, the main characteristics are the novelty of the product or service, R&D intensity of the production or service, qualifications of employees and the company belonging to some research-intensive industry sectors. Besides the mentioned characteristic features, HSMEs are defined as those companies that are contributing to the 'creation of high-technology new knowledge themselves, this knowledge is unique and creates competitive advantage on the market' (Mets, 2012: 169).

These tech start-up companies able to internationalise or globalise from inception are called 'international new ventures' (INVs), or explicitly 'born global' (BG) or 'hi-tech' new ventures. Governments and non-governmental organisations are interested in supporting the entrepreneurial ecosystems where tech start-ups are created and developed. Preliminary evaluation of the contribution of BGs into job creation and welfare in Europe (Eurofound, 2012) shows that about one-fifth of young enterprises in Europe are BGs; for example, less than 10 per cent in Hungary and up to 50 per cent in Romania, Belgium or Denmark. The main conclusion is: 'little is known about the full economic potential of these companies and how best to support them' (ibid.: 1).

This situation creates the need to learn more about entrepreneurs together with their BGs, prior conditions and development trajectories of tech start-ups. However, the situation is a dynamic one. On the one hand, entrepreneurs are continually adapting their businesses; on the other hand, the ecosystem in which they are operating is also changing. As a consequence, it is impossible to find cases that are identical to others.

The chapter aims to study the internationalisation trajectories of BGs in regional development and entrepreneurial ecosystem frameworks of the emerging knowledge economy. This means creating the model and mapping globalisation processes of BGs in different timeframes and environments. However, it also means generalising findings and creating a better understanding of the needs of BGs and their potential to contribute to regional development.

This chapter is structured as follows. First, the concept of the entrepreneurial ecosystem, and its components influencing hi-tech BGs, are revisited. Next, a brief literature overview and analysis of internationalisation trajectories of BGs under the influence of an ecosystem are given. The context of regional development embedded in international new ventures is then disclosed. Following that, the methodology and a short description of the three case study sample companies are presented. After that, the chapter presents the empirical findings, discussion of the results and policy implications. A conclusions section brings the chapter to an end.

BORN GLOBALS MAKING PERIPHERY GLOBAL

The Ecosystem around Born Globals

The concept of ecosystems in business studies was introduced by Moore (1993). Now, the concept is more widely used partly in (hi-tech) entrepreneurship development and research. For the successful creation of ecosystems, one of the myths in the high-tech sector is that it is enough to have technology (usually coming from a university), entrepreneurs, the capital and sunshine. Another belief says, 'luck alone was the driver' that generated the 'critical mass' in the Silicon Valley ecosystem around Stanford University in California in the United States. However, Isenberg (2010) warns public leaders in emerging economies not to emulate Silicon Valley despite the fact that it is the home of Intel, Oracle, Apple and others.

Entrepreneurial ecosystems around new (growth) ventures consist of tangible and intangible components and actors, which include (Foster et al., 2013):

- Accessible markets: domestic and foreign, with large companies, SMEs and public sector as customers.
- Human capital or workforce, including management and technical talents with entrepreneurial business experience, outsourcing availability (networks).
- Funding and finance: friends and family, angel investors, private equity, venture capital and access to debt.
- Support system: mentors and advisors, professional services, incubators or accelerators, network of entrepreneurial peers.
- Regulatory framework and infrastructure: ease of starting business, tax incentives, business-friendly legislation and policies, access to elementary infrastructure (for example, water, electricity), access to telecommunications and Internet and to transport.
- Education and training: available workforce with (pre-)university education and entrepreneurship-specific training.
- Major universities as catalysts, including promoting entrepreneurship and entrepreneurial culture, playing a key role in idea formation for new businesses and preparing graduates for new companies.
- Cultural support of tolerance for risk and failure, preference for self-employment, success stories and role models, research culture, positive image of entrepreneurship and celebration of innovation.

The components of an entrepreneurial ecosystem, as specified above, can be criticised by appearing static rather than dynamic, influenced by the omission of any reference to the growth context. As a consequence, it is necessary to add a temporal dimension to the spatial dimension, in order that both aspects are included as part of the context for entrepreneurship in technology-based start-ups and BGs. A further element in the context of these BG companies are sector-specific aspects which could include different conditions for market entry and different opportunities to hire a workforce in various regions. Nowadays physical infrastructure is not the critical factor it once was, and virtual technology is used to link networks of high-tech innovators. These networks link research institutions, science and technology parks, and technology and production businesses. This can be seen from the example of Living Labs (LL) where users in the innovation process are given the opportunity to contribute and test new ideas, prototypes and final products (Varblane and Lepik, 2010).

Traditionally such ecosystems have partly been embedded in networks of regional development. These networks are linking research institutions, science and technology parks, and technology and production villages with financial capital and (local) governmental development agencies. Important parts of this network are business incubators facilitating new ventures and training novice entrepreneurs. Since 2005, incubators have been transferred into a more intensive form: business accelerators.

The creation of accelerators (schools for start-ups) by governmental enterprise institutions for the speeding up of all start-up entrepreneurial (learning) processes (*The Economist*, 2014) has profoundly widened the meaning and geography of ecosystems. On a competitive basis, start-up entrepreneurs from countries worldwide are becoming tenants of these accelerators. After an intensive learning event, they leave the community and place, but (virtual) networks remain as part of the ecosystem. Of course, entrepreneurs' ideas and ambitions, and ecosystems, are undergoing dynamic change; there never can be absolute pertinence and accordance between the actors and components of ecosystems.

Formulations of the following hypotheses of seven intangibles of regional technological entrepreneurship by Venkataraman (2004) are based on the guess that the tangible components of the ecosystem already exist:

1. Focal points producing novel ideas. The author points to top-tier universities and R&D laboratories being 'the incubators of a steady flow of novel technical ideas' (ibid.: 155).
2. The need for the right role models. If someone has already succeeded in creating a successful new business, combining novel ideas and finding capital for investment, then this encourages others to follow

that model. The role models prove there is a chance for entrepreneurial success.

3. The informal forums of entrepreneurship. The access to role models can occur in informal forums such as incubators, classrooms, meetings and other informal events.
4. The need for the creation of region-specific ideas. The central question is how to build region-specific knowledge and convert that knowledge into original new products, processes and services.
5. The need for safety nets. That means the need to cope with failure; a genuine part of novelty is the risk of not succeeding. Is the environment tolerant enough not to ruin an entrepreneur morally and materially?
6. The need for gateways to vast markets. That means easy access to product markets for tech start-ups as well as an easy exit from the markets for investors.
7. The need for executive leadership. Usually leaders have been thought of as visionaries, but executive leadership and relevant competencies are even more significant.

Both of the descriptions of the entrepreneurial ecosystem disclosed above are based on some government-supported infrastructure in its maturity; that is, all these features are already functioning. Isenberg (2010) recommends engaging in such an ecosystem's private sector with public–private partnership from the start, and the private buy-out options later. Only in this way will it work efficiently.

Different spatial and industry sector ecosystems exist simultaneously, such as university, regional and global ecosystems, or information technology (IT) and biotech ecosystems. These ecosystems overlap each other, and of course can be in different phases of maturity depending on economic development of the region and industry in the area. This also means that, depending on the timing and location, a start-up entrepreneur can be a member of different ecosystems and can get different (level) support for their aspirations. Start-ups together with suppliers' and customers' networks can create and run within ecosystems reaching far beyond their neighbourhood boundaries.

What Born Global HSMEs Do Differently

Traditionally internationalisation is a slow, incremental or gradual resource-intensive process acknowledged as the Uppsala model ('U-model') of internationalisation (Johanson and Vahlne, 1977). The next development, the innovation-related 'I-model', links the gradual internationalisation of the company to internal and external actors, and to factors including push and pull mechanisms. The obstacles derived usually from slow and resource-consuming processes of becoming international have been overcome by the born global HSMEs (Gabrielsson and Kirpalani, 2004). However, overcoming this is not an automatic process per se.

According to Gabrielsson and Kirpalani (2004) there are necessary channels for BGs' existence; these are the following:

- multinational companies (MNCs) (as systems integrators) somehow integrating BGs;
- MNCs as distributors of BGs' products and services;
- networks;
- the Internet;
- a combination of (all or some of) the above channels.

These channels can appear to be based on established, incrementally new and radically new emerging value systems. From the analysis of both Israeli and Finnish knowledge-intensive BGs, the authors conclude that (start-up) companies striving for new business space in international markets must use the channels outlined above. The authors also suggest that borrowing and building resources leads to slow development paths (ibid.). The value systems (or value chain) and channels are part of the general entrepreneurial business ecosystem, described above. Hereby it could also be argued that even large multinationals are not entirely independent of using the same or similar channels, or other components of the ecosystem. So what do born globals do differently?

Several researchers refer to internationalisation as an entrepreneurial process. The entrepreneurial process and the entrepreneurial characteristics have similar importance for venture creation in international entrepreneurship as well as in entrepreneurship studies generally, but the BG/INV form can be found to be a competitive advantage. It has also has been found that the earlier intention of internationalisation and greater knowledge intensity are associated with the INV, exhibiting a higher level of international and industry experience than domestic new ventures (Autio et al., 2000).

Entrepreneurs scan the (global) environment for opportunities before launching their own global business, which means there is a chance to satisfy customers' existing and new needs and create value for customers globally. In the literature the process approach has been found to be fragmented, inadequately reflecting the early entrepreneurial stages of the non-linear internationalisation process (Keupp and Gassmann, 2009). Furthermore, within these early stages the entrepreneurial learning and business model (BM) development for BG HSMEs is insufficiently covered.

As a generalisation of several studies, the BM concept describes how the company transfers its inputs into value, provides that value to the customer, and earns the revenue. Chesbrough and Rosenbloom (2002) argue that the BM unlocks latent value from technology. Teece (2010) points out the importance of the skills related to the intellectual property (IP) in designing the BM. This also means that the IP aspects play a crucial role in the entrepreneurial process of HSMEs. At the same time, the business model is not a strategy: the central issue is the fit between the strategy and the business model aspects.

Hedman and Kalling (2003) present the BM as functioning between the the suppliers' market and the customers' market, including the resources (resource-based view, RBV) and activities (process-based view) on an organisational level. The BM has been seen as the result of the appearance of the BG phenomenon in companies' behaviour, presuming 'knowledge and experience accumulation – that is, [the] entrepreneurial learning period, which is leading to' the (global) business (breakthrough) opportunity recognition and the invention of the leveraging BM to implement that opportunity (Mets, 2012: 186).

From that concise overview and analysis could be proposed the following issues of how the BG (hi-tech) new ventures differ from the other SMEs. They differ by:

a)   The larger share of intellectual and knowledge assets embedded into their entrepreneurial process and business model.
b)   The bigger role of business model innovation in the entrepreneurial process, from the opportunity discovery to the opportunity exploitation.
c)   The higher importance of intellectual capital, product and business model co-development in their opportunity exploitation.

To conclude, entrepreneurial opportunities are embedded in ecosystems whilst also being influenced by the capabilities of the technology entrepreneur (Kudina et al., 2008). Besides the home conditions, other factors leading to early internationalisation are new market conditions, technological advantages and entrepreneurial (managerial) learning (ibid.). The roles of the ecosystem and entrepreneurial skills in various business development stages are different; only in very rare cases are all these aspects equally balanced in favourable proportions, leading to immediate success.

Regional Aspects of New International Ventures

Regional aspects of economic development in Estonia have a twofold meaning. First, Estonia, a small country regaining independence from Soviet occupation in 1991, is located in the European periphery and far from large markets for technology products. Second, although a small country, Estonia has its own periphery, with regions far from the capital city of Tallinn. Regional development and regional policy under market economy conditions has been the topic of the first strategy documents from the concept of Estonia's economic autonomy since the 1980s. The Estonian government implemented cohesion policy, and regional convergence took place in 1994–98 (Raagmaa et al., 2014). Until the accession to the European Union (EU) in 2004 the European programmes' (Phare; Instrument for Structural Policies for Pre-Accession, ISPA) funding supported convergence of Estonian national and EU spatial policies. Further programmes funded by the EU did not achieve the aim of balanced regional development in Estonia, and in fact regional differences increased if anything (ibid.). The dominance of the capital region of Harju County in share of Estonian population is more than 41 per cent; the proportion of gross domestic product (GDP) of the county grew from 53 per cent in 1996 to 61.1 per cent in 2009, and the trend is growing (Raagmaa et al., 2014). In 2011, 12–33 per cent of the population of the neighbouring counties were employed in Tallinn and the capital region of Harju County (Ristkok, 2014).

Imbalance of regional development is sometimes expressed in different and paradoxical ways. In the period 2005–10, GDP of the Võru County, which is the farthest from the capital region, surpassed that of the Rapla County, which is a neighbour to the Tallinn region of Harjumaa County (MB, 2014). There is no clear explanation for this phenomenon. It can only be supposed that the first entrepreneurship development centre, founded with the support of the Swedish Development Agency (NUTEK) in Võru 1993, played a role.

Similarly, evidence of the role of the University of Tartu and Tartu Science Park in counterbalancing industrial capital north of Estonia is difficult to find. Located in the mostly rural south, the University of Tartu is a multidisciplinary classical research university established in 1632. Now it belongs to the Coimbra Group of European classical universities, of a high international standard, together with such universities as Cambridge, Uppsala, Heidelberg, Bologna, Barcelona and Lyon (http://www.coimbra-group.eu). Only recently, the University of Tartu raised the topic of how better to contribute to the economy and regional development of Estonia. Tartu Science Park, founded in 1992, is the oldest science park in the

Baltic States. It replaced the disappearing former Soviet military and space programmes-oriented science-based industry, and helped to retain hi-tech competencies in Tartu. The founders of the Tartu Science Park were enthusiasts working in the period when the Estonian government had no strategy or resources to develop a knowledge-based economy in the region.

Besides internal regional imbalances, Estonia faces the challenge of catching up to innovation-based economies such as neighbouring in Finland, across the Baltic Sea. To achieve a similar structure of employment (and economy) as Finland, in Estonia approximately 30 000 highly qualified jobs are lacking in the technology field (Männik and Pärna, 2013). Although several technology development centres of bigger international corporations such as Skype of Microsoft, and the Estonian Mobile Telephone (EMT) of TeliaSonera, are located in Tallinn, these are mainly creating highly qualified jobs and producing knowledge for the multinational corporations, not for Estonian high-tech products to export.

In a situation where natural resources are lacking, the main way for an economy to grow at both the regional and national levels is through exporting its products and services. Former competitive advantages based on lower costs of subcontracting (Smallbone et al., 1998) are no longer advantages in traditional fields. This means that there is a need to create products with higher added value. For that purpose, in a small country, knowledge-based BG start-ups are one of the best solutions, to reach markets worldwide. Particularly in South Estonia, a traditional rural area, the role of science parks, incubators and new technology ventures linking the university competence and regional economy to global markets cannot be overestimated.

CONCEPTUAL FRAMEWORK AND RESEARCH METHODOLOGY

As discussed in the preceding sections, the empirical research is based on the process theory and general ecosystem framework of the globalisation of technology SMEs. The approach is mainly focused on the business model (BM), and the product development and role of both knowledge and IP (usually results of R&D) in this process. The knowledge (sometimes IP) is the basis for product development as well as for operations development in reaching a global market. The role of the ecosystem in that process is also studied. The hypotheses by Venkataraman were used as a basis for mapping case companies' growth trajectories and further analysis.

Globalisation is understood not simply as becoming international: it is reaching other continents. This also implies the need to analyse changes in the complexity of knowledge in globalisation. What is happening with (product) knowledge complexity in that process? What is the timeframe for the accumulation of the necessary competences for globalisation, and how is it related to the internationalisation process – is there a so-called 'pre-history'? Can entrepreneurial learning in the globalisation BM development process be identified? Moreover, what are the consequences of customer involvement for competitive advantage, business model, IP, and strategy?

Case studies were used to map the main factors affecting the internationalisation process of BG HSMEs. The main criteria for the selection of a case study company were as follows:

- Small-country (Estonia) origin of the company.
- The case should be relevant to a success story of HSME, that is, it should be already global.
- The main growth track of the company could be examined.
- Core part of knowledge and technology is created in the start-up's homeland.
- Timing of entrepreneurial processes of the BGs should correspond to different shapes of ecosystem maturity.
- The companies represent a capital city region as well as regions in the periphery.
- The companies represent technologies of different fields.

The case studies represent the HSMEs located in the Estonian capital city Tallinn as well as the leading town of the province, Tartu, 185 km away. The headquarters of Defendec is in Tallinn Technology Park, and that of Click & Grow is in Tartu Science Park (see also Table 6.1). Both businesses have their production unit in Estonia and both are good examples of tenancy in science or technology parks, homes to high-potential technology companies. Mobi Solutions, as an early starter, has its headquarters in Tartu. A candidate for a case study was also a software company, MassMedia, situated approximately 70 km south of Tartu and 260 km from Tallinn in a small county town, Võru, which is considered as the absolute periphery of Estonia. The only reason to exclude MassMedia from the sample was its quite narrow business focus: software production in Estonia and sales in the United States. Another, HSME Surface Labs International from Võru, was also excluded as it was a company in the very early stages of growth. Both the businesses indicate the potential for globalisation by hi-tech companies of rural area origin.

The case studies presented in this chapter are based mainly on public information from the media, company websites, and the official databases

Table 6.1 Global HSMEs

	Mobi Solutions	Defendec	Click & Grow
Company name, founders, founding data, location, business support structure	Mobi Solutions, IT and business students, October 2000; spin-off Fortumo, 2007; spin-off Messente Communications, 2013; Tartu	Defendec (until 2010, Smartdust Solutions OÜ), Jaanus Tamm, Tauri Tuubel, Jürgo-Sören Preden, 2006; Tallinn; Tallinn Technology Park	Click & Grow (C&G), inventor Mattias Lepp, 2009; Tartu; Tartu Science Park
Product/service, launched, date	SMS voting, 2001; SMS ticket, 2002; M-business/services	Wireless sensors networks and monitoring system (for border protection), 2009	Intelligent houseplant pot, Smartpot, 2011
Domestic period	Until 2002 (first export)	Very short period after winning the bid for Estonian Border Guard, 2009–10	Did not exist, the first shipment was exported to Sweden, autumn 2011
Lessons learned before globalisation	Testing > 200 products/services on local or close markets	International business and technology development experience of the team	Business and technology experience of the inventor
Globalisation	Own offices, associates and subsidiaries: Canada, 2006; China, 2008; USA, 2011	2011, branches and representatives worldwide	Sales to USA, 2011; product promoted in *Wired Magazine*, *Fast Company* and *New York Times*
Product development	> 200 services tested. Tracking customers' reactions in SMS voting and other market tests	Smartdec system launched 2010 improved permanently, version 3.0 in 2013	From NASA-inspired idea concept of Smartpot created; 2nd generation: Smart Herb Garden; 3rd: Smart Farm; university scientists involved
Production	Software, copyright	Production in Estonia; ISO 9001:2008 31 October 2011	Production in Estonia; international subcontractors for chip production
Number of clients	> 300 mobile operators; > 80000 developers-service providers, 2013; reachable to 4 billion mobile users	N/A	150000 Smartpots sold, 2013; expected sales of Smart Herb Garden 300000, 2014

Table 6.1 (continued)

Company name, founders, founding data, location, business support structure	Mobi Solutions, IT and business students, October 2000; spin-off Fortumo, 2007; spin-off Messente Communications, 2013; Tartu	Defendec (until 2010, Smartdust Solutions OÜ), Jaanus Tamm, Tauri Tuubel, Jürgo-Sören Preden, 2006; Tallinn; Tallinn Technology Park	Click & Grow (C&G), inventor Mattias Lepp, 2009; Tartu; Tartu Science Park
Target markets (countries)	> 80 countries worldwide; prognosis digital market US$268 billion, 2015	European Union, Eastern Europe, Eastern Asia, South America, USA	USA, United Arab Emirates, Russia, Great Britain, Germany, France, Canada, Brazil, China and Japan
Details about business model (BM)	B2B; partnering with Ericsson; clients: Skype, Paymentwall, TravianGames, Barn Buddy, Rovio (Angry Bird)	Business-to-business (B2B); Direct sales leveraging globally own IP	Retailing chains, incl. Virgin Megastore
Competitive edge	Easy to use; no fees (from concrete service only); worldwide reachability	R&D base; international experience; patented solutions (IP)	First-mover, emotional attractiveness of the product
Intellectual property	Software	Patent(s); IP contracts with employees – requirement of the investor	Patent(s); R&D in collaboration with universities in Estonia, France, the Netherlands and Russia
Involving of customers in product/business development	Partly Living Lab methodology implemented	Direct negotiations with customers	Kickstarter campaign, 2013, > 10000 backers, with expectations of > US$600 000 return on the new product
Networking	Leverage via subsidiaries and mobile operators	Own offices and resellers worldwide, lobbying governments	Networking with traders interested in collaboration, no aggressive marketing
Strategy	Integrating customers' BM with their own BM	Focus on concrete technology application, leverage based on IP	Focus on concrete technology application, leverage based on IP

Sources: The author; websites and Annual Reports of the companies; Tamm (2011), Tambur (2014), Rohelaan and Põlendik (2013), Olmaru (2014), Mets (2012) and Lunden (2013).

of the Commercial Registry, including Annual Reports of the companies and other secondary data. First of all, the author's experience and knowledge were used; then a search for research publications was carried out using Google Scholar. This gave the possibility to learn from previous research on the case companies. Then historical facts and general overviews were collected from previous studies and the media (see, e.g., Tänavsuu, 2013). After that, the websites and the Annual Reports of the companies were studied. The facts obtained during the previous studies, as well as current research, were evaluated in the context of the theoretical framework. Aspects not covered before, and newer facts, were mapped. Also, some interpretations were checked against public interviews with entrepreneurs in the media.

FINDINGS

Mobi Solutions

For Mobi Solutions (Table 6.1) the journey to its business model was not smooth, despite the fact that it was able to follow the technology and business model example of the Estonian Mobile Telephone (EMT) company. EMT launched the mobile parking and payment system in Estonia on 1 July 2000.

The team lacked courage and any idea of going global at the beginning. They started from mobile marketing together with Ericsson and EMT. Mobi became more recognised in the region for its mobile voting and M-Ticket (mobile ticket) projects. However, after several years of local and regional testing of various services, Mobi Solutions reached its model leading to the global market. Now Mobi, via its spin-off and subsidiary Fortumo (founded in 2007), offers a 'specific "easy to use," "pay after receiving money" and "pay only as much as you use" business model to its clients' (Mets, 2012). By creating a business model 'ready for use' for its clients, Fortumo has created its own business renting out the business model to customers. In this way, mediators (mobile network owners) and customers are co-creating their businesses with Fortumo. In addition, Fortumo became very popular as a mobile payment provider in the regions of Asia where credit card penetration is low.

During some periods, Fortumo needed additional investment for product development, but venture capitalists did not trust the company enough. In 2009 external investors were ready to join the company, but Fortumo no longer had a need for them. In 2011, Mobi Solutions merged with Indilo Wireless, another SME experienced in the mobile field and with

75 applications for iPhone and iPad. By the end of 2012, Mobi employed 69 people.

Mobi seems to be a good example of a 'learning global' company. Although the implementation of its services needs the mediation of a local mobile operator, the spreading of Fortumo's services is entirely free. The Internet potentially offers a revenue environment of service for businesses. The market and the value chain of Fortumo are dependent on the interest of mobile operators, as well as Fortumo's capabilities to negotiate and create networks with them whilst attracting some key supplier companies like Rovio with the 'Angry Bird' game. Mobi's decision to involve customers in the new product development process, whereby the LL concept was introduced, was unique at the time. However, now with global experience, the Mobi team is involved in Enterprise Estonia's cluster initiatives to develop the LL experience in the Estonian information and communication technology (ICT) sector (Varblane and Lepik, 2010).

In February 2013, Fortumo announced that it had involved Intel Capital and Greycroft Partners as its first external shareholders. TechCrunch reported a deal for approximately US$10 million. Fortumo's co-founder Rain Rannu explained the reasons for involving new investors: 'Working with Intel Capital and Greycroft will help us to pursue additional growth opportunities, including strategic partnerships and acquisitions' (Lunden, 2013).

Prospects for Fortumo appear challenging. In 2014 mobile billing became available to more than 4 billion mobile users worldwide, and prognosis of the digital market in 2015 reached US$268 billion. Fortumo's competitor Bango reported a loss of US$3.8 million within the nine months to 31 December 2012. Rannu confirms that Fortumo is 'the only mobile payment provider who has been profitable and is profitable' (ibid.). By combining mobile telecommunication and the Internet environment in its business model, Mobi Solutions demonstrates how starting from idea generation and real team creation can create a new profitable global business with very modest investments. Mobi's mobile payment system has created a real business co-creation environment for its customers; a virtual network of thousands of companies. Mobi is now already an investor into the new business ideas of new ventures in Estonia.

Defendec

Unlike the first case of Mobi Solutions, the initial technology idea of the Defendec company came from university researchers (Table 6.1). In 2006, two classmates and friends, Jaanus Tamm and Tauri Tuubel, looked for ideas for the application of new 'smart dust' technology. Tamm had made an exit from his software company two years earlier; Tuubel had experience of product development with international teams (Tamm, 2011). Further development efforts started from an ambitious vision that 'smart dust' technology can change the world. Still a doctoral student at the Tallinn University of Technology, and with international private business and technology experience from Silicon Valley, California, USA, Jürgo-Sören Preden proved the best specialist in the field and, moreover, the candidate for the chief technology officer (CTO) position. Initially, when founded in 2006, the company's name was Smartdust Solutions. Many applications of sensor systems were tested before reaching the central idea: remote premises surveillance technology. The result was several patent applications on monitoring systems. Product development required much money and, fortunately, two Estonian venture capital companies (Springcapital and WNB Project) joined Defendec as investors in 2009.

The breakthrough came with the order placed by the Estonian Border Guard Department in 2009. The company was renamed Defendec (2010). The company defines its product in the following way: 'Smartdec is a cost-effective and energy-efficient perimeter intrusion detection system that is used daily to thwart global threats of terrorism, narcotics smuggling, and human trafficking making it the technology of choice of border guards around the world'. In December 2010 the European Venture Summit contest's jury awarded Defendec the accolade of the 'fifth best promising company in Europe'.

The Smartdec technology has proved its efficiency in protecting the borders of the European Union and North Atlantic Treaty Organization (NATO) countries, detecting and signalling the motions of illegal subjects around the border area. Tens of incidents were blocked during the first year on the Estonian border (Berendson, 2011). This has been a strong argument for further clients among the public and private institutions worldwide. Marketing and networking have included attending military and space fairs and exhibitions, but also accompanying the President and Prime Minister of Estonia on state visits. Dr Preden has become an expert not only within his professional associations but also for the Estonian Ministry of Defence as a member of the science council, and as the Estonian national representative in the NATO task groups. Defendec is very proud to be contributing its own software to the Estonian space project; Estonia became the 41st space nation after launching Estonia's first (students' of the university of Tartu) satellite ESTCube-1 to orbit the Earth on 7 May 2013 at 05:06.

Now Defendec has branch business offices in Asia and the Americas (see also http://www.defendec.com/contact). The number of members in the development team has reached more than 18. Production is organised by the company internally whilst using suppliers worldwide.

Click & Grow

In 2005, Mattias Lepp, inventor and the company's founder and chief executive officer (CEO) (Table 6.1), by education a choirmaster, happened to read the National Aeronautics and Space Administration (NASA) report about aeroponics (air and mist) technology, which makes it possible to cultivate plants in outer space (Tambur, 2014). With experience already in (not a very successful) software business he decided to try again. Lepp participated in the entrepreneurship competition 'Brainhunt', which started in autumn 2009. In the final stage of the competition, the following spring, the winner of 'Brainhunt' (Lepp) already had his own business and prototype of the product, and the first investment from WNB Project was agreed. The core idea of Click & Grow's Smartpot and garden system is 'to automatically provide the correct water, and nutrient balance needed for indoor plants to grow' (Tambur, 2014). This idea led Mattias Lepp to develop inventions that were protected by patents worldwide. The Click & Grow (C&G) system consists of two parts: the pot (including pumps, processor, primary circuit, alert lights, environment sensors, water reservoir and batteries) and the plant cartridge (including seeds and fertiliser, growing medium and a growth software program circuit). The pot is reusable; the cartridge is specially designed to grow a particular plant and can be used only once. Production is organised on Hiiumaa, an island in West Estonia, supporting new job creation in a rural area.

Now, from the initial idea, the third-generation concept of smart farming is being developed in collaboration with scientists of the universities of Tartu, Estonia, as well as universities in France, the Netherlands and Russia. Already its technology allows people to cultivate food plants four to five times faster than in soil (Tambur, 2014). C&G smart products also use significantly less water (up to ten times less) than is required for ordinary agricultural production.

Lepp started the promotion and marketing of the product in a way marketing experts usually do not recommend: publication of the idea and product in *Wired Magazine*, *Fast Company* and the *New York Times*. The product development was not yet finalised, but the market accepted that. The first sales were made not in the home market but with a Swedish trader, who took the first shipment for cash in autumn 2011. The products of C&G are now sold by the retailing chain Virgin Megastore, and in one of the world's largest shopping centres, Dubai Mall in the United Arab Emirates (UAE). Currently, the product's bigger markets are the USA, the UAE and Russia. Mattias Lepp sees tremendous potential in the C&G technology because the world's population is growing, and food and water resources are expected to become scarcer in the future. His ambition for the company is to develop C&G into a world-leading technology company for producing food in towns. He sees an enormous need for the technology, for example in Japan where 80 per cent of food is imported. High dependence is a challenge for national food security and a solution could be reached using the C&G technology (Rohelaan and Põlendik, 2013). Currently, Click & Grow employs ten workers, and according to *Äripäev* (Business Daily) the company's own estimation of its overall value is well above €16.4 million (Olmaru, 2014).

DISCUSSION

In starting the analysis of the entrepreneurial ecosystem of the case companies, it should be mentioned that Estonia is a small, open economy, even smaller than Finland, Israel or Sweden which have been previously described in this way by other authors (Gabrielsson and Kirpalani, 2004). Since 1992, in order to overcome backwardness inherited from Soviet occupation and to attract foreign investments, the Estonian government 'has practiced a liberal economic policy and has opened the Estonian market to foreign goods and capital' (Mets, 2012: 182). As a liberal, but also comparatively weak economy in the 1990s, Estonia has supported neither technology-based companies nor any start-ups as strongly as neighbouring Scandinavian countries and Finland could do. Therefore, the primary survival condition for Estonian start-up companies has been a balance between costs and revenues. Even after accession to the European Union in 2004, Estonia had quite a modest investment climate for high-tech companies. The investment climate became much more favourable after Skype was sold to eBay in September 2005 for US$2.6 billion. The four Estonian core team members earned about US$42 million each (Tänavsuu, 2013), and themselves became investors in other enterprises. Very soon after that, domestic venture capital or angel investor companies, as well the public venture fund (Estonian Development Fund), began to invest into new technology projects.

Although Tartu Science Park, the oldest science park in Estonia and the Baltics, had been active since regaining Estonian independence in 1991, significant resources for tech start-up development became available after 2006–08. The 'Brainhunt' start-up competition was launched in 2008, and some years later start-up accelerators were made available for Estonian hi-tech entrepreneurs.

In the entrepreneurship ecosystem context one can see how long the globalisation period was for Mobi. It was a period of learning from the EMT's mobile payment method about how to reach its own global product. In this context, the globalisation process of Defendec was faster. Good role models already existed and the leaders were experienced, but in the product development period until 2009 both Mobi and Defendec lacked investment capital. Much easier was the funding process for C&G, which started several years after Defendec. C&G is also an example of a success story for the Estonian entrepreneurial ecosystem. Besides funding, proper training and mentoring services by business accelerators were available.

Preliminary technology ideas for all three companies were available during the inception period, both from the business environment (Mobi) and from the international technology literature (Defendec and C&G). Product development by Defendec and C&G resulted in their filing patents, and further technology development required the involvement and contribution of university researchers available in the region.

The availability of a qualified workforce, especially in the IT field in Estonia, is partly supported by the Estonian government launching the IT-Tiger programme in the 1990s. A growing number of IT companies now means stronger competition for the better talent.

In terms of their production, Defendec is focused on electronic sensor and network systems and C&G combines plastic, IT and agricultural products. Both demonstrate the integration of different technology fields (with C&G specifically innovating agriculture technology) and both are in the leading position globally in their own area of product development. Their lead role in a new technology, as well as IP, is their competitive advantage in their business field. Until the appearance of competitors the main advantage for Mobi/Fortumo was their business model. Now their competitive edge is their coverage of the global market and the eminent global investors Intel Capital and Greycroft as their strategic partners.

Defendec started with the technology for a wide field of applications but, due to limited resources, had to decide between the options. A choice between these options was made by looking at the challenge for usage by local people with a high level of competence in ad hoc networks. This enabled patenting of the method and system for perimeter intrusion detection; the product development and production processes are International Organization for Standardization (ISO) certified.

With his invention Mattias Lepp, founder of C&G, opened up new perspectives for the cultivation system to grow food plants; the Smart Farming System technology has high potential to solve food production problems of societies with limited space and water supply. Currently, the Smartpot product has become very popular among people cultivating plants at home. Lepp has demonstrated an excellent competence in integrating the IT (software and hardware) and nanotechnology with the plant cultivation, extending the orientation of a traditional industry (agriculture) to hi-tech application.

In evaluating the development trajectories of these case study companies, one can mention that they follow the logic presented by Gabrielsson and Kirpalani (2004) above. MNCs are their partners in their distribution networks and, of course, the Internet is a part of their business models, as it is for traditional MNCs.

The success stories of the start-up entrepreneurs have demonstrated their competence in creating a vision of new global businesses as well as their skills in leading HSMEs to global markets. In the case of Mobi/ Fortumo the young (student) entrepreneur team started earlier, and in less favourable ecosystem conditions, than the other firms analysed here. Also, the world market was not mature enough for their product at the beginning of the 2000s. The breakthrough came only with the invention of their own business model that was 'ready to use' for their client businesses (Mets, 2012: 183). Realising their visionary models, as well as attaining executive competence, was the result of a long learning journey for them as they started from the very beginning as just undergraduate students. Mobi and Defendec illustrate how important the multidisciplinary teams (real communities) have become in creating a new synergy. Defendec and C&G both demonstrate how start-ups can begin with their leader-entrepreneurs' global vision: the global ambition existed from inception.

IMPLICATIONS FOR POLICY AND PRACTICE

Since the economic recession years 2008–10, public opinion has become more favourable towards entrepreneurs in Estonia, more so than in other East European emerging countries (GEM, 2013). The media, publishing information on entrepreneurship events, has supported positive changes in public opinion and has propagated entrepreneurial behaviour among young people. Seed-funding in the early stage of new projects has also helped to create safer conditions for tech start-ups.

However, GEM (2013) data show a somewhat discouraging decrease in the level of the Total Early-Stage Entrepreneurial Activity (TEA) index among the Estonian population, from 14.3 per cent in 2012 to 13.1 per cent in 2013. Warning signals have come from the 'Brainhunt' competition, where a decrease in the number of new ideas and a reduction in the number of participants that are ready to launch a venture based on their own ideas demonstrates that a willingness to engage in this type of enterprise is not limitless (Villig, 2014). All in all, there are certain warning signs that the entrepreneurship bubble in Estonia may have burst.

Moreover, poor models and knowledge of the entrepreneurial (venture launch) process can appear as a barrier to creating better policy, training and support systems for future knowledge-driven, innovative, high-potential entrepreneurship SMEs and new ventures (Eurofound, 2012), in order to drive a smart specialisation economy. All these aspects may point to the need for better long-term entrepreneurship (education) policy, which should be based on a more comprehensive understanding than a GEM survey can produce.

The case study companies, as well as examples of technology start-ups from rural Võru County, demonstrate that a contemporary knowledge-based society and open economy do not have traditional barriers of regional location and market distance, as experienced by 'old economy' SMEs before them. If there is evidence that new ventures in the technology sector induce five times more jobs than in other sectors (Moretti, 2012), then born global start-ups have high potential to become the engine of regional development even in rural areas.

CONCLUSIONS

The three case studies in this chapter demonstrate different globalisation trajectories of start-ups depending on the maturity of the entrepreneurial ecosystem in an emerging small country. A poor business environment at start-up is part of the explanation for the 'long journey' of Mobi Solutions to becoming global after several years of product and business model (co-)development efforts. The case of Defendec demonstrates how limited resources can contribute to extending the period of product development in the field of high-complexity systems. The case of Click & Grow shows how a developed entrepreneurial ecosystem can accelerate the growth of the born global start-up. All these cases also demonstrate that the appearance of the 'born global' phenomenon among start-ups presumes a knowledge and experience accumulation period: that is, a period of entrepreneurial learning. This learning can take place before the formal founding of a company as well as in an already functioning company.

Development of the start-up environment and new success stories have provoked questions about the economic sustainability of new venture creation in Estonia. Recently Estonians sold the outstanding hi-tech business, CrabCad, founded in 2010, to Stratasys Ltd (NASDAQ: SSYS), which is a leading global provider of three-dimensional (3D) technology solutions, for approximately US$100 million (Lunden, 2014). Opinions vary within Estonia about the importance of Estonians losing control of this business. A *Forbes* observer said that it is not important for the Estonian economy to have such businesses because ordinary people never experience a better standard of living as a result of such technology (Majandus24, 2014). Estonians themselves are more optimistic about the impact of technology entrepreneurship on the Estonian economy (Lepik, 2014).

The cases of born global start-ups from Estonia, a small emerging country, demonstrate that the entrepreneurial ecosystems are more or less attaining the shape and features suggested by researchers and policy advisors, as described in the overview above. However, in the globalisation context the case companies even exceed the boundaries of these earlier expectations. They overcome the spatial and distance limitations that traditional SMEs have; they make the Estonian periphery, and Estonia as a European periphery country, global. In conclusion, it can be proposed that shortening the start-up period, increasing the number of success stories, and increasing the intensity of creation of new start-ups indicate the maturity of the entrepreneurial ecosystem; and that the ecosystem itself has become more global than ever before.

NOTE

*   An earlier version of this chapter was presented at the Small Enterprise Association of Australia and New Zealand 27th Annual SEAANZ Conference, Sydney, 16–18 July 2014 under the title 'How "born global" SMEs are born: small emergent country cases'.

REFERENCES

Autio, E., H.J. Sapienza and J.G. Almeida (2000), 'Effects of age at entry, knowledge intensity, and imitability on international growth', *Academy of Management Journal*, **43**, 909–24.
Berendson, R. (2011), 'Eesti-Vene maismaapiiri valvab elektrooniline süsteem', *Postimees*, 12 October, available at http://www.postimees.ee/594482/eesti-vene-maismaapiiri-valvab-elektrooniline-susteem (accessed 25 May 2014).
Chesbrough, H. and R.S. Rosenbloom (2002), 'The role of the business model in capturing value from innovation: evidence from Xerox Corporation's technology spin-off companies', *Industrial and Corporate Change*, **11** (3), 529–55.
The Economist (2014), 'Tech startups. Special report', 18 January.
Eurofound (2012), 'Born global: the potential of job creation in new international businesses', Luxembourg: Publications Office of the European Union.
Foster, G. et al. (2013), *Entrepreneurial Ecosystems Around the Globe and Company Growth Dynamics. Report Summary for the Annual Meeting of the New Champions 2013*, Geneva: World Economic Forum.
Gabrielsson, M. and V.H.M. Kirpalani (2004), 'Born globals: how to reach new business space rapidly', *International Business Review*, **13**, 555–71.
Global Entrepreneurship Monitor (GEM) (2013), *Estonian GEM 2013 Data*.

Hedman, J. and T. Kalling (2003), 'The business model concept: theoretical underpinnings and empirical illustrations', *European Journal of Information Systems*, **12**, 49–59.

Isenberg, D.J. (2010), 'How to start an entrepreneurial revolution', *Harvard Business Review*, June, 41–50.

Johanson, J. and J.E. Vahlne (1977), 'The internationalization process of the firm – a model of knowledge development and increasing foreign market commitments', *Journal of International Business Studies*, **8** (1), 23–32.

Keupp, M.M. and O. Gassmann (2009), 'The past and the future of international entrepreneurship: a review and suggestions for developing the field', *Journal of Management*, **35** (3), 600–633.

Kudina, A., G. Yip and H. Barkema (2008), 'Born global', *Business Strategy Review*, Winter, 38–44.

Lepik, K. (2014), *Miks GrabCADi tehing on oluline Eesti jaoks*, available at http://memokraat.ee/2014/09/miks-grabcadi-tehing-on-oluline-eesti-jaoks/ (accessed 19 December 2014).

Lunden, I. (2013), *Fortumo Raises ~$10M From Intel Capital, Greycroft to Take on Bango and More in Carrier Billing; Inks Deals with China Mobile and Vodafone*, available at http://techcrunch.com/2013/02/21/fortumo-raises-10m-from-intel-capital-greycroft-to-take-on-bango-and-more-in-carrier-billing-inks-deals-with-china-mobile-and-vodafone/ (accessed 13 April 2014).

Lunden, I. (2014), '3D printing company Stratasys is buying GrabCAD for around $100m, beating out Autodesk, Adobe', available at http://techcrunch.com/2014/09/16/3d-printing-company-stratasys-is-buying-grabcad-for-around-100m/ (accessed 19 December 2014).

Luostarinen, R. and M. Gabrielsson (2004), 'Finnish perspectives of international entrepreneurship', in L.-P. Dana (ed.), *Handbook of Research on International Entrepreneurship*, Cheltenham, UK and Northampton, MA, USA: Edward Elgar, pp. 383–403.

Maaettevõtluse Büroo (MB) (2014), *Regionaalne SKP piirkondade ja majandussektorite järgi*, Põllumajandusministeerium.

Majandus24 (2014), 'Forbes'i kolumnist: Eestit kiitev statistika ei tähenda eestlaste jaoks midagi', available at http://majandus24.postimees.ee/1300594/forbes-i-kolumnist-eestit-kiitev-statistika-ei-tahenda-eestlaste-jaoks-midagi/ (accessed 19 December 2014).

Männik, K. and O. Pärna (2013), '"Estonia – the business paradise": Kuidas ühendada jõud, et muuta Eesti rahvusvahelise äritegemise keskuseks – talendikate inimeste, tasuvate töökohtade ja väärtust loovate välisinvesteeringute sihtriigiks? Lõppraport', available at www.technopolis-group.com (accessed 19 December 2014).

Mets, T. (2012), 'Creative business model innovation for globalizing SMEs', in T. Burger-Helmchen (ed.), *Entrepreneurship – Creativity and Innovative Business Models*, Rijeka: InTech, pp. 169–90.

Moore, J.F. (1993), 'Predators and prey: a new ecology of competition', *Harvard Business Review*, **71** (3), 75–86.

Moretti, E. (2012), *The New Geography of Jobs*, Boston, MA and New York: Mariner Books.

Olmaru, J. (2014), 'Mattias Lepp – nutika lillepoti ristiisa', *Postimees*, 1 March, available at http://tartu.postimees.ee/2746084/mattias-lepp-nutika-lillepoti-ristiisa (accessed 24 May 2014).

Raagmaa, G., T. Kalvet and R. Kasesalu (2014), 'Europeanization and de-Europeanization of Estonian regional policy', *European Planning Studies*, **22** (4), 775–95.

Ristkok, P. (2014), *Eesti riik, kohalik omavalitsus ja ettevõtluse areng*, Tallinn: Siseministeerium.

Rohelaan, K. and K. Põlendik (2013), 'Kosmilise lennuga leiutaja', *Äripäev* (*Business Daily*), 16 August.

Smallbone, D., B. Piasecki, U. Venesaar, K. Todorov and L. Labrianidis (1998), 'Internationalisation and SME development in transition economies: an international comparison', *Journal of Small Business and Enterprise Development*, **5** (4), 363–75.

Tambur, S. (2014), 'Click a button and grow herbs – the story of Estonian startup Click & Grow', *Estonian World*, 15 April, available at EstonianWorld.com (accessed 24 May 2014).

Tamm, J. (2011), 'Defendec: äri, mis raputab maailma', *Director*, **2**, February, 56–9. available at http://www.director.ee/defendec-ri-mis-raputab-maailma/ (accessed 22 May 2014).

Tänavsuu, T. (2013), 'How can they be so good? The strange story of Skype', available at http://arstechnica.com/business/2013/09/skypes-secrets/ (accessed 17 April 2014).

Teece, D.J. (2010), 'Business models, business strategy and innovation', *Long Range Planning*, **43**, 172–94.

United Nations (UN) (2014), 'GDP', available at http://unstats.un.org/unsd/snaama/dnltransfer.asp?fID=2 (accessed 20 May 2014).

Varblane, U., D. Dyker and D. Tamm (2007), 'How to improve the national innovation systems of catching-up economies?', *TRAMES*, **11** (2), 106–23.

Varblane, U. and A. Lepik (2010), 'How to speak the same language with European innovation-policy in terms of living labs?', *Discussions on Estonian Economic Policy*, **18**, 215–32.

Venkataraman, S. (2004), 'Regional transformation through technical entrepreneurship', *Journal of Business Venturing*, **19**, 153–67.

Villig, M. (2014), 'Ajujahi finalist Taxify: üllatavalt vähe noori tahavad ettevõtet teha', *Postimees*, 7 May, available at http://e24.postimees.ee/2786262/ajujahi-finalist-taxify-ullatavalt-vahe-noori-tahavadettevotet-teha (accessed 24 May 2014).

PART III

Entrepreneurial Activity and Regional
Development

7. Entrepreneurial activity of the Russian population: factors of cross-regional diversity – methodology, indicators, preliminary findings

Alexander Chepurenko, Vladimir Elakhovsky and Ekaterina Popovskaya[1]

INTRODUCTION

The entrepreneurial activity of a population is, first, one of the core sources of economic and social development of any region or settlement. Second, its density is as such a complex indicator of the business climate and pro-entrepreneurial structural conditions in the related territory. Hence, the differences in entrepreneurial activity of the population between territories can tell us much about the regional context of entrepreneurship as well as varying economic prospects.

Until the establishment of projects such as the Global Entrepreneurship Monitor (GEM) researchers did not possess much reliable data for cross-country investigations of entrepreneurial activity. The GEM data for 2006–13 show that the entrepreneurial activity of Russia's population is lower compared with most formerly socialist Central and Eastern European (CEE) countries. Meanwhile, being a huge country where regions have different geographical features, economic structure and cultural heritage, Russia should have a very diverse level of entrepreneurial activity across regions. However, additional data are needed in order to determine this. Such data were collected for the first time during a pilot project conducted with the direct participation of the authors in 2011. This chapter deals with the analysis of the results.

What are the factors explaining the uneven dissemination of entrepreneurial activity in Russia's regions? Are these the same factors explaining the entrepreneurial activity of other large countries under transition, such as in established market economies, or is there a different set of factors that we should take into consideration? This chapter is a first attempt to explore these questions using relevant empirical data.

CONCEPTUAL FRAMEWORK

There are different approaches in the literature, based on labour market analysis (factors such as unemployment and skills), firms' ecology (industrial structure of the regional economy by size and industrial sector), demography (population density and growth, human capital) and financial infrastructure (availability of financing, and so on), to the characteristics which significantly influence regional variation in new firm birth rates.

In several empirical surveys it was shown that economic growth and performance of the regional economy influences the density of already established small and medium-sized enterprises (SMEs), and that the latter also affect entrepreneurial activity (Reynolds et al., 1994; Foelster, 2000; Audretsch and Fritsch, 2002). In the 2000s, some progress was achieved regarding some of the questions raised earlier. However, most papers dealt with the impact of entrepreneurial activity on differing levels of growth and prosperity in different regions (Audretsch and Keilbach, 2004; Fritsch and Mueller, 2004; Van Stel and Storey, 2004; Mueller et al., 2008). Fewer studies analysed the regional factors that influence the level of entrepreneurial activity within specific regions. However, this chapter is concerned with the impact of the characteristics of regions and regional differences on the pattern of entrepreneurial activity across Russia.

In recent years, some headway has been achieved in explaining cross-regional disparity in entrepreneurial activity by using measurements of social capital along with the traits and values of the population (Audretsch et al., 2008; Westlund and Adam, 2010; Westlund et al., 2014; Kibler et al., 2014). Such person-related variables include the so-called variables influencing perception (opportunity cognition, self-efficacy, fear of failure), education level and practical experience, and prior employment in a small firm or self-employment experience (Zhao and Seibert, 2006; Rauch and Frese, 2007; Zhao et al., 2010; Storey and Greene, 2011; Sorgner and Fritsch, 2013; Caliendo et al., 2014). For instance, regions with a high share of people inclined to become entrepreneurial, or regions with a significant role of small firms in the employment structure, could have higher entrepreneurial entry rates (Obschonka et al., 2013).

Two more approaches are important for this chapter. First, Bergmann (2004), using multivariate data analysis with ten German regions, showed that regional start-up activities – when determined by demand and agglomeration – depend, in a more direct way, on the attitudes and self-efficacy of novice entrepreneurs; which mediate the objective state of the economy and infrastructure and other structural conditions of a particular region. Similar evidence was found by Bosma and Schutjens (2011) who compared the data for 127 regions in 17 European countries participating in the GEM, linking institutional factors and economic and demographic attributes to variations in regional entrepreneurial attitude and activity. The authors found entrepreneurial attitudes (the fear of failure in starting a business, perceptions of start-up opportunities in the place of residence, and self-assessment of personal capabilities to start a firm are among them) to especially influence differences in the Total Early-Stage Entrepreneurial Activity (TEA) index and related indicators.

Recently the Kibler et al. (2014) paper has shown how differing levels of the social legitimacy of entrepreneurship affect the formation of new businesses in different regions. The authors stress that a better attitude towards entrepreneurship 'can give those with entrepreneurial intentions the final impulse needed to turn their intentions into actual start-up behaviour' (Kibler et al., 2014: 16).

To summarise, from the existing literature it is known that to explain differences in entrepreneurial activity among regions the level of the population's economic well-being and the structure of the regional economy exert an influence. Both agglomeration (higher density of population) and access to external financing positively affect entrepreneurial activity, whilst unemployment does not. Furthermore, regions and settlements with higher levels of human capital show higher entrepreneurial activity. Finally, variables influencing perception (perceived opportunities to become an entrepreneur, self-efficacy, fear of failure) correlate with entrepreneurial activity in a region.

It is important to stress, however, that all these effects can be found *ceteris paribus* primarily in established market economies. Meanwhile, in this chapter we identify whether some of the factors explored in the literature play any explanatory role when discussing disparities in entrepreneurial activity of the Russian population by region and type of settlement.

METHODOLOGY

The main principles of the explanatory model of the Global Entrepreneurship Monitor (see Reynolds et al., 2005) were used while constructing a regionally representative sample to study and measure entrepreneurial activity in Russian regions. A database was established employing standard methods for observing entrepreneurial activity. Based on the

GEM approach, a set of 18 questions were integrated into the omnibus Georating survey by the Public Opinion Foundation (POF), Moscow. From these 18 questions, eight were related to the socio-demographic characteristics of respondents (gender, age, education, main source of income in last month, its amount, professional occupation, labour market status, family well-being), and ten special questions identified the engagement of the interviewee in entrepreneurial activity (nascent, novice or established business owner – three different questions to define), self-estimation of ability and capability to run a business, single owner or co-owners, social capital, sources of financing, the innovativeness of products, motivation, and a general estimation of entrepreneurial structural conditions in the settlement where they reside.

The POF used a three-step stratified household sampling procedure. In the first step, administrative districts were selected; in the second step, concrete locations; in the third step, concrete households. The survey was conducted in May 2011. The main characteristics of the sampling are as follows:

- 79 Russian regions (of 82 in total), with 139.9 million inhabitants, or 98.6 per cent of the total population of the Russian Federation;
- adults aged 18 years and older;
- total sample of 56 900 respondents, 800 respondents in each of 58 regions and 500 respondents in each of 21 regions;
- 2335 settlements: 77 capitals of republics, *krays* and *oblasts* including Moscow and St Petersburg, 683 cities, 282 small towns (official status: 'town-like villages') and 1293 villages; of 2372 cities and 'town-like villages' in these 79 regions, 1042 were included in the sample;
- statistical error did not exceed 5.5 per cent in regions with 500 respondents and 4.6 per cent in regions with 800 respondents; in total for all 79 regions statistical error did not exceed 1 per cent.

For Russia on weighted average, the TEA index value was between 4.8 and 5.2 per cent (taking into consideration the ultimate sample error and a probability standard of 0.95). The range of variation of the TEA across regions was 7.8 per cent (from the minimal value of 0.4 per cent in the Republic of Karelia, up to the maximal value of 8.2 per cent in the Republic of Dagestan). The variation coefficient, as a characteristic of the degree of homogeneity of regions, is 54.3; hence regional disparities are extremely high.

The special subindexes for each entrepreneurial cohort also show a high differentiation (Table 7.1). For instance, the values of the nascent

*Table 7.1   Dispersion of some indicators of early entrepreneurial activity
in Russia, by region*

Indicator	Main characteristics of respective indicator				
	Mean (+/− sample error)	Minimum	Maximum	Standard deviation	Coefficient of variation (%)
Total Early-Stage Entrepreneurial Activity (TEA) index	2.4–2.6	0.4 Republic Karelia	8.2 Republic Dagestan	1.4	54.3
Nascent entrepreneurship index	1.30–1.49	0.0 Magadan oblast	4.7 Republic Dagestan	0.9	75.0
New business owner (NBO) index	1.19–1.38	0.0 Jewish autonomous oblast	3.6 Republic Sakha (Jakutia)	0.7	52.4
Established business owner (EBO) index	1.39–1.59	0.4 Republic Karelia	4.3 Republic Northern Ossetia–Alania	0.8	52.2

Source: POF (2011).

entrepreneurship index in the top 10 per cent of regions by level of development is nine times higher than in the 10 per cent of regions with the
lowest nascent entrepreneurship index. As regards the new business owners
(NBOs), the differentiation is somewhat lower, but even in this case the
highest and lowest index groups differ by nearly eight times.

Such a big differentiation in entrepreneurial activity among regions,
combined with the rather moderate general level of entrepreneurial activity
in Russia, is an explanatory challenge. As we know (Reynolds et al., 1994;
Foelster, 2000; Audretsch and Fritsch, 2002), regions with more developed
SMEs also score better with regard to the entrepreneurial activity of the
population. Hence:

H1:   The higher the density of already existing SMEs in the region, the
higher the prevalence of opportunity-driven entrepreneurship.

Keeble and Walker (1994) argued that the state of urban agglomeration is
one of the key factors influencing the diversity of entrepreneurial activity
on a regional level. Hence, we test this under:

H2:   The bigger the settlement, the higher the TEA (H3.1) as well as the
prevalence of opportunity-driven entrepreneurship (H3.2).

In spite of the argument made by Naude et al. (2008), that the level of unemployment does not play a significant role in explaining necessity-driven entrepreneurship, we test both the role of unemployment and the role of the well-being in the structure of incentives (dominance of push or pull factors), as follows:

H3: In locations with a higher than median level of unemployment the share of necessity-driven early entrepreneurship is higher than the median.

H4: In regions with a higher level of well-being per capita, both TEA (H4.1) and the prevalence of opportunity-driven early entrepreneurship (H4.2) are higher.

Because it is recognized that factors influencing perception affect the readiness of adults to engage in entrepreneurial activity (see, e.g., Arenius and Minniti, 2005), levels of entrepreneurial activity of the population in different regions may correlate with them. That is:

H5: The lower the fear of failure, the higher the perceived opportunities to start a new venture (H5.1), and self-efficacy leads to a higher TEA in respective regions and types of settlement (H5.2).

Data Analysis

First, a database of SMEs was created, based on the last (2010) SME census. A database was established for 79 Russian regions where the Georating survey was conducted in 2011 (four regions did not participate in this survey) which contained indicators such as the number of jobs and the number of enterprises in each region.

Second, we took data on the economically active population in Russian regions, based on the 2010 Russian population census. Third, a database on early entrepreneurial activity (Georating) was used to measure indexes of TEA for each region and groups of regions, entrepreneurial motivation, and the prevalence of opportunity entrepreneurship in each region.

Moreover, two separate indexes were measured, reflecting the share of employment in the economically active population of the respective region for, respectively, groups of small and medium-sized enterprises. After dividing the regions into three groups, we obtained the results shown in Tables 7.2 and 7.3.

The correlation between employment in both small and medium-sized enterprises and the prevalence of opportunity-driven entrepreneurs is

Table 7.2 Medium-sized enterprises' share of employment in regions, and the prevalence of opportunity-driven entrepreneurship, by groups of regions

Medium-sized enterprises Groups of regions by the share of employed in SMEs (in the regions' economically active population as a whole)	Prevalence of opportunity-driven entrepreneurs (%)
Lower than Russian median (0.7–3.0)	6.2
Average (3.0–4.0)	24.6
Higher than Russian median (4.0–6.0)	12.6
Empirical correlation coefficient	0.30
Analysis of variance (ANOVA) results: F (p)	3.88 (0.012)

Source: POF (2011).

Table 7.3 Small enterprises' share of employment in regions, and the prevalence of opportunity-driven entrepreneurship, by groups of regions

Small-sized enterprises (without micro enterprises) Groups of regions by the share of employed in SME (in the regions' economically active population as a whole)	Prevalence of opportunity-driven entrepreneurs (%)
Lower than Russian median (2.0–10.0)	3.3
Average (10.0–13.0)	19.7
Higher than Russian median (13.0–19.0)	6
Empirical correlation coefficient	0.19
ANOVA results: F (p)	1.39 (0.25)

Source: POF (2011).

relatively weak. The lowest prevalence rate is characteristic of regions with the lowest employment share; the highest rate of prevalence is found in regions with average employment share. Regions with a higher than average level of employment in both medium-sized as well as small enterprises show a far more moderate prevalence of opportunity-driven entrepreneurship. The delineation of regions on median number of employees in medium-sized enterprises and the values of opportunity-driven TEA are shown in Table 7.4.

Furthermore, it was also assumed that the type of settlement influences early entrepreneurial activity and its 'quality', or the prevalence of opportunity-driven entrepreneurship.

*Table 7.4   Medium-sized enterprises' median number of employees, TEA
              and prevalence of opportunity-driven entrepreneurs, by groups
              of regions*

Medium-sized enterprises Groups of regions by the number of employees per one enterprise	TEA
Lower than Russian median (170–199)	3.15
Average (200–219)	2.40
Higher than Russian median (220)	2.96
Empirical correlation coefficient	0.23
ANOVA test: F (p)	2.10 (0.11)

Sources: POF (2011) and Federal State Statistics Service (2010).

Meanwhile, as Table 7.5 shows, there is neither a direct nor an inverse correlation between the type of settlement and the TEA; the TEA levels vary between different types of settlements in a random fashion. Yet in regard to the prevalence of opportunity-driven entrepreneurship, it tends to diminish with the reduction in settlement size; however, the correlation is not strong. In general, in urban areas the opportunity-driven entrepreneurship is dominant, while in villages there is an inverse picture: necessity-driven entrepreneurs dominate.

It was assumed, also, that in locations with a higher than average level of unemployment the share of necessity-driven early entrepreneurship is higher than average. Regrettably, official statistics in Russia provide data on unemployment only for two big groups: cities and villages. In these types of locations the unemployment rate differs: in cities in 2010 it was 6.4 per cent, whilst in villages the rate was 10.8 per cent. Of course, the difference between types of cities might be rather large, and may be bigger than that between cities and villages, but it is not possible to obtain data to check this.

Regarding the correlation between unemployment and necessity-driven early entrepreneurial activity in different types of settlements (Table 7.6), the results are uneven. In approximately 40 per cent of cities the share of necessity-driven entrepreneurs among early entrepreneurs does not differ from the average.

In general, it was observed that in settlements with an unemployment rate higher than average the level of necessity-driven entrepreneurs is also higher. This is true both for cities and villages, but in villages it occurs in a clearer way. However, the empirical correlation coefficient and ANOVA test results are very encouraging.

Table 7.5   TEA and prevalence of opportunity-driven entrepreneurs, by type of settlement

Type of settlement	TEA	Prevalence of opportunity-driven entrepreneurs (%)
Cities with > 1 million inhabitants	3.16	47.8
Cities with 0.5 to 1 million inhabitants (large cities)	2.61	59.5
Cities with 0.250 to 0.500 million inhabitants (somewhat large cities)	2.52	27.4
Cities with 0.100 to 0.250 million inhabitants (medium-sized cities)	2.95	16.5
Cities with 0.050 to 0.100 million inhabitants (small cities)	2.61	23.9
Cities with < 0.050 million inhabitants (towns)	2.90	30.9
Urban villages (from < 0.003 to 0.020 million inhabitants, while > 85% are employed in non-agriculture)	2.21	1.5
Villages (from < 0.010 to 0.020 million inhabitants employed mostly in agriculture)	2.37	−30.6
Empirical correlation coefficient	0.12	0.48
ANOVA test: F (p)	8.21 (0.000)	89.58 (0.000)

Source: POF (2011).

Table 7.6   Unemployment level and share of necessity-driven entrepreneurship, by type of settlement

Unemployment level, 2010*	Share of necessity-driven early entrepreneurship, by type of settlement	
	City	Village
Lower than median for Russia	28.8	42.2
Higher than median for Russia	34.2	54.0
Empirical correlation coefficient	0.12	0.17
ANOVA test: F (p)	1.14 (0.32)	2.23 (0.11)

Source: * Rosstat (2011).

Table 7.7   Factual final consumption of households in 2010 and TEA and prevalence of opportunity-driven entrepreneurship in 2010, by groups of regions

Factual final consumption of households per capita, 2010*	Share of regions (%)	TEA, 2010	Prevalence of opportunity-driven early entrepreneurs (%)
FFC lower than median for Russia	82	2.49	3.4
FFC higher than median for Russia	18	3.23	34.0
Empirical correlation coefficient		0.24	0.30
ANOVA test: F (p)		3.21 (0.046)	7.77 (0.001)

Source: * Rosstat (2012).

Furthermore, it was supposed that in regions with a higher than average level of well-being, both the TEA as well as the share of opportunity-driven early entrepreneurship is higher than average. To prove this hypothesis we decided to use not the gross regional product (GRP), which measures the production level, but rather to use the factual final consumption of households (FFC) per capita. This indicator reflects the consumption of households established on the regions' territory, including both incomes and state and public organisations' transfers (Table 7.7).

Table 7.7 shows that, in regions with higher than average FFC, both the TEA and opportunity-driven entrepreneurship prevalence are higher than in the opposite group of regions.

Using the FFC with a one-year lag changed the results on TEA and opportunity-driven entrepreneurship prevalence, as a higher level of well-being encourages people to become entrepreneurial after a certain period, but the basic tendency remained (see Table 7.8). The changes between 2009 and 2010 result from the fact that during this one-year period the set of regions with higher and lower than average FFC per capita changed.

Even when using a less detailed indicator such as GRP per capita (Table 7.9), the results are similar. In regions with a higher than average level of GRP per capita the TEA (correlation is not significant) and the prevalence of opportunity-driven entrepreneurship are higher as well.

As the set of regions belonging to each group remained the same, the usage of the GRP per capita for the previous year did not affect the early entrepreneurial activity indicator, TEA.

Table 7.8   Factual final consumption of households in 2009 and TEA and prevalence of opportunity-driven entrepreneurship in 2010, by groups of regions

Factual final consumption of households per capita, 2009	Share of regions (%)	TEA, 2010*	Prevalence of opportunity-driven early entrepreneurs (%)
FFC lower than median for Russia	82	2.51	4.2
FFC higher than median for Russia	18	3.19	32.7
Empirical correlation coefficient		0.22	0.28
ANOVA results: F (p)		2.69 (0.07)	6.65 (0.002)

Note: * Some modest difference between Table 7.8 and Table 7.9 TEA 2010 data occurred because of a minor change of sets of regions belonging to each group in 2009 and 2010, respectively.

Source: Rosstat (2012).

Table 7.9   GRP per capita in 2010 and TEA and prevalence of opportunity-driven entrepreneurship in 2010, by groups of regions

GRP per capita, 2010	Share of regions (%)	TEA	Prevalence of opportunity-driven early entrepreneurs (%)
Lower than median for Russia	82	2.59	5.1
Higher than median for Russia	18	3.12	39.2
Empirical correlation coefficient		0.16	0.34
ANOVA results: F (p)		1.61 (0.21)	9.89 (0.000)

Source: Rosstat (2012).

We also tested whether differences in the state of factors influencing perception across regions, such as perceived opportunities, self-efficacy and the fear of failure, affect the entrepreneurial activity of the population in different regions. The assumption was that the lower the fear of failure and the higher both the perceived opportunities to start a new venture

Table 7.10   Level of perceived opportunity and TEA, by groups of regions

Level of perceived opportunity (*PercOpp*)	Share of regions in each group (%)	TEA
Below median (< 2%)	38	2.34
Median (2–3%)	28	2.75
Above median (> 3%)	34	3.21
Empirical correlation coefficient		0.26
ANOVA results: F (p)		2.81 (0.045)

Source: POF (2011).

Table 7.11   Level of self-efficacy and TEA, by groups of regions

Level of self-efficacy (*SelfEff*)	Share of regions in each group (%)	TEA
Below median (< 5%)	33	1.85
Median (5–7%)	32	2.39
Above median (> 7%)	35	3.48
Empirical correlation coefficient		0.49
ANOVA results: F (p)		11.91 (0.000)

Source: POF (2011).

and self-efficacy, respectively, the higher the TEA should be in respective regions and settlement types.

Among variables influencing perception, data for perceived opportunity (*PercOpp*) as well as self-efficacy (*SelfEff*) have a positive correlation with TEA indexes (Tables 7.10 and 7.11). Meanwhile, fear of failure has a weak negative correlation with regional TEA indexes (Table 7.12).

As was revealed, the TEA of regions correlates positively with the level of perceived opportunities in the respective region ($r = 0.474$), as well as with self-efficacy ($r = 0.314$). Fear of failure, however, has a negative correlation with the regional TEA ($r = -0.498$) only in the regions with the highest self-efficacy values (higher than average plus standard deviation). In other regions no impact was found of this variable on the TEA level. The analysis of variance (ANOVA) results are stronger when explaining the correlation between self-efficacy and the TEA in different groups of regions.

When looking for differences among settlement types we used three groups: largest cities, all other urban settlements, and rural settlements.

Table 7.12   Level of fear of failure and TEA, by groups of regions

Level of fear of failure (*FearFail*)	Share of regions in each group (%)	TEA
Below median (< 20%)	24	2.32
Median (20–30%)	52	2.73
Above median (> 30%)	24	2.88
Empirical correlation coefficient		0.15
ANOVA test: F (p)		0.82 (0.49)

Source: POF (2011).

Table 7.13   Perceptional variables, as by types of settlements

Type of settlement	Level of perceived opportunity (*PercOpp*)	Level of self-efficacy (*SelfEff*)	Level of fear of failure (*FearFail*)	TEA
Biggest cities (> 1 million inhabitants)	1.78	7.48	28.0	3.16
Other urban settlements	2.56	6.93	27.0	2.68
Villages	2.70	2.70	27.0	2.37
Empirical correlation coefficient	0.014	0.085	0.006	0.013
ANOVA test: F (p)	5.80 (0.006)	206.28 (0.000)	0.98 (0.399)	4.73 (0.003)

Source: POF (2011).

As may be seen from Table 7.13, the perception variables show different trends, and their correlation with TEA in settlements belonging to respective groups is not significant. However, ANOVA test results – especially for self-efficacy – are notable.

These findings merely coincide with the general reasoning that in urban areas with a higher level of human capital and better infrastructure, as well as higher competition on markets and higher market entry barriers, the objective constraints for any start-up activity might be higher, too; whilst in rural areas the level of economic constraints for entrepreneurial activity is lower, but the set of human and physical capital available is much scarcer.

RESULTS AND DISCUSSION

H1 is not confirmed: a higher density of SMEs does not guarantee a better quality of entrepreneurship, in terms of the prevalence of opportunity-driven entrepreneurs. This may look confusing when compared with the observation made in established market economies, but in economies such as Russia's, in regions with established SMEs, entrepreneurial opportunities are restricted to niches for necessity-driven entrepreneurs, because of issues such as unfair competition or restricted demand typical of imperfect market economies. This means that convincing results in promoting entrepreneurship in Russian regions cannot be achieved with a supply-driven entrepreneurship policy alone. Demand-side policies, such as prevention of local and regional monopolies, promotion of the establishment of local business associations, as well as any policy shaping incentives to transform savings into supply and investments of households, should be facilitated too.

H2.1 is not confirmed: only a rather low correlation between the level of urbanisation and the general TEA level could be found. Yet H2.2 is confirmed: the higher the level of urbanisation, the higher also the prevalence of opportunity-driven early entrepreneurship. These results do not support the mainstream literature findings about the importance of human capital, high population density and cultural diversity for entrepreneurial activity. Perhaps this can be explained by the combination of a wide range of possibilities facing individuals, that include working in a state-owned sector and starting a new venture in bigger urban settlements, combined with rather restrictive entrepreneurial framework conditions. The fact that urban settlements are characterised by a higher prevalence of opportunity-driven entrepreneurs supports this idea, as only those driven by the idea of improvement and possessing high human and social capital may be inclined to start up a business under such environmental constraints. When big cities and urban areas in general provide not only concentrated physical infrastructure but also opportunities for the free choice of economic activity and support for people's creativity, Russian urban landscapes will become friendlier for entrepreneurs.

H3, about the role of unemployment, is not confirmed: the correlation between unemployment and the share of necessity-driven early entrepreneurship, in both urban and rural settlements, is insignificant. This, again, contradicts many observations in established market economies and even in economies in the early stages of transition (Earle and Sakova, 2000). Yet this fact only reflects the generally low level of unemployment in most of the Russian regions as well as, in lieu of starting up a new business, the possibilities to work in state-funded sectors or to engage in subsistence in smaller towns or informal work in bigger settlements (Round et al., 2010; Williams and Round, 2010; Chepurenko, 2014). However, the stagflation which occurred in the Russian economy in 2013–14 may both diminish the opportunities to find a secure job in state services as well as increase the role of the informal sector. The federal state and regions should intervene with proactive measures, shaping possibilities for improvement of the knowledge and skills needed for start-ups, which usually strengthens self-efficacy and diminishes the fear of failure among nascent entrepreneurs, thus transforming them toward opportunity motives and away from necessity orientations.

H4.2 is not denied: the level of well-being correlates with the share of opportunity-driven early entrepreneurship on the regional level. However, the correlation between both well-being (expressed in terms of factual consumption as well as GRP per capita) and the TEA is not significant. Hence, the level of general entrepreneurial activity in a region may be low even if the well-being is relatively high; in other words, factors other than well-being are important to pull people into entrepreneurial activities. H4.1 is denied. In fact, this evidence reflects one of the core issues of the economic system established in Russia in the first decade of the twenty-first century: namely, the low correlation between the engagement in entrepreneurial activity and the level of well-being, as well as the poor state of entrepreneurship structural conditions (World Bank and IFC, 2012). Under such circumstances, the more prosperous regions are not necessarily more entrepreneurial, and vice versa. Here, only the evolution of the whole system of economic incentives and political power may bring any significant change.

H5.1 is confirmed on the regional level for two variables influencing perception (but not for fear of failure). When both perceived opportunities to start a new venture and self-efficacy (especially) are higher, the TEA in respective regions is higher as well. On the other hand, the analogous H5.2 for settlement types was denied; hence, the transparency of the economic policy of regional authorities may influence positive change in opportunity perceptions. Meanwhile, the establishment of a full-fledged system of courses on entrepreneurship and related themes may support the enhancement of self-efficacy among adults and thereby also support their readiness to establish a new venture.

In a non-homogenous economy there are different possible factors, including non-economic factors and models for explaining the entrepreneurial activity of the population. The results support the proposition that one size does not fit all, but rather models of entrepreneurship need to be sensitive to the context in which they are operating, which includes both the formal and informal sectors. As a consequence, it is impossible to facilitate the same models of entrepreneurship promotion in different types of regions in Russia. Rather, there should be different models of SME and entrepreneurship policy invented to support entrepreneurial activity within its regionally and locally specific constraints.

For instance, there is no definite correlation between the SME density in the region and the level of opportunity-driven entrepreneurial activity. Hence, a smart entrepreneurship policy should focus on an in-depth analysis of the structure of the sector and early entrepreneurship when formulating policies, rather than on quantitative data based only on the number or density of SMEs.

Generally speaking, while checking most of our hypotheses we found that for the whole sample the statistical correlation is either absent or very low. Some tendencies can be seen only among some specific groups of regions or settlements. These groupings, however, are based merely on individual criteria (population size, estimations of well-being, and so on), and we assume that more robust correlations could be found when constructing typologies based also on socio-cultural items, which could give more insight into not only the level but also the type of entrepreneurial activity in different Russian environments.

Further insights could be gained if particular sets of variables could be found to represent different mixes of economic, social and psychological characteristics that would explain the diversity of entrepreneurial activity, not across all regions but within specific groups of regions and settlements. Taking into consideration the high degree of heterogeneity of Russia's society and economy, this approach should be promising.

Nevertheless, the above results show that the high level of heterogeneity of Russian regions demands a more fine-tuned focus on the part of researchers as well as policy-makers. In terms of SME and entrepreneurship support policy, an approach that simply disseminates from the centre to the periphery, while co-financing the same set of measures and mechanisms in different Russian regions without taking into consideration the different quality and quantity of resources, skills and institutions, is unlikely to reduce regional imbalances in entrepreneurship.

NOTE

1. The data analysed in this chapter are from a 2011 project in which the authors participated: the Georating survey by the Public Opinion Foundation (POF), Moscow. It was realised with financial support of the Center of Fundamental Research of the National Research University Higher School of Economics, Moscow.

REFERENCES

Arenius, P. and M. Minniti (2005), 'Perceptual variables and nascent entrepreneurship', *Small Business Economics*, **24** (3), 233–47.

Audretsch, D.B., W. Boente and M. Keilbach (2008), 'Regional entrepreneurship capital and its impact on knowledge diffusion and economic performance', *Journal of Business Venturing*, **23** (1), 687–98.

Audretsch, D.B. and M. Fritsch (2002), 'Growth regimes over time and space', *Regional Studies*, **36** (2), 113–24.

Audretsch, D. and M. Keilbach (2004), 'Entrepreneurship capital and economic performance', *Regional Studies*, **38** (8), 949–59.

Bergmann, H. (2004), 'Gründungsaktivitäten im regionalen Kontext: Gründer, Gründungseinstellungen und Rahmenbedingungen in zehn deutschen Regionen', *Kölner Forschungen zur Wirtschafts- und Sozialgeographie*, **57**, 234.

Bosma, N. and V. Schutjens (2011), 'Understanding regional variation in entrepreneurial activity and entrepreneurial attitude in Europe', *Annals of Regional Science*, **47** (3), 711–42.

Caliendo, M., F. Fosen and A. Kritikos (2014), 'Personality characteristics and the decision to become and stay self-employed', *Small Business Economics*, **42** (4), 787–814.

Chepurenko, A. (2014), 'Informal entrepreneurship under transition: causes and specific features', in Dieter Boegenhold (ed.), *Soziologie des Wirtschaftlichen*, Dordrecht: Springer VS, pp. 361–82.

Earle, J.S. and Z. Sakova (2000), 'Business start-ups or disguised unemployment? Evidence on the character of self-employment from transition economies', *Labour Economics*, **7** (5), 575–601.

Federal State Statistics Service (ed.) (2012), 'Results of full-scale Federal statistical observation on activities of subjects of small and medium entrepreneurship in 2010', Moscow: Statistics of Russia (in Russian).

Foelster, S. (2000), 'Do entrepreneurs create jobs?', *Small Business Economics*, **14** (2), 137–48.

Fritsch, M. and P. Mueller (2004), 'The effects of new firm formation on regional development over time', *Regional Studies*, **38** (8), 961–75.

Keeble, D. and S. Walker (1994), 'New firms, small firms and dead firms: spatial patterns and determinants in the United Kingdom', *Regional Studies*, **28** (4), 1–27.

Kibler, E., T. Kautonen and M. Fink (2014), 'Regional social legitimacy of entrepreneurship: implications for entrepreneurial intention and start-up behaviour', *Regional Studies*, **48** (6), 995–1015.

Mueller, P., A. Van Stel and D.J. Storey (2008), 'The effects of new firm formation on regional development over time: the case of Great Britain', *Small Business Economics*, **30** (1), 59–71.

Naude, W., T. Gries, E. Wood and A. Meintjies (2008), 'Regional determinants of entrepreneurial start-ups in a developing country', *Entrepreneurship and Regional Development*, **20** (2), 111–24.

Obschonka, M., E. Schmitt-Rodermund, S.D. Gosling and R.K. Silbereisen (2013), 'The regional distribution and correlates of an entrepreneurship-prone personality profile in the United States, Germany, and the United Kingdom: a socioecological perspective', *Journal of Personality and Social Psychology*, **105** (1), 104–22.

Public Opinion Foundation (POF) (2011), 'Georating' (monitoring project), Moscow, available at http://bd.fom.ru/report/cat/cult/sci_sci/ans_sociology/georating.

Rauch, A. and M. Frese (2007), 'Let's put the person back into entrepreneurship research: a meta-analysis on the relationship between business owners' personality traits, business creation, and success', *European Journal of Work and Organizational Psychology*, **16** (4), 353–85.

Reynolds, P.D., D.J. Storey and P. Westhead (1994), 'Cross national comparison of the variation in new firm formation rates', *Regional Studies*, **28** (4), 443–56.

Reynolds, P., N. Bosma, E. Autio, S. Hunt, N. De Bono and I. Servais et al. (2005), 'Global entrepreneurship monitor: data collection design and implementation 1998–2003', *Small Business Economics*, **24** (3), 205–31.

Rosstat (ed.) (2011), 'Population employment survey 2010', Moscow (in Russian).

Rosstat (ed.) (2012), 'Russian National Accounts in 2004–2011', Moscow (in Russian).

Round J., C. Williams and P. Rodgers (2010), 'The role of domestic food production in everyday life in post-Soviet Ukraine', *Annals of the Association of American Geographers*, **100** (5), 1197–1211.

Sorgner, A. and M. Fritsch (2013), 'Occupational choice and self-employment – are they related?', Jena Economic Research Papers, 001.

Storey, D.J. and F.J. Greene (2011), *Small Business and Entrepreneurship*, London: Pearson.

Van Stel, A. and D.J. Storey (2004), 'The link between firm births and job creation: is there a Upas Tree effect?', *Regional Studies*, **38** (8), 893–909.

Westlund, H. and F. Adam (2010), 'Social capital and economic performance: a meta-analysis of 65 Studies', *European Planning Studies*, **18** (6), 893–919.

Westlund, H., J.P. Larsson and A.R. Olsson (2014), 'Start-ups and local entrepreneurial social capital in the municipalities of Sweden', *Regional Studies*, **48** (6), 974–94.

Williams, C. and J. Round (2010), 'Spatial variations in the character of off-the-books entrepreneurship: some lessons from a study of contrasting districts of Moscow', *International Journal of Entrepreneurship and Small Business*, **10** (2), 287–300.

World Bank and IFC (2012), 'Doing Business in Russia 2012', available at http://www.russianlawonline.com/law-firms-publications/doing_business_russia_2012.pdf (accessed 28 July 2013).

Zhao, H. and S.E. Seibert (2006), 'The big-five personality dimensions and entrepreneurial status: a meta-analytical review', *Journal of Applied Psychology*, **91** (2), 259–71.

Zhao, H., S.E. Seibert and G.T. Lumpkin (2010), 'The relationship of personality to entrepreneurial intentions and performance: a meta-analytic review', *Journal of Management*, **36** (10), 381–404.

8. Entrepreneurial perceptions and entrepreneurial activity in core and peripheral regions in Estonia

Urve Venesaar and Merle Küttim

INTRODUCTION

Entrepreneurship is widely acknowledged as a main driver of regional development, but previous research has shown that there exist substantial and persistent differences in entrepreneurial activity across nations and regions (Sternberg, 2009; Fritsch and Mueller, 2006; Bosma and Schutjens, 2011). Researchers have carried out a multitude of studies with the aim of explaining the factors affecting the discovery and exploitation of business opportunities (Shane and Venkataraman, 2000), and promoting the entrepreneurial activities in regions (e.g. Grilo and Irigoyen, 2006; Sternberg, 2009; Stuetzer et al., 2014). Empirical research has explained regional variation in entrepreneurship and its persistency by determinants that exert an influence on the individual decision to launch a start-up and the frequency of start-ups within regions. These determinants have been explained at different analytical levels (Bosma and Schutjens, 2009; Sternberg, 2009) considering the central role of the individual in decision-making (personal characteristics, perceptions, attitudes) and the importance of regional contextual factors influencing the decision-making process. Bosma and Schutjens (2009) have explained the regional aspect in entrepreneurship through specific regional economic attributes (job or market opportunities), a regional demographic component (individuals with high levels of entrepreneurial spirit and behaviour) and an institutional component encompassing informal (for example, attitudes towards self-employment) and formal (regulations) factors.

The cognitive approach for explaining entrepreneurship at different levels (for example, individual, aggregate) has become important nowadays (e.g. Arenius and Minniti, 2005; Fernández et al., 2009; Krueger et al., 2000). Previous research has shown that both potential and existing entrepreneurs capture the influence of the external environment through their motivations and perceptions, generating attitudes and intentions which determine behaviours (Fernández et al., 2009). Here, entrepreneurial perceptions include individual perceptions, perceptions on economic opportunities and socio-cultural perceptions. There is a widely held view that entrepreneurial perceptions precede entrepreneurial activity (e.g. Arenius and Minniti, 2005; Freytag and Thurik, 2007). But studies have also confirmed that the perception of opportunities for start-ups and that of (matching) personal capabilities do not necessarily represent the key determinant of making the step to entrepreneurial activity; and a mixture of individual, social and contextual factors impact on the individual's decision-making process when it comes to venturing into entrepreneurial activity (Amoros and Bosma, 2014). Considering the important role of entrepreneurial attitudes, perceptions and motivation in an individual's decision-making process (Krueger, 2003), it will be necessary to know how entrepreneurs in different phases of entrepreneurship perceive the regional characteristics for entrepreneurship. This knowledge could be a basis for the development of national policies to promote entrepreneurship in regions with lower entrepreneurial activity.

Several studies using different databases have explained the relationships between entrepreneurial perceptions and entrepreneurial activities in countries or regional contexts, particularly among potential and nascent entrepreneurs (e.g. Fernández et al., 2009; Shinnar et al., 2012; Stuetzer et al., 2014). Fewer studies have been dedicated to the comparison and connection of entrepreneurial perceptions among all phases of entrepreneurship, and specifically in core and peripheral regions of countries; nor searched for the connections between entrepreneurial perceptions and entrepreneurial activities. The Global Entrepreneurship Monitor (GEM) includes a number of cognitive items which makes it possible to study regions with different contextual characteristics. This was also the inspiration for conducting the research on Estonia presented in this chapter.

Estonia, where this study was carried out, has been a member state of the European Union (EU) since 2004, and has harnessed a free market and pro-business economic environment since the year of its re-independence. The case is interesting as Estonia represents those accession countries (like other Baltic countries) in Eastern Europe where entrepreneurship was fully restricted (or illegal) until the late 1980s. Then fundamental reforms were implemented in early 1990s, supported by the liberal economic policy that opened Estonia to foreign markets. Influenced by various processes of socio-economic restructuring after regaining national independence, there appeared marked regional imbalances in business development that to a large extent were inherited from the past. For example, considerable regional differences can be found in Estonia when comparing the metropolitan area and the rest of the country (which in this chapter are called core and peripheral regions).

The capital, Tallinn, and the surrounding area (that is, core region) had 50 per cent of enterprises and 38 per cent of the total population in 2000 (Statistics Estonia). Whilst gross domestic product (GDP) per capita in the core region represented 51 per cent of the relevant EU level, GDP in other regions (that is, peripheral regions) varied at around 22–25 per cent of the EU level. In 2012, the proportion of enterprises in the core region was 57 per cent and 43 per cent of the total population lived there (Statistics Estonia). GDP per capita in the core region represented 106 per cent of the relevant EU level in 2011, and GDP in other regions (that is, peripheral regions) varied at around 42–47 per cent of the EU level.

This shows that despite the openness of Estonia to foreign markets (for example, export of goods and services exceeding 95 per cent of GDP), liberal economic policy and rapid economic growth (6–7 per cent annual growth from 2000 until the economic crisis), the regional differences between the core and peripheral regions have remained almost intact. From here the question arises of how to decrease regional differences in Estonia and increase the level of well-being in peripheral regions. This question has been and is currently relevant also in many other countries (e.g. Amoros et al., 2013; Bosma and Schutjens, 2011).

In this context, the aim of this chapter is to identify and compare individuals' entrepreneurial perceptions in core and peripheral regions, and assess their connection with entrepreneurial activity in different phases of entrepreneurship. In this regard the analysis follows the cognitive approach of explaining entrepreneurship. Since entrepreneurial activity in regions depends largely on the regional characteristics and trends in the development of entrepreneurship in Estonia, these can be seen as a background factor for understanding the differences of entrepreneurial activities in core and peripheral regions. To fulfil the aim of the study the following research questions have been formulated:

- What are the main differences in the entrepreneurial perceptions of individuals in core and peripheral regions of Estonia, and in different phases of entrepreneurship?
- How are different individuals' entrepreneurial perceptions connected with entrepreneurial activity in core and peripheral regions of Estonia?

The chapter contributes to the current literature by explicitly focusing on better understanding the reasons for differences in entrepreneurship between core and peripheral regions in Estonia as a post-socialist country in transition from efficiency-based to innovation-based economy. The chapter presents the results of Global Entrepreneurship Monitor (GEM) research, which was conducted in Estonia in 2013. The total sample consists of 1741 respondents including micro, small and medium-sized enterprises. The empirical study is based on various questions about entrepreneurial perceptions and activities in different phases of entrepreneurship.

The remainder of the chapter is organised as follows. First the theoretical framework is presented and indicators are derived to characterise entrepreneurial perceptions to assess their impact on entrepreneurial activities. In the next section the study design, data and methodology are described. And in the subsequent section the results of the analyses are provided. Finally the results of the research are discussed and conclusions are drawn.

THEORETICAL FRAMEWORK

Entrepreneurial Perceptions and Entrepreneurial Activity

Entrepreneurship is seen primarily as a local event where the connectivity, local availability of finance and space, and local institutional environment influence the decision to start and run a business (Hofer and Welter, 2011; Feldman, 2001). It has also earlier been confirmed by Johannisson (2000: 287) that entrepreneurship is 'a generically social, a collective phenomenon' influenced by, among other determinants, the regional environment.

According to Sternberg (2009) a region is an important unit for understanding the most immediate factors affecting entrepreneurship. So in order to develop regional entrepreneurship it is necessary to assess factors that affect the behaviour of entrepreneurs in finding business opportunities and making choices between becoming self-employed or working as an employee. This may be conditioned and influenced by personality and demographic characteristics, as well as different contextual factors of regions (such as resources, institutional context, socio-cultural attitudes). From a person-focused perspective these regional characteristics may operate as background factors, in that they affect proximal predictors of entrepreneurial behaviour (Stuetzer et al., 2014). This means that regional characteristics have an effect on the individual perception of business opportunities, which in turn can predict start-up intentions and activity or encourage continuing (or growing) existing businesses.

The connection between the region and individual described above can be explained through perceptions of regional characteristics, which generate attitudes and intentions and may trigger entrepreneurial behaviour in the region (Stuetzer et al., 2014). According to cognitive psychology, perceptions reflect the external environment around individuals, captured through their senses and elaborated in their mind (Krueger, 2003).

The perceptions of regional characteristics may be divided into three groups (according to the classification of Fernández et al., 2009 and supported by GEM data): individual perceptions (role model, self-efficacy and risk aversion), perceptions of economic opportunities, and socio-cultural perceptions (perceptions about the social legitimation of entrepreneurship, including desirability of career choice, status of and respect for new businesses, preference for a typical living standard, and public media publicity for successful enterprises). Socio-cultural perceptions express a population's attitude towards entrepreneurship, which may impact on entrepreneurial intention and their activities in the region.

The empirical research has shown that at the regional level positive relationships exist between entrepreneurial perceptions and entrepreneurial activity, demonstrating that regions with a higher level of personal entrepreneurial perceptions show higher levels of entrepreneurial activity (Bosma and Schutjens, 2009). But it has also been found that an individual's attitude (or perception) may not have a direct link with entrepreneurial activity, because different barriers in regions (for example, laws, regulations) may hinder people from starting businesses or the continuation and growth of established businesses (Bosma and Schutjens, 2009).

From an individual's cognitive perspective, perceptions are the most important factor in the intention to start a business (Krueger, 2003); entrepreneurial intentions are the most relevant elements leading to starting up a new venture. Intentions are classically defined as the cognitive state temporally and causally prior to action (e.g. Krueger, 2000), therefore in the context of entrepreneurial activities this means the state of an individual prior to the decision to start a business (Krueger, 2003).

It is argued that intentions models predict behaviour better than both individual (for example, personality) and situational (for example, employment status) variables (Krueger et al., 2000). Several studies (Kolvereid, 1996; Tkachev and Kolvereid, 1999; Autio et al., 1997; de Pillis and Reardon, 2007) have examined entrepreneurial intentions predicting entrepreneurial behaviour in different countries (the United States, France, Russia, Norway, Sweden, and so on). In current research, intention is defined as an individual's expectation to start a business in the next three years, which according to the GEM concept identifies potential entrepreneurship. The study of the role of different perceptions in the formation of intentions towards start-up activities in different regions (Krueger, 2000) may help to better understand the external environment around individuals through their cognitive biases.

Fernández et al. (2009) have studied the influence of cognitive aspects (individual perceptions, entrepreneurial opportunities and socio-cultural perceptions) of entrepreneurial intentions and have concluded that the three kinds of perceptions, but especially self-efficacy and role model as components of individual perceptions, have significant influence on intentions. The influence of entrepreneurial opportunities was not as high as was expected, and the results of socio-cultural perceptions were found to be the weakest. While comparing Scandinavian and Mediterranean sub-samples the most important differences were found to exist in terms of some demographic variables (work status and education) and some individual perceptions (role model and self-efficacy), but not in perceptions about entrepreneurial opportunities and in socio-cultural perceptions. The question arises of whether the influence of the same cognitive aspects of entrepreneurial intentions may differ in different regional contexts, for example in the core and peripheral regions.

Entrepreneurship in Core and Peripheral Regions

Taking into account the strong connection entrepreneurship has with the region where entrepreneurs operate daily, regional differences exert a direct influence for the behaviour of enterprises. Furthermore, existing research clearly reveals that there are pronounced regional differences in start-up activity (e.g. Armington and Acs, 2002; Bosma et al., 2009), which are remarkably persistent over time (Fritsch and Mueller, 2005). Several authors have noted that, especially, the prevalence rate of nascent and young businesses varies widely across regions (e.g. Andersson and Koster, 2011; Bosma and Schutjens, 2009; Stuetzer et al., 2014).

In terms of regional aspects, significantly more entrepreneurship activities are found in urban regions, particularly in cities, compared with other regions of the same country (Sternberg, 2009). Studies of different developed countries in Western Europe have shown that core regions exhibit more strengths for fostering entrepreneurial activities (Van Stel and Suddle, 2008; Burke et al., 2009) due to different positive phenomena in these regions. For example, the general economic advantage of highly dense urban areas is explained by the agglomeration effect (Van Stel and Suddle, 2008; Florida, 2003). This is attributed to the density of potential entrepreneurs, a highly educated population, a large potential market, and knowledge spillovers from universities.

There is also the opportunity of sharing information with research organisations and easier diffusion of (tacit) knowledge (Werner and Athreye, 2004). Also, Minniti (2005) has concluded that areas with a higher density of entrepreneurs have a stronger entrepreneurial culture, which encourages entry. Parker (2004) suggests that regions with a strong entrepreneurial tradition have an advantage if they are able to perpetuate it over time and across generations.

The role of small firms as seedbeds for new business formation on the regional level has been analysed in several studies (e.g. Fritsch and Mueller, 2005; Audretsch and Fritsch, 1994), and the empirical evidence confirms that a high population of young and small firms in a region increases the individual propensity to transit to self-employment. This evidence may be one of the explanations for the persistence of differences between the core and periphery, as entrepreneurial activity is often higher in core regions.

Peripheral, and especially rural, areas are usually economically weaker or even deprived (Cannarella and Piccioni, 2006). This phenomenon has been demonstrated throughout several empirical studies conducted in different countries, both underdeveloped (Lanjouw, 2001) and developed (Polese and Shearmur, 2006; Kalantaridis, 2009; Smallbone et al., 1999). Entrepreneurship is seen as a source of economic development in peripheral regions.

At the same time, the studies of entrepreneurship in peripheral regions have emphasised several factors in the division of resources and in the behaviour of entrepreneurs that distinguish entrepreneurship in core and peripheral regions. In many cases these differences have been explained through an uneven distribution of human, social and financial capital in a nation, reinforced by migration and the tendency for individuals to form groups on the basis of similarity (Bosma et al., 2009).

Previous studies have also shown that a lack of entrepreneurial role models has acted as a key institutional factor exerting a negative influence on venture development by rural economic agents (Lang et al., 2014). Differences in entrepreneurship in the core and peripheral regions mentioned in previous studies indicate the need to look for the reasons for the different behaviour of entrepreneurs in various regional environments. The studies also show that in addition to regional differences, the behaviour of entrepreneurs is influenced by several cognitive factors such as entrepreneurial perceptions and other aspects, which in turn influences regional entrepreneurial activity (e.g. Bosma and Schutjens, 2009; Stuetzer et al., 2014).

Based on previous studies the economic level of development of regions also has to be taken into account as it could influence entrepreneurial activity. For example, it has been pointed out in GEM studies that entrepreneurial activity has a causal relationship with a country's level of economic development (e.g. Wennekers et al., 2005; Sternberg and Wennekers, 2005; Bosma et al., 2009). Based on the methodology of the 2011 GEM survey, countries are divided into three groups according to their stages of economic development, as described in Porter's typology (Porter et al., 2002): factor-, efficiency- and innovation-driven economies (Kelley et al., 2012). This division reflects the influence of the entrepreneurial environment on a country's entrepreneurial activity at various stages of economic development.

There are also groups of countries that are in transition from one stage to another. For example, Estonia, along with Hungary, Latvia, Lithuania, Poland and Croatia, belong to the group of European countries that are in transit from efficiency-based economies to innovation-based ones. The results of a current study based on the case of Estonia should give some insights for explaining the differences in entrepreneurship development among this group of countries, considering the connections between entrepreneurial perceptions and entrepreneurial activity in core and peripheral regions.

METHOD AND SAMPLE

Study Design

The study is based on the survey carried out by the GEM in 2013. The GEM measures individuals' perceptions of entrepreneurship, their involvement in entrepreneurial activity, and their aspirations in relation to this (Bosma et al., 2012). Primarily Estonian GEM data are used in the study reported in this chapter, but comparisons are also drawn with other countries and country groups. The data were collected though standardised questionnaires involving an adult population aged 18–64.

In the study a differentiation is made between core and peripheral regions of Estonia. The core region includes the capital of Estonia and its surrounding area (that is, Harju County). The peripheral regions include the rest of Estonia (that is, 14 counties besides Harju County). The reason for this selection of regions is justified by the quite significant and persistent differences of entrepreneurial activity in these two regions, and because of a need to understand better how different perceptions are influencing the variation of entrepreneurial activity in the selected regions.

The study looks also at differences between various phases of entrepreneurial activity in the two regions. The phases of entrepreneurial activity include: potential entrepreneurs who express entrepreneurial intentions (expecting to start a business within the next three years), nascent entrepreneurs (undertaking steps to start a business during the last 12 months, or being in business less than three months), new entrepreneurs (being in business longer than three months, but less than three and a half years), early-stage entrepreneurs (grouping together nascent and new entrepreneurs, being in business less than three and a half years) and established entrepreneurs (being in business more than three and a half years).

Sample

In terms of entrepreneurial activity, the sample is divided into potential, nascent, new and established entrepreneurs in core and peripheral regions. The total population of working age included in the Estonian sample consists of 1741 respondents, of whom 668 are entrepreneurs (Table 8.1). The proportion of potential, nascent and new entrepreneurs in the sample is higher in the core region (which is also statistically significant), while the proportion of established entrepreneurs is higher in the peripheral region of Estonia.

As to gender, the proportion of men is higher in all phases of entrepreneurial activity, but the difference is largest in the case of established entrepreneurs (statistically significant for potential and nascent entrepreneurs). The average age tends to be higher in the peripheral region, but it is quite similar for potential, nascent and new entrepreneurs in the core region (33–35 years) and in the peripheral region (36–38). Established entrepreneurs, however, are somewhat older (45 years in the core, and 51 years in the peripheral region).

Educational level is highest among nascent and new entrepreneurs as among them there is the largest proportion of those respondents who have some form of post-secondary education. In the case of both potential and established entrepreneurs about two-thirds have a secondary degree or lower educational attainment (statistically significant for potential and nascent entrepreneurs). The proportion of respondents with graduate education is higher in almost all phases of entrepreneurship in the peripheral region; and post-secondary and graduate education together dominate in the core region. Higher educational attainment refers to a labour force with higher levels of professional skills in the core region and, at the same time, also refers to activities that require a somewhat less-educated workforce in the periphery.

As to the level of income, new and established entrepreneurs are financially better off than other types of entrepreneurs. There are, however, among the established entrepreneurs, quite a large proportion of those who belong to the lowest 33 percentile of income. At the same time, the proportion of established entrepreneurs who belong to the middle tile is lower than in case of other entrepreneurs. The highest 33 percentile of income is characteristic of all phases of entrepreneurship in the core region, except new entrepreneurs. The lowest 33 percentile is higher amongst potential and established entrepreneurs in the periphery.

Table 8.1 Division of entrepreneurs by phases and their demographic characteristics in core and peripheral regions

	Potential entrepreneurs		Nascent entrepreneurs		New entrepreneurs		Established entrepreneurs	
	Core	Peripheral	Core	Peripheral	Core	Peripheral	Core	Peripheral
No. of entrepreneurs (N)	202	147	89	64	45	34	41	46
% by phases of activity	57.9	42.1	58.2	41.8	57.0	43.0	47.1	52.9
Gender, %								
Male	69.2	55.8	68.2	52.3	70.5	62.9	73.8	69.6
Female	30.8	44.2	31.8	47.7	29.5	37.1	26.2	30.4
Age, average	33	36	34	37	35	38.0	45	51
Education, %								
None		0.7				2.9		
Some secondary	4.0	5.5	1.1	3.1	4.5	14.7	2.4	2.2
Secondary degree	57.2	65.1	44.9	60.9	43.2	52.9	52.4	71.7
Post-secondary	25.9	13.7	38.2	17.2	34.1	17.6	16.7	10.9
Graduate experience	12.9	15.1	15.7	18.8	18.2	11.8	28.6	15.2
Income, %								
Lowest 33% tile	14.3	25.2	22.1	10.6	9.4	10.3	12.5	27.0
Middle 33% tile	34.8	38.7	26.5	48.9	34.4	24.1	28.1	29.7
Highest 33% tile	50.9	36.1	51.5	40.4	56.3	65.5	59.4	43.2

In conclusion, the nature of the sample indicates that the results of the study see the typical entrepreneur more often as a male with secondary or post-secondary education. Early-stage entrepreneurs are younger (aged 34–36 years) and operate more in the service sector. Established entrepreneurs are older (on average 48 years old) and operate more in the primary and secondary sectors. The nature of the sample is taken into account when interpreting the results of the study.

Data Analysis and Variables

Entrepreneurial activity is analysed by using frequency distributions and cross tables. Entrepreneurs at different stages are studied, including potential, nascent and new (making up the early-stage entrepreneurship) and established entrepreneurs. In addition to entrepreneurial activity, motivation of early-stage entrepreneurs to enter into entrepreneurship (that is, opportunity- and necessity-driven entrepreneurship) is analysed.

The active entrepreneurs, both early-stage and established, are analysed also in terms of their developmental aspirations using cross tables. This analysis is justified by the fact that entrepreneurial activity is characterised in the long run by the extent that the entrepreneurs are employing strategies that support their development (internationalisation, innovation, job growth). Internationalisation measures the proportion of entrepreneurs that export outside the country boundaries; innovation brings with it new and better products and services and markets; the intention to create new jobs characterises the growth potential (Kelley et al., 2012).

The four groups of entrepreneurs (potential, nascent, new and established) are also analysed in terms various personal characteristics and perceptions to find out regional disparities in each entrepreneurial phase by using logistic regression.

The specific variables included in the regression model are as follows:

1. Potential entrepreneurship or entrepreneurial intentions (dependent variable): expects to start a business in the next three years (0 = No, 1 = Yes).
2. Nascent entrepreneurship (dependent variable): involved in starting a business less than three months old (0 = No, 1 = Yes).
3. New entrepreneurship (dependent variable): manages and owns a business that is less than three and a half years old (0 = No, 1 = Yes).
4. Established entrepreneurship (dependent variable): manages and owns a business that is more than three and a half years old (0 = No, 1 = Yes).
5. Personal characteristics:

    a. Gender: (0 = Female, 1 = Male).
    b. Age: age at time of survey (in years).
    c. Education level: highest educational attainment (0 = none, 1 = up to some secondary education, 2 = secondary degree, 3 = post-secondary, 4 = graduate experience).

6. Individual perceptions:

    a. Risk perception: fear of failure would prevent from starting a business (0 = Yes, 1 = No).
    b. Self-efficacy: has the knowledge, skill and experience required to start a new business (0 = No, 1 = Yes).
    c. Role model: knows a person who started a business in the past two years (0 = No, 1 = Yes).

7. Perceptions on entrepreneurial opportunities: in the next six months there will be good opportunities for starting a business in the area where I live (0 = No, 1 = Yes).

8. Socio-cultural perceptions:

    a. Equal living standard: preference for similar standards of living in the country (0 = No, 1 = Yes).
    b. Desirable career choice: in my country most people consider starting a new business a desirable career choice (0 = No, 1 = Yes).
    c. Status and respect: in my country those successful at starting a new business have a high level of status and respect (0 = No, 1 = Yes).
    d. Public media: in my country you will often see stories in the public media about successful new businesses (0 = No, 1 = Yes).

9. Control variables:

    a. Household size: (0 = 1 member, 1 = 2 members, 2 = 3–4 members, 3 = 5–6 members, 4 = 7–10 members).

Limitations of the Study

The main limitation is connected to the size of the Estonian sample. Although the original sample was relatively large and covered the working-age population randomly, the number of entrepreneurs, especially established entrepreneurs, is quite low. This becomes an issue when conducting a detailed analysis of specific phases of entrepreneurial activity. In the case of a small sample, the results of analysis may be affected by the proportions of different types of entrepreneurs in the sample of regions.

RESULTS

Entrepreneurial Activity in Estonian Core and Peripheral Regions

Entrepreneurial activity, especially potential and early-stage entrepreneurship, tends to be influenced by the level of economic development of a country (Amoros and Bosma, 2014). Entrepreneurial activity in Estonia is higher in all phases of entrepreneurship compared with the average of countries in transit from efficiency-driven to innovation-driven economies, except in the case of established entrepreneurs, where the Estonian indicator is lower than that of the comparable group average (Table 8.2).

Taking into account the possible change related to the transfer to an innovation-based economy, it could be expected that the rate of potential and early-stage entrepreneurship will continue to decrease in Estonia. At the same time, what is worrying is the low rate of established entrepreneurship (5 per cent), which is constantly lower (in 2012 and 2013) than the average of countries in transition from efficiency- to innovation-driven, as well as that of countries of innovation-driven economies. Comparing entrepreneurial activity in core and peripheral regions, the indicators in the core region tend to be higher in all phases of entrepreneurship. The difference is most noticeable in terms of potential and early-stage entrepreneurs (also statistically significant).

However, in terms of the established entrepreneurs who have been in business for a longer time (more than three and a half years) the difference between core and peripheral regions is much smaller. So the survival rate of enterprises in the peripheral region is higher than that in the core region (0.6 in the peripheral and 0.4 in the core region), and higher than the Estonian average (0.4) (Venesaar et al., 2014). Entrepreneurial activity in the core region is also higher, although more entrepreneurs have discontinued their activities there.

Regarding the motivation to commence early-stage entrepreneurship, in Estonia opportunity-based entrepreneurship is somewhat higher and necessity-based entrepreneurship is lower compared with the average of countries in transition from efficiency- to innovation-driven economy. There is nearly two times more opportunity-based entrepreneurship in the core region, and an approximately similar level of necessity-based entrepreneurship in the periphery.

In terms of the development of entrepreneurship it is important to increase the proportion of those enterprises that are competitive because of their growth, innovation and exporting capabilities. Entrepreneurs with higher developmental aspirations in the areas of higher entrepreneurial propensity exert a more profound influence on the economy compared to

Table 8.2 Entrepreneurial activity in Estonian core and peripheral regions compared with average in country groups according to the level of their economic development, % respondents

Phase of entrepreneurial activity	Estonian regions		Total Estonia	Average of countries in transit from efficiency to innovation-driven economy	Average of countries of innovation-driven economies
	Core	Peripheral			
Potential entrepreneurship (expects to start up in the next three years)	29.4	17.5	22.9	20.4	11.6
Nascent entrepreneurship (actively involved in start-up effort up to three months)	11.2	6.7	8.8	6.2	3.9
New entrepreneurship (manages and owns a business that is up to 42 months old)	5.7	3.6	4.5	4.1	2.8
Established entrepreneurship (manages and owns a business that is older than 42 months)	5.2	4.8	5	6.0	6.6
Early-stage opportunity-based entrepreneurship	13.9	7.4	10.4	9.3	6.2
Early-stage necessity-based entrepreneurship	1.9	2.0	1.9	3.1	1.4

Table 8.3   Developmental aspirations of early-stage and established entrepreneurs

	Early-stage entrepreneurs		Total	Established entrepreneurs		Total
	Core	Peripheral		Core	Peripheral	
Internationalisation/export intensity						
More than 75	11.3	9.9	10.7	11.9	6.8	9.3
25 to 75	12.9	18.7	15.3	11.9	4.5	8.1
Under 25	51.6	29.7	42.3	40.5	45.5	43.0
None	24.2	41.8	31.6	35.7	43.2	39.5
Innovation						
New product market combination	32.8	37.1	34.6	22.0	10.9	16.1
Expected job growth in 5 years						
Decreases	0.8		0.4		4.3	2.3
Remains stable	27.5	37.5	31.7	73.2	71.7	72.4
Increases	71.8	62.5	67.8	26.8	23.9	25.3

areas with lower levels of entrepreneurial activity, but equally high development aspirations (Xavier et al., 2013). The developmental aspirations of enterprises consist of their endeavours to internationalise, innovate, and grow in terms of the number of employees, and are studied separately for early-stage and established entrepreneurs.

As to the level of internationalisation, in the case of both early-stage and established entrepreneurs the majority are exporting (68 per cent and 60 per cent, respectively) (Table 8.3). The proportion of highly international enterprises (that have more than 75 per cent of customers abroad) is somewhat higher in the core region (distribution is significant for early-stage entrepreneurs). In the case of enterprises that are not internationally oriented, there are more of those that are not exporting but working for local markets in the peripheral region.

In terms of innovative activities that comprise new product–market combination (that is, the product/service is new for some or most of the clients, and a few or none of the other enterprises are offering the same product/service), early-stage entrepreneurs are more innovative than established entrepreneurs (35 per cent and 16 per cent, respectively), particularly in the peripheral region (37 per cent). In the case of established entrepreneurs there are more innovative entrepreneurs in the core region. This indicates that in addition to positive perceptions affecting entrepreneurship (for example, risk perception), new product and market innovation are factors that enable the future growth of entrepreneurship potential in the periphery.

As to the job growth that entrepreneurs expect in the next five years, this is higher in the core region, where a larger proportion of both early-stage and established entrepreneurs anticipate employment growth. More specifically 68 per cent of early-stage and 25 per cent of established entrepreneurs foresee growth in the number of their employees. The difference between enterprises in different phases of development is that the majority of early-stage entrepreneurs foresee job growth, while most of the established entrepreneurs think that the number of people they employ will remain largely the same. It follows that the established entrepreneurs are not only more experienced but also more cautious about development possibilities. In a way, growth aspirations are the prerogative of younger enterprises as the trend is that they are more growth-oriented.

When comparing the developmental aspirations of Estonia with the average for all countries in transition from efficiency- to innovation-driven economies, Estonian indicators are higher in internationalisation and innovation, but lower in growth aspirations. The developmental aspirations of entrepreneurs in the peripheral region are usually lower, especially in the case of established entrepreneurs. At the same time, peripheral early-stage entrepreneurs having a higher aspiration for innovation as a combination of new market and product supports the positive perceptions of regional characteristics, which may envisage a prerequisite for the increase of entrepreneurial activity of peripheral regions in the future. The following analysis of entrepreneurial perceptions of regional characteristics should help to explain the differences between entrepreneurial activity in core and peripheral regions.

Perceptions Affecting Entrepreneurs of Different Stages in Core and Peripheral Regions

Logistic regression was performed separately for potential, nascent, new and established entrepreneurs in core and peripheral Estonian regions to see whether there are similar and/or different characteristics of entrepreneurs that may explain their activity levels. Their perceptions were analysed in terms of individual perceptions, perceptions of entrepreneurial opportunities and socio-cultural perceptions.

The analysis shows that personal characteristics are important in the case of potential and nascent entrepreneurs (Table 8.4). They tend to be more often males, especially in the case of potential entrepreneurs where the regression coefficient is higher and statistically significant. In terms of regional variation, males dominate more in the core region in the case of potential entrepreneurs. New and established entrepreneurs are also more likely to be male, but this is statistically significant only in the case of established entrepreneurs in the periphery. As to age, potential and early-stage entrepreneurs tend to be younger, whereas established entrepreneurs are older, especially in the periphery. Regarding human capital, potential and early-stage entrepreneurs in the core region tend to have a higher level of education than their counterparts in the periphery.

In terms of individual entrepreneurial perceptions, the analysis shows that risk perception is not a factor that influences new venture creation, meaning that both potential and nascent entrepreneurs are not afraid of failing while starting a business. As to regional differences, nascent entrepreneurs in the periphery are more confident. Also new and established entrepreneurs do not think that risks are an obstacle for business activities, and the coefficients are higher than for potential and nascent entrepreneurs. In terms of regional differences, while new entrepreneurs are more confident in the periphery, established entrepreneurs are less afraid of failure in the core region. This implies that the greater experience of established entrepreneurs helps them to be more confident about being able to run a business in the highly competitive environment of the core region.

In terms of self-efficacy, potential and nascent entrepreneurs perceive that they have the necessary knowledge and skills to start a business. This perception is higher in the case of nascent entrepreneurs, who have already undertaken steps to found a business, than among potential entrepreneurs, who are still considering it. In terms of regional differences, potential and established entrepreneurs in the peripheral region are more likely to think that they have the knowledge and skills to run a business than their counterparts in the core region, whilst in the case of nascent and new entrepreneurs the pattern is reversed.

Having a role model is important for potential, nascent and new entrepreneurs, meaning that they know someone who has recently started a business. As to regional differences, having a role model is more important in the core region than in the periphery. In the case of established entrepreneurs, having a role model is not important. Established entrepreneurs have already developed their routines and may not be looking for new contacts.

Perceptions of entrepreneurial opportunities are important for potential entrepreneurs in the periphery, where they contribute positively towards the intention of starting a business. Except in the case of established entrepreneurs in the periphery, other groups foresee good opportunities for entrepreneurship, although the difference is not statistically significant.

Socio-cultural perceptions are not so important for different groups of entrepreneurs. Potential entrepreneurs in the core regions and periphery

Table 8.4　　*Personal characteristics and entrepreneurial perceptions by different phases of entrepreneurship in core and peripheral regions*

	Potential entrepreneurs				Nascent entrepreneurs		
	Core		Periphery		Core		Periphery
	Coef.	Std. err.	Coef.	Std. err.	Coef.	Std. err.	Coef.
Personal characteristics							
Gender	0.667**	0.241	0.503*	0.250	0.461	0.340	0.532
Age	−0.042***	0.010	−0.050***	0.010	−0.038*	0.015	−0.039**
Education	0.092	0.148	0.037	0.151	0.404*	0.206	0.281
Individual perceptions							
Risk perception	0.093	0.241	0.305	0.255	0.195	0.345	0.585*
Self-efficacy	0.720**	0.240	0.958***	0.263	1.663***	0.398	1.174**
Role model	0.598*	0.236	0.261	0.261	0.561*	0.330	0.243
Perceptions on opportunities							
Entrepreneurial opportunities	−0.207	0.248	0.525*	0.258	0.509	0.387	0.438
Socio-cultural perceptions							
Equal living standard	−0.150	0.230	−0.468*	0.250	−0.514	0.313	0.411
Desirable career	−0.083	0.230	−0.074	0.258	−0.017	0.310	−0.215
Respect	0.171	0.240	0.191	0.262	0.076	0.313	−0.438
Public media	0.148	0.233	0.123	0.262	−0.059	0.312	0.643*
Control variables							
Household size	0.059	0.135	−0.073	0.137	−0.056	0.177	−0.061
N	404.44		494.38		464.98		540.36
Constant	0.402	0.680	0.362	0.710	3.531	0.964	3.094
R-squared (Nagelkerke)	0.192		0.226		0.244		0.202
Log likelihood	466.883		421.389		294.519		276.305
Chi-square	60.981***		76.509***		65.442***		52.186***

Note:　Significance levels: *** significant at $p < 0.001$, ** significant at $p < 0.01$, * significant at $p < 0.1$.

do not think that there should be equal living standards. Active entrepreneurs believe more that the living standard should be equal as compared to potential entrepreneurs (but it is not statistically significant).

　　The impact of perceiving entrepreneurship as a good career choice and perceiving entrepreneurs as having a high status in society is for the most part not statistically significant. However, the entrepreneurs perceive that those active in business do not have a high status and respect in society. In terms of media coverage, nascent and new entrepreneurs in the periphery

| | New entrepreneurs | | | | Established entrepreneurs | | | |
| | Core | | Periphery | | Core | | Periphery | |
Std. err.	Coef.	Std. err.	Coef.	Std. err.	Coef.	Std. err.	Coef.	Std. err.
0.329	0.355	0.475	0.579	0.533	0.329	0.494	0.843*	0.486
0.013	−0.013	0.021	−0.039*	0.020	0.067**	0.022	0.091**	0.027
0.196	0.212	0.299	−0.878*	0.384	0.019	0.284	0.094	0.284
0.354	0.960	0.599	1.731*	0.776	1.387*	0.661	0.235	0.485
0.358	3.037**	1.069	2.041**	0.688	2.147**	0.676	3.860***	1.073
0.346	2.510**	0.786	0.960	0.626	−1.015*	0.509	−0.180	0.551
0.345	0.364	0.588	0.319	0.541	0.542	0.527	−0.442	0.569
0.336	0.392	0.448	0.867	0.571	−0.012	0.461	0.371	0.504
0.334	0.507	0.441	−0.582	0.547	−0.225	0.472	−0.004	0.484
0.334	−0.486	0.441	0.154	0.544	0.095	0.482	−1.119*	0.510
0.340	−0.256	0.448	1.032*	0.557	0.980*	0.477	−0.453	0.556
0.178	−0.088	0.251	−0.476	0.304	0.567*	0.295	0.749*	0.296
	464.98		540.36		464.98		540.36	
0.971	8.332	1.813	3.545	1.702	9.584	1.693	11.607	2.202
	0.348		0.342		0.277		0.411	
	152.208		120.232		145.275		131.310	
	65.093***		53.316***		45.735***		75.826***	

tend to think that the media often covers business success stories, while established entrepreneurs find this in the core region.

It can be concluded from the preceding analysis that although entrepreneurial activity is, in all phases, higher in the core region than in the peripheral region, there are nevertheless some variations based on personal characteristics of entrepreneurs and entrepreneurial perceptions. In terms of personal characteristics the dominance of males is rather similarly important among potential entrepreneurs in both the core and peripheral regions, who intend to start a business within the next two years. Also, whereas potential and new entrepreneurs tend to be younger, established entrepreneurs tend to be older.

There are regional differences that allow conclusions to be drawn on how entrepreneurial perceptions are connected with entrepreneurial activities. Risk perception or being afraid of failure does not prevent potential entrepreneurs from wanting to start a business in the peripheral region. This applies to an even greater degree for nascent and new entrepreneurs. Entrepreneurs feel that they have the necessary knowledge and skills, and it is natural that confidence grows with the age of the enterprise. Established entrepreneurs in the periphery assessed their knowledge and skills to be higher than in the core region. Role models are more important in the core region, though unimportant for established entrepreneurs. Socio-cultural perceptions are more essential in the periphery, but they are less important than individual perceptions.

DISCUSSION AND CONCLUSIONS

On the whole, Estonian entrepreneurial activity is higher than the average of countries in transition from efficiency-driven economies to innovation-driven economies. Taking into account the relationship between entrepreneurial activity and the level of economic development of a country, it could be expected that entrepreneurial activity will continue to decrease in Estonia.

Entrepreneurial activity in Estonia is characterised by relatively high opportunity-based entrepreneurship, which exceeds the average indicators of countries at the same economic development level (Amoros and Bosma, 2014). When analysing entrepreneurial perceptions in terms of entrepreneurial opportunities, we found that good entrepreneurial opportunities for starting a business are perceived the most by potential entrepreneurs in the periphery. Here perceptions of opportunities should contribute positively towards the intention of starting a business in the periphery. This statement is also supported by previous studies (e.g. Arenius and Minniti, 2005). But entrepreneurial activity is low in the periphery, and we can presume that realising the intention to start a business is problematic due to restrictions stemming from other perceptions (for example, socio-cultural), or other formal and informal factors. These factors may also influence lower developmental aspirations of entrepreneurs in the peripheral region, especially in terms of internationalisation and economic growth intentions in the case of established entrepreneurs.

In the case of the developmental aspirations toward innovation, new product and market combinations were reported more often by established entrepreneurs in the core region, but more often by early-stage entrepreneurs in the periphery. So in the case of innovation, the pattern of developmental aspirations being lower in the periphery does not apply, implying that younger enterprises can be also innovative in peripheral regions, but perhaps with incremental and regional innovations rather than with radical and international ones.

Entrepreneurial activity in the peripheral region is supported by a somewhat smaller gender difference than in the core region, in terms of both early-stage and established entrepreneurs. Entrepreneurs in the peripheral region also tend to be older, but are characterised by lower educational attainment as less respondents in the periphery hold a post-secondary degree. Furthermore, the income level of entrepreneurs in the periphery is lower, especially in the case of established entrepreneurs. The issue here is how to make the periphery attractive for potential and early-stage entrepreneurs (who tend to be younger and better-educated) as more than half of them seem to prefer the core region.

Entrepreneurial perceptions analysed in the current study are rather different across the various phases of entrepreneurship and in core and peripheral regions, which gives us the opportunity to explain the connections between entrepreneurial perceptions and entrepreneurial activity. Individual entrepreneurial perceptions, particularly self-efficacy and role models, seem to have the highest influence on entrepreneurial intentions (that is, potential entrepreneurship), as well as on the entrepreneurial activities in other phases (that is, early-stage and established) of entrepreneurship. Having a role model was an important factor in the core region for potential entrepreneurs, but role models are less important in the periphery. This confirms the results of previous studies (Lang et al., 2014) and indicates that the lack of role models may lead to lower entrepreneurial activity.

In addition, potential entrepreneurs in the periphery show a higher propensity to report entrepreneurial opportunities than other entrepreneurs in the periphery. This shows that while there is much less opportunity-based entrepreneurship in the peripheral region than in the core region, perceiving entrepreneurial opportunities and self-efficacy in the periphery are very important and influence entrepreneurial intentions. And there is a need to promote the turning of these intentions into activity through policies that promote entrepreneurship.

For early-stage entrepreneurs in the core region individual perceptions were significant in terms of self-efficacy and role model, as well as lower risk perception for established entrepreneurs. This could explain the higher entrepreneurial activity in the core region. As not perceiving risk self-efficacy was also important for early-stage and established entrepreneurs in the periphery, this shows again that the region has high potential for entrepreneurial activities. The high level of perception of self-efficacy of entrepreneurs means that perceiving themselves to have knowledge, skills and experience is supporting their entrepreneurial intentions that, in the Estonian case, are resulting in short-term (nascent and early-stage) entrepreneurship.

The level of self-efficacy seems to be insufficient for long-term entrepreneurship, because the proportion of established entrepreneurship is very low in Estonia. Although self-efficacy is highest among established entrepreneurs in the periphery, other types of perceptions (for example, risk perception, role models and socio-cultural aspects) are not sufficiently supporting the developmental aspirations of established entrepreneurs in the periphery.

Overall, socio-cultural perceptions had no significant effect on entrepreneurial activities. However, the attention by the media towards successful new businesses is important for nascent and new entrepreneurs in the periphery, and established entrepreneurs in the core region. Established entrepreneurs in the periphery also think that entrepreneurs are perceived by society in terms of a high level of status and respect. These aspects should be considered more strongly in designing relevant policy measures. Estonian public bodies responsible for the development of entrepreneurship have already made efforts in fostering entrepreneurial activity and promoting an entrepreneurial mind-set as a way out of unemployment and job insecurity. Apparently the creation of a supportive socio-cultural environment for entrepreneurship through relevant policy and activities requires a longer time to change the population's attitudes and mind-set, considering the historical background of Estonia.

In conclusion, in the presence of overall high entrepreneurial potential, high early-stage entrepreneurship and a low level of established entrepreneurship in Estonia, significant differences have been found in the role of entrepreneurial perceptions at different phases of entrepreneurship, and in core and peripheral regions. The results of the analysis of entrepreneurial perceptions show a need to support the promotion of entrepreneurship in the peripheral region through evolving role models and supporting the lowering of risk perceptions. In addition, socio-cultural factors help to create a favourable environment for raising the level of entrepreneurial activities. The sustainability of enterprises could be supported through increasing their self-efficacy, which means the development of entrepreneurship education and training, and widening the accessibility of training particularly for potential and early-stage entrepreneurs. Socio-cultural aspects should also be included, to support the development of sustainable entrepreneurship.

Future research on entrepreneurship activities in core and peripheral regions may be extended to deepen the investigation of a population's cognitive aspects as well as other formal and informal aspects using secondary data and the opinion of experts. Considering the rapid changes in countries in transition from efficiency-driven to innovation-driven economies, additional value would be found from the comparison of entrepreneurial perceptions and entrepreneurial activities in these countries over a longer period of development.

REFERENCES

Amoros, J.E. and N. Bosma (2014), *GEM 2013 Global Report*, available at http://www.gemconsortium.org/docs/3106/gem-2013-global-report.

Amoros, J.E., C. Felzensztein and E. Gimmon (2013), 'Entrepreneurial opportunities in peripheral vs. core regions in Chile', *Small Business Economics*, **40**, 119–39.

Andersson, M. and S. Koster (2011), 'Sources of persistence in regional start-up rates – evidence from Sweden', *Journal of Economic Geography*, **11** (1), 179–201.

Arenius, P. and M. Minniti (2005), 'Perceptual variables and nascent entrepreneurship', *Small Business Economics*, **24**, 233–47.

Armington, C. and Z. Acs (2002), 'The determinants of regional variation in new firm formation', *Regional Studies*, **36**, 33–45.

Audretsch, D.B. and M. Fritsch (1994), 'The geography of firm births in Germany', *Regional Studies*, **28** (7), 359–65.

Autio, E., R. Keeley, M. Klofsten and T. Ulfstedt (1997), 'Entrepreneurial intent among students: testing an intent model in Asia, Scandinavia, and USA', in D.L. Sexton and J.D. Kasarda (eds), *Frontiers of Entrepreneurial Research*, Wellesley, MA: Babson College Publications, pp. 133–47.

Bosma, N.S., Z.J. Acs, E. Autio, A. Coduras and J. Levie (2009), *Global Entrepreneurship Monitor 2008, Executive Report*, Babson Park, MA, USA; Santiago, Chile; London, UK: Global Entrepreneurship Research Consortium.

Bosma, N., A. Coduras, Y. Litovsky and J. Seaman (2012), 'GEM Manual. A report on the design, data and quality control of the Global Entrepreneurship Monitor', available at www.gemconsortium.org.

Bosma, N.S. and V. Schutjens (2009), 'Determinants of early-stage entrepreneurial activity in European regions: distinguishing low and high ambition entrepreneurship', in D. Smallbone, H. Landstrom and D. Evans Jones (eds), *Making the Difference in Local, Regional and National Economies: Frontiers in European Entrepreneurship Research*, Cheltenham, UK and Northampton, MA, USA: Edward Elgar Publishing, pp. 49–77.

Bosma, N. and V. Schutjens (2011), 'Understanding regional variation in entrepreneurial activity and entrepreneurial attitude in Europe', *Annals of Regional Science*, **47** (3), 711–42.

Burke, A.E., F.R. Fitzroy and M.A. Nolan (2009), 'Is there a North–South divide in self-employment in England?', *Regional Studies*, **43** (4), 529–44.

Cannarella, C. and V. Piccioni (2006), 'Dysfunctions and sub-optimal behaviours of rural development networks', *International Journal of Rural Management*, **2** (1), 29–57.

de Pillis, E. and K.K. Reardon (2007), 'The influence of personality traits and persuasive messages on entrepreneurial intention', *Career Development International*, **12** (4), 382–96.

Feldman, M.P. (2001), 'The entrepreneurial event revisited: firm formation in a regional context', *Industrial and Corporate Change*, **10**, 861–91.

Fernández, J., F. Liñán and F.J. Santos (2009), 'Cognitive aspects of potential entrepreneurs in Southern and Northern Europe: an analysis using GEM-data', *Revista de economía mundial*, **23**, 151–78.

Florida, R. (2003), 'Entrepreneurship, creativity, and regional economic growth', in D.M. Hart (ed.), *The Emergence of Entrepreneurship Policy*, Cambridge: Cambridge University Press, pp. 39–58.

Freytag, A. and R. Thurik (2007), 'Entrepreneurship and its determinants in a cross-country setting', *Journal of Evolutionary Economics*, **17** (2), 117–31.

Fritsch, M. and Mueller, P. (2005), 'Regional growth regimes revisited – the case of West Germany', *Advances in Interdisciplinary European Entrepreneurship Research*, **2**, 251–73.

Fritsch, M. and P. Mueller (2006), 'The evolution of regional entrepreneurship and growth regimes', in M. Fritsch and J. Schmude (eds), *Entrepreneurship in the Region: International Studies in Entrepreneurship*, **14**, 225–44.

Grilo, I. and J.-M. Irigoyen (2006), 'Entrepreneurship in the EU: to wish and not to be', *Small Business Economics*, **26**, 305–18.

Hofer, A.R. and F. Welter (2011), 'The local dimension of entrepreneurship policy: the example of East Germany', in F. Welter and D. Smallbone (eds), *Handbook of Research on Entrepreneurship Policies in Central and Eastern Europe*, Cheltenham, UK and Northampton, MA, USA: Edward Elgar Publishing, pp. 19–33.

Johannisson, B. (2000), 'Modernising the industrial district: rejuvenation or managerial colonisation', in M. Taylor and E. Vatne (eds), *The Networked Firm in a Global World: Small Firms in New Environments*, Ashgate: Aldershot, pp. 283–45.

Kalantaridis, C. (2009), 'SME strategy, embeddedness and performance in East Cleveland, North East England', *International Small Business Journal*, **27** (4), 496–521.

Kelley, D.J., S. Singer and M. Herrington (2012), *Global Entrepreneurship Monitor (GEM) 2011 Global Report*, Babson Park, MA, USA; Santiago, Chile; Kuala Lumpur, Malaysia; London, UK: Global Entrepreneurship Research Association.

Kolvereid, L. (1996), 'Prediction of employment status choice intentions', *Entrepreneurship Theory and Practice*, Fall, 47–57.

Krueger, J. (2000), 'The projective perception of the social world: a building block of social comparison processes', in J. Suls and L. Wheeler (eds), *Handbook of Social Comparison: Theory and Research*, New York: Kluwer Academic/Plenum Publishers, pp. 323–51.

Krueger, N.F. (2003), 'The cognitive psychology of entrepreneurship', in Z.J. Acs and D.B. Audretsch (eds), *Handbook of Entrepreneurship Research: An Interdisciplinary Survey and Introduction*, London: Kluwer, pp. 105–40.

Krueger, N.F., M.D. Reilly and A.L. Carsrud (2000), 'Competing models of entrepreneurial intentions', *Journal of Business Venturing*, **15**, 411–32.

Lang, R., M. Fink and E. Kibler (2014), 'Understanding place-based entrepreneurship in rural Central Europe: a comparative institutional analysis', *International Small Business Journal*, **32** (2), 204–27.

Lanjouw, J.O. (2001), 'The rural non-farm sector: issues and evidence from developing countries', *Agricultural Economics*, **26**, 1–23.

Minniti, M. (2005), 'Entrepreneurship and network externalities', *Journal of Economic Behaviour and Organization*, **57** (1), 1–27.

Parker, S.C. (2004), *The Economics of Self-Employment and Entrepreneurship*, Cambridge: Cambridge University Press.

Polese, M. and R. Shearmur (2006), 'Why some regions will decline: a Canadian case study with thoughts on local development strategies', *Papers in Regional Science*, **85** (1), 23–36.

Porter, M.E., J.J. Sacjs and J. McArthur (2002), *Executive Summary: Competitiveness and Stages of Economic Development. The Global Competitiveness Report 2001–2002*, New York: Oxford University Press.

Shane, S. and S. Venkataraman (2000), 'The promise of entrepreneurship as a field of research', *Academy of Management Review*, **25** (1), 217–26.

Shinnar, R.S., O. Giacomin and F. Janssen (2012), 'Entrepreneurial perceptions and intentions: the role of gender and culture', *Entrepreneurship Theory and Practice*, **36** (3), 465–93.

Smallbone, D., D. North and C. Kalantaridis (1999), 'Adapting to peripherality: a study of small rural manufacturing firms in northern England', *Entrepreneurship and Regional Development: An International Journal*, **11** (2), 109–27.

Statistics Estonia (n.d.), Statistics Estonia website, http://www.stat.ee/ (accessed 18 November 2014).

Sternberg, R. (2009), 'Regional dimensions of entrepreneurship', *Foundations and Trends in Entrepreneurship*, **5** (4), 211–340.

Sternberg, R. and S. Wennekers (2005), 'Determinants and effects of new business creation using Global Entrepreneurship Monitor data', *Small Business Economics*, **24**, 193–203.

Stuetzer, M., M. Obschonka, U. Brixy, R. Sternberg and U. Cantner (2014), 'Regional characteristics, opportunity perception and entrepreneurial activities', *Small Business Economics*, **42** (2), 221–44.

Tkachev, A. and L. Kolvereid (1999), 'Self-employment intentions among Russian students', *Entrepreneurship and Regional Development*, **11** (3), 269–80.

Van Stel, A. and K. Suddle (2008), 'The impact of new firm formation on regional development in the Netherlands', *Small Business Economics*, **30** (1), 31–47.

Venesaar, U. et al. (2014), *Globaalne ettevõtlusmonitooring 2013. Eesti raport* (Global Entrepreneurship Monitor 2013. Estonian report), Tallin: Eesti Arengufond.

Wennekers, S., A. van Stel, R. Thurik and P. Reynolds (2005), 'Nascent entrepreneurship and the level of economic development', Discussion Papers on Entrepreneurship, Growth and Public Policy, Max Plank Institute for Research into Economic Systems Group Entrepreneurship, Growth and Public Policy, Jena, Germany.

Werner, C. and S. Athreye (2004), 'Marshall's disciplines: knowledge and innovation driving regional economic development and growth', *Journal of Evolutionary Economics*, **14**, 505–23.

Xavier, S.R., D. Kelley, J. Kew, M. Herrington and A. Vorderwülbecke (2013), *Global Entrepreneurship Monitor (GEM) 2012 Global Report*, Babson Park, MA, USA; Santiago, Chile; Kuala Lumpur, Malaysia; London, UK: Global Entrepreneurship Research Association.

9. The capitalisation of new firms: exploring the influence of entrepreneurial characteristics on start-up finance

Paul Robson, Tyler Chamberlin and Mark Freel

INTRODUCTION

Those who endeavour to stimulate innovation and regional development are frequently concerned with the availability of financial capital for new ventures. It has long been recognised that the initial capitalisation of new ventures positively influences both survival prospects and firm growth (see for example Parker, 2004 for a discussion). The relationship between survival and capitalisation is often rationalised in terms of 'buying time' (Bates, 2005): allowing the entrepreneur time to learn how to run the business and meet unexpected challenges. Undercapitalised firms, in contrast, lack this buffer and may more quickly be forced to close as a result of liquidity problems. Thus, in regions where financial capital is relatively plentiful, entrepreneurs may be better afforded the opportunity to learn, to innovate and to prosper.

However, whilst it is common to note the relationships between start-up financing and survival or growth, and more occasionally to understand their bases, a significant prior step is typically neglected. That is, whilst asking why better-capitalised firms enjoy better survival prospects (having first observed that they do) is an important question, it is equally important to ask why some firms are better capitalised (or, indeed, the reverse). Attempts to answer this latter question are relatively rare and tend to emphasise structural factors (such as industry affiliation), which are unlikely to be readily amenable to policy intervention or entrepreneurial action, and are limited in their ability to explain the observed within-industry heterogeneity in start-up size. However, following Colombo et al. (2004) and Åstebro and Bernhardt (2005), and drawing on UK survey data, we are able to shine further light on the role of human capital variables in determining initial firm size.

In short, the current study is concerned with understanding those human capital factors which predict higher or lower levels of start-up financing. A better appreciation of these issues may improve the survival prospects of new firms. At present many firms may fail due to limited capitalisation rather than limited entrepreneurial capability.

Specifically, we use United Kingdom (UK) data drawn from 234 new ventures in a variety of industries. The data address both structural aspects of the businesses and characteristics of the lead entrepreneurs. Importantly, the data record the amount of financing available at start-up. From this, we are able to explore associations between levels of start-up financing and a range of human capital variables. In so doing, we use two main techniques: firstly, we present simple cross-tabulations (and report the results of χ^2 independence tests). This essentially descriptive analysis provides the reader with a 'feel' for the data set and the apparent relationships between initial capitalisation and the explanatory variables of interest. Thereafter, we formally model the determinants of start-up finance using a series of linked ordered-logit models.

The chapter is structured as follows. It first provides a brief overview of human capital theory as it relates to the initial financing of new ventures. This contextualisation provides the basis for the derivation of our hypotheses. The next section presents our data, including some discussion of the data collection process and the relationship with similar endeavours outside of the UK. This section also details the manner in which the variables used in the analyses were composed and measured. The chapter then presents both the brief descriptive analysis and the regression models. Finally, we offer some concluding remarks and discuss both the implications of our results and the limitations in our research.

HUMAN CAPITAL AND START-UP SIZE

The idea of 'human capital' is an old one. Adam Smith identified its essence as one of four 'articles' of fixed capital:[1]

> the acquired and [economically] useful abilities of all the inhabitants or members of the society. The acquisition of such talents, by the maintenance of the acquirer during his education, study, or apprenticeship, always costs a real expense, which is a capital fixed and realized, as it were, in his person. (Smith, [1776] 1998: 166)

However, the concept enjoyed something of a renaissance in the second half of the twentieth century, following the pioneering work of Jacob Mincer and Gary Becker, amongst others (see, e.g., Mincer, 1958; Becker, 1962). More contemporary usage of the term 'human capital' shares much with Smith's idea, though it is perhaps a little broader in scope. In the standard reference work, Becker (1964), for instance, details investments in human capital to include 'schooling, on-the-job-training, medical care, migration, and searching for information about prices and incomes'. Whilst much of the work on human capital has been in relation to incomes and income growth, our concern is with human capital in relation to entrepreneurship. To the extent that human capital theory holds that higher levels of human capital increase individuals' efficiency and proficiency, it seems likely, all other things being equal, that it will also better position individuals for entrepreneurship. As Davidsson and Honig (2003: 305) note: 'if profitable opportunities for new economic activity exist, individuals with more or higher quality human capital should be better at perceiving them'; and, one would suppose, be better placed to exploit them.

Crucially, human capital is not thought to be uniform. In particular, human capital acquired in one activity may be more or less valuable in performing other activities. This observation leads to the important distinction between general and (firm-)specific human capital (Parsons, 1972). The former may be thought of as capital which is productive in a variety of situations (or firms), whilst the latter is productive in only one situation (or firm) (Lazear, 2003).

General Human Capital

In this vein, and in the current context, general human capital may be taken to encompass key socio-demographic characteristics such as age, gender, ethnicity and education[2] (see Becker, 1975; Cooper et al., 1994). Of course, the first three of these are, at best, indirect measures of human capital. In the case of age, for instance, we take this to proxy the accumulation of both experience and assets or wealth. That is, other things being equal, older entrepreneurs are likely to have acquired greater experience and accumulated greater assets (including social assets such as networks) and wealth, affording or attracting higher amounts of start-up finance (Mata, 1996). On the other hand, it is likely that age also correlates with attitudes to risk, as greater family responsibilities initially place greater demands upon financial resources (Holtz-Eakin et al., 1994). In this way, the relationship between age and start-up finance may not be linear and, in addition to the log of the age of the entrepreneurs, we include a quadratic term in age in our later regression models.

In a similar way to age, the gender of the entrepreneur may be thought to indirectly influence initial funding through a variety of human capital mechanisms. For instance, to the extent that women enjoy fewer labour market opportunities, receive lower salaries or record career discontinuities, they are likely to accumulate less wealth and less experience at management levels (Verheul and Thurik, 2001). Additionally, evidence suggests that risk aversion may be higher amongst prospective female entrepreneurs (Wagner, 2007), resulting in smaller start-ups as a way to limit downside risk. Certainly, empirical evidence that businesses started by female entrepreneurs are relatively undercapitalised is longstanding (e.g. Carter and Rosa, 1998; Verheul and Thurik, 2001); and this evidence persists irrespective of sectoral considerations.[3]

Education, in contrast, is a more direct measure of general human capital. Education is undoubtedly the most researched aspect of human capital (Becker, 1975) and one which is consistently included as an explanatory variable in multivariate analyses. As with our other measures of general human capital, level and type of education are likely to both directly and indirectly influence initial start-up size. Directly, one anticipates that education will correlate with past earnings and, through this, will lower the extent of financial constraint associated with imperfections in financial markets (Colombo et al., 2004). Less directly, highly educated individuals are likely to hold higher reservation wages and, as such, are only likely to enter self-employment where the promised rewards are commensurate (Storey, 1994), which in turn is likely to require larger initial size. Indirectly, education presumably relates to 'knowledge, skills, problem-solving ability, discipline, motivation, and self-confidence' (Cooper et al., 1994: 376), all of which may be thought to be attractive to providers of external capital and other relevant stakeholders.

Whilst it is common to proxy education-based human capital by recording whether or not the individual holds a bachelor's degree (or equivalent; see, e.g., Cooper et al., 1994), there is some evidence that education in specific areas is particularly associated with increasing initial size. For instance, Colombo et al. (2004) distinguish between technical education and economic education, finding that only the former has any relationship with initial size. Similarly, Verheul and Thurik (2001) find financial management expertise to be positively related to the amount of start-up capital. In addition to the education effects discussed above, financial expertise is likely to result in potential entrepreneurs being better informed about the sorts of capital available at start-up and the individuals who can help in accessing it. Accordingly, our models incorporate measures of both general education (an undergraduate degree or higher) and the presence of specific financial qualifications.

This foregoing discussion of general human capital yields the following hypotheses:

H1a: Older entrepreneurs are more likely to have a larger amount of start-up finance compared to younger entrepreneurs.

H1b: Businesses owned by female entrepreneurs are less likely to have a larger amount of start-up finance compared to male-owned businesses.

H1c: Entrepreneurs with a university degree, or higher degrees, are more likely to have a larger amount of start-up finance compared to those entrepreneurs without a degree.

H1d: Entrepreneurs with financial qualifications or training are more likely to have a larger amount of start-up finance compared to those without financial qualifications or training.

Specific Human Capital

The second classic type of human capital is specific human capital. Frequently, this is rendered as 'firm-specific human capital', 'which results from training, search, and transfer investments of peculiar value to a particular firm' (Parsons, 1972: 1120). However, since our entrepreneurs are involved in new firms, firm-specific human capital is unlikely to be easily measured. Accordingly, it may make more sense to talk about 'task-specific' human capital, that is, human capital which is 'specific to the task being performed, as opposed to being specific to the firm' (Gibbons and Waldman, 2004: 203). One source of task-specific human capital is likely to apply directly to entrepreneurship. That is, to the extent that entrepreneurship is concerned with owner-management, one might anticipate that prior experience with business ownership and management would better position prospective entrepreneurs for start-up success (including success in securing initial finance).

Prior ownership experience is likely to prepare prospective entrepreneurs. Following the early work of Scott and Rosa (1996) and Westhead and Wright (1998), it has become common to distinguish between novice, serial and portfolio entrepreneurs on the basis of their prior, and continuing, business ownership experience; the latter two collectively termed 'habitual' entrepreneurs. Much of this work directly relates ownership experience to resource acquisition. For instance, drawing on data collected from 354 Scottish entrepreneurs, Westhead et al. (2003) record that, on average, the total initial capital used to establish, inherit or purchase their current business was substantially greater for portfolio (£99 600) and serial (£99 648) entrepreneurs, compared to novice (£41 346) entrepreneurs. Similar findings were reported by Alsos et al. (2006) using Norwegian data: recording that serial (4.43) and portfolio (4.22) entrepreneurs were able to raise significantly more capital for investment in the new business compared to novice (3.37) entrepreneurs, where the values in parentheses are the mean scores of start-up finance.[4] These findings are typically rationalised in terms of the dual effects on wealth and resource acquisition discussed above, such that: '[s]uccessful habitual entrepreneurs may be expected to have larger amounts of personal capital, and greater access to external sources of funds than novice entrepreneurs' (Ucbasaran et al., 2006: 381).

Beyond this direct measure of task-specific human capital, our models include two further proxies for specific human capital: exporting and innovation. Clearly, exporting and innovation are directly elements of firm strategy rather than entrepreneurial human capital. However, to the extent that the new firm is built around the entrepreneur (Cooper et al., 1994), operating in exporting markets or introducing innovations at such an early stage in the firm's life is likely to signal ambition, capability or relevant prior experience on the part of the entrepreneur(s). As Westhead et al. (2001: 342) note, 'more capital allows a firm to pursue a broader range of activities as well as more ambitious projects'. This is likely to hold both for financial capital, directly, and for human capital. Indeed, a primary contention here is that the latter generates the former.

At the very least, incorporating measures of exporting and innovation control for the (initial) firm size implications of these strategies. Evidence from empirical studies consistently records positive firm size–exporting and firm size–innovation relationships (see, e.g., Kalantaridis, 2004; Fritsch and Meschede, 2001, respectively). Both exporting and innovation imply a sunk cost to the firm newly engaging in them. However, there is some recent evidence that at least some engagement in exporting and innovation acts as a positive signal to providers of external finance (again, respectively, Beck et al., 2003; Freel, 2007).

This foregoing discussion of specific human capital yields the following hypotheses:

H2a: Prior owner management experience is likely to be positively related to the amount of start-up finance.

H2b: Exporting is likely to be positively related to the amount of start-up finance.

H2c: Innovating is likely to be positively related to the amount of start-up finance.

It is important to note that in all of the above we remark upon a dual effect of human capital on start-up finance. These effects may be termed the 'wealth effect' and the 'entrepreneurial ability effect' (Colombo et al., 2004). Unfortunately our data do not allow us to disentangle the relative valence of these two effects. The danger, then, is that we are simply observing the effects of prior wealth on initial firm size. However, in a rare study, Cressy (1996) shows that there is no correlation between wealth and business survival after human capital effects have been controlled for. In other words, both wealth and ability appear to result from human capital. In a similar vein, whilst much of the rhetoric of supporting small firms bemoans the existence of financial constraints, there is quite compelling evidence that firms are more likely to be constrained by human capital than financial capital. Where firms face financial constraints it typically reflects weaknesses in human capital (Cressy, 1999, 2008). In short, though we are unable to separately determine the effects of wealth and ability, we are confident that in both we are observing, to a greater extent, the effects of human capital.

DATA AND MEASURES

The UK Survey of SME Finances

The data employed in this chapter were collected as part of the UK Survey of SME Finances 2007. This project was undertaken by the Centre for Business Research at the University of Cambridge on behalf of a consortium of UK public and private sector organisations led by the Department for Business, Enterprise and Regulatory Reform (Cosh et al., 2008). This UK project shares similarities in style and motivation with the National Survey of Small Business Finances in the United States (see, e.g., Levenson and Willard, 2000) and with the SME Financing Data Initiative in Canada (e.g., Orser et al., 2006). The 2007 UK survey was intended as a follow-up to the 2004 survey of small and medium-sized organisation (SME) finances undertaken by Fraser (see Fraser, 2005). Consistent with the 2004 survey, the sample design adopted a stratified approach based upon size (number of employees) and, within size, industry sector (two-digit) and region (UK NUTS 1). Larger-sized businesses and smaller-sized sectors and regions were oversampled relative to their proportion of the population. Clearly such stratification will inevitably distort aggregate observations but, if this is borne in mind, the legitimacy of the analysis presented in this chapter ought not to be compromised.

In total, 2514 SME respondents completed the questionnaire, representing a 10 per cent response rate (see Cosh et al., 2008 for more details). To limit bias arising from the fallibility of informants' memories, questions relating to start-up finance were only administered to firms less than two years from founding. This resulted in a subset of 276 'new firms'. These are the focus of our analysis.

Measures

Dependent variable

The dependent variable of interest measures the amount of start-up finance by category. Respondents reported the amount of money used to start their business in the following categories: <£5000, £5000–£9999, £10000–£49999, £50000–£99999, £100000–£499000, £500000–£999999, £1 million–£4.9 million, and £5 million or more. Predictably, there were few observations in the larger categories. Accordingly, and to limit the number of empty cells in the statistical analyses, the larger five categories were combined together. Figure 9.1 records the distribution of responses in each of the resulting categories. The distribution we report is broadly consistent with prior research. Fraser (2005), for instance, uses a similar research methodology and data from the earlier UK SME Finances survey to estimate initial start-up finance in a sample of new small firms, finding that mean initial capitalisation was £71 000, while the median amount was just over £15 000. As Figure 9.1 makes clear, the tendency is to very small start-up size.

Independent and control variables

Table 9.1 details the variables used in both the descriptive and the regression analyses. In terms of brief descriptive statistics, 28.9 per cent of the sample firms were led by female entrepreneurs. A large minority of sample entrepreneurs (37.4 per cent) possessed a degree and (30.1 per cent) had undertaken some specific financial qualification or training. Remarkably, 48.4 per cent of the entrepreneurs were novices engaged in their first entrepreneurial venture, whilst 51.6 per cent of the entrepreneurs were habitual.[5] A relatively small proportion of the firms were exporters (10.6 per cent) or innovators (18.7 per cent).

In addition to the variables developed to test our hypotheses, the analyses include important structural controls. To this end, industry sector and firm size are 'usual suspects'. Firms starting in industries with higher fixed capital requirements will inevitably be larger than firms with lesser requirements (for example, manufacturing versus service firms). Similarly, firms which engage

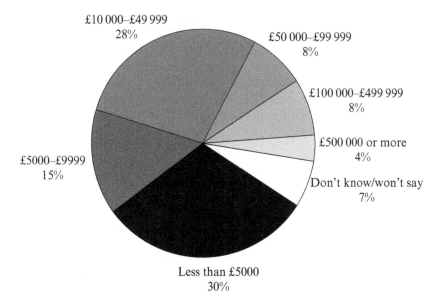

£10 000–£49 999
28%

£50 000–£99 999
8%

£100 000–£499 999
8%

£500 000 or more
4%

Don't know/won't say
7%

£5000–£9999
15%

Less than £5000
30%

Source: Authors' own calculations based on the UK Survey of SME Finances 2007 (Cosh et al., 2008).

Figure 9.1   Distribution of start-up funds

more employees as start-up are likely to require greater initial funding. In the former case, the data allow us to classify firms by their principal industrial activity. Figure 9.2 records this distribution. As one would expect, service firms dominate and, in broad terms, the distribution is similar to the population of firms, as proxied by value-added tax (VAT) registrations.

Firm employment also follows an expected distribution: 129 of the firms recorded zero employees; 75 were micro firms (1–9 employees); 39 were small firms (10–49 employees); and only three were medium-sized (50–25 employees). For analytical purposes, these medium-sized firms were collapsed into our small firm category in the cross-tabulations.

Finally, we include a measure of firm location. The data provided information on the location of respondents at the level of government office region (GOR): NUTS 1 regions. Firms were present for each of the 12 GORs. However, given the relatively small sample size (and the relative small size of some of the regions), it was not possible to explore responses in all regions. Rather, in recognition of the strength of the core economies of London and the South East, these two NUTS 1 regions were combined (61 observations) and compared with all other regions (185 observations).

Table 9.1   Variables used in the analyses

Variable	Measurement	Anticipated effect
General human capital		
Gender	Binary: If the business was male-led it was assigned a value of 1, 0 otherwise.	+
Age of Entrepreneur	Continuous in regressions; categorical in cross-tabulations (categories 18–30 years, 31–39 years, 40–49, 50+).	+
Higher Education	Binary: Assigned a value of 1 if the owner held a degree-level qualification or higher, 0 otherwise.	+
Financial Qualifications	Binary: Assigned a value of 1 if the owner recorded holding a financial qualification or undertaking financial training, 0 otherwise.	+
Specific human capital		
Habitual Entrepreneur	Binary: Respondents indicating prior (or additional) owner-management experience were assigned a value of 1, 0 otherwise.	+
Exporting	Binary: Respondents indicating sales outside of the UK were assigned a value of 1, 0 otherwise.	+
Innovation	Binary: A value of 1 was assigned to firms indicating a novel product innovation, 0 otherwise.	+
Control variables		
Location	Binary: Firms located in London and the South-East of England were assigned values of 1; firms located elsewhere in the UK were recorded as 0.	+
Sector	Categorical capturing industrial sector at the two-digit level, with real estate, etc. as the reference category.	Various
Firm Size	Employment-based categories, with zero employees as the reference group. Continuous in the regressions.	+

Source: Authors' own calculations based on the UK Survey of SME Finances 2007 (Cosh et al., 2008).

ANALYSES

We begin our analyses with simple cross-tabulations between the amount of initial capital employed and the range of variables used in our regression

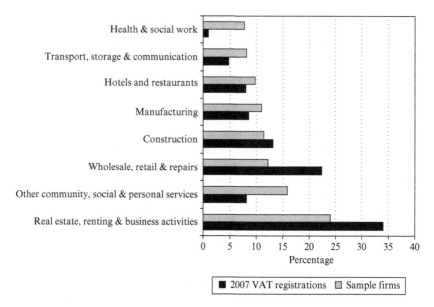

Source: Authors' own calculations based on the UK Survey of SME Finances 2007 (Cosh et al., 2008).

Figure 9.2 Sectoral distribution of sample firms

models. Table 9.2 presents the patterns of association in the data. As can be seen, the relationships are largely as anticipated. For instance, 45.1 per cent of female-led businesses were started with less than £5000, compared with 28 per cent of male-led businesses. Young entrepreneurs are also more likely to start their businesses with limited capital, with 44.9 per cent of young entrepreneurs (18–30 years) starting with less than £5000 compared with 17.3 per cent of the over-50s. A similar pattern is apparent amongst those with prior owner-management experience. Habitual entrepreneurs were significantly more likely to have launched their businesses with more capital than their novice counterparts. Education also seems to matter, although it is the more specific form indicated by financial training, rather than the general form indicated by higher education, which associates with larger amounts of start-up financing. Finally, initial strategy also associates with initial capitalisation, at least insofar as exporting is concerned. The data suggest that early exporters are better capitalised than non-exporters.

In summary, our cross-tabulations suggest associations between both direct and indirect measures of an entrepreneur's human capital and the initial capitalisation of their firms that are broadly consistent with our

Table 9.2   Cross-tabulations of initial capitalisation

	< £5000	£5000–£9999	£10000–£49000	≥ £50000	p	N
All	32.9	15.9	30.5	20.7		246
Employment						
0	51.9	22.5	20.9	4.7	**< 0.001**	129
1–9	14.7	12.0	48.0	25.3		75
10+	7.1	2.4	28.6	61.9		42
Location						
L/SE	36.1	18.0	23.0	23.0	0.138	61
Elsewhere	31.9	15.1	33.0	20.0		185
Gender						
Female	45.1	18.3	22.5	14.1	**0.028**	71
Male	28.0	14.9	33.7	23.4		175
Age						
18–30	47.6	16.7	28.6	7.1	**< 0.001**	42
31–39	44.9	13.0	24.6	17.4		69
40–49	25.3	13.3	34.9	26.5		83
50+	17.3	23.1	32.7	26.9		52
Education						
Degree	32.6	15.2	26.1	26.1	0.392	92
No degree	33.1	16.2	33.1	17.5		154
Financial qual.						
Yes	10.8	16.2	37.8	35.1	**< 0.001**	74
No	42.4	15.7	27.3	14.5		172
Experience						
Habitual	18.9	12.6	35.4	33.1	**< 0.001**	127
Novice	47.9	19.3	25.2	7.6		119
Exporter						
Yes	19.2	11.5	19.2	50.0	**0.002**	26
No	34.5	16.4	31.8	17.3		220
Innovator						
Yes	28.3	13.0	32.6	26.1	0.682	46
No	34.0	16.5	30.0	19.5		200

Notes: Results in bold are significant by conventional standards based upon χ^2 independence tests. Percentages are shown for presentational purposes. Raw cell frequencies were used in the tests.

Source: Authors' own calculations based on the UK Survey of SME Finances 2007 (Cosh et al., 2008).

hypotheses. Specifically they provide preliminary support for H1a, H1b and H1d, but not for H1c; and for H2a and H2b, but not H2c. However, these findings may simply reflect the co-relation of initial capitalisation and our range of variables either with each other or with the structural variables that the literature has shown to relate to the scale of start-up financing. For example, the relationship between gender and start-up financing may simply reflect established patterns of variation by industry sector between male- and female-led businesses. Given our interest in the marginal contribution of each of these variables to explaining initial capitalisation, a multivariate framework is appropriate.

Given the nature of the dependent variable, ordered logit models were used to identify the combination of variables which were associated with increasing start-up finance. In common with other regression techniques, ordered logits are sensitive to correlations amongst predictor/independent variables. On the basis of simple correlation tests,[6] there is no evidence of multicollinearity in the data. Beyond collinearity concerns, a variety of measures may be used to provide an indication of goodness of fit in ordered logit regression models. Here we record two of the most commonly used: Nagelkerke R^2 and the log likelihood, which provide benchmarks in assessing goodness of fit (see the bottom of Table 9.3). In both cases, the statistics suggest satisfactory fit; with all the log-likelihood in all models improving upon the constant only model and the pseudo R^2 indicating explained variance between 14 per cent and 22 per cent.

The full results of these analyses are shown in Table 9.3. In the first instance (model 1), we present a base model which contains the control variables only. In model 2 we add variables relating to general human capital. In models 3–5, we separately add the three measures of specific innovation. Finally, we present a model of the combined control, general and specific human capital variables. The change in R^2 which is associated with each of our models of start-up finance and the sequential building up of independent variables is observed. All six models were statistically significant at the 1 per cent level.

Model 1 has a Nagelkerke R^2 of 0.142. The log likelihood in model 1 was −284.12. Unsurprisingly, the results indicated that larger-sized firms were more likely to have larger amounts of start-up finance compared to those firms with fewer numbers of employees. There is some evidence of a non-linear relationship. Indeed, both the size dummy and the size squared variables included in the model 1 were statistically significant at the 1 per cent level; perhaps indicating some levelling off. Beyond size, two of the sector dummies are statistically significant at the 5 per cent level: manufacturing, and hotels and restaurants. Again this may be expected given the capital costs in establishing a venture in either sector. As with

Table 9.3 Ordered logit regression models relating to the amount of start-up finance (n = 246)

	Model 1	Model 2	Model 3	Model 4	Model 5	Model 6
Control variables						
Size	**0.18 (0.03)**[a]	**0.16 (0.03)**[a]	**0.14 (0.03)**[a]	**0.15 (0.03)**[a]	**0.16 (0.03)**[a]	**0.14 (0.03)**[a]
Size²	**−0.00 (0.00)**[a]	**−0.00 (0.00)**[a]	**−0.00 (0.00)**[a]	**−0.00 (0.00)**[a]	**−0.00 (0.00)**[a]	**−0.00 (0.00)**[b]
Manufacturing	**0.92 (0.43)**[b]	**1.02 (0.44)**[b]	**1.07 (0.44)**[b]	**1.06 (0.45)**[b]	**1.06 (0.45)**[b]	**1.12 (0.45)**[b]
Construction	−0.33 (0.43)	−0.23 (0.45)	−0.40 (0.46)	−0.11 (0.46)	−0.19 (0.46)	−0.28 (0.47)
Wholesale/Retail	**0.74 (0.41)**[c]	**0.86 (0.43)**[b]	**0.76 (0.44)**[c]	**0.98 (0.43)**[b]	**0.87 (0.43)**[b]	**0.88 (0.44)**[b]
Hotels & Restaurants	**1.29 (0.52)**[b]	**1.29 (0.52)**[b]	**1.18 (0.53)**[b]	**1.47 (0.53)**[a]	**1.33 (0.53)**[b]	**1.35 (0.53)**[b]
Transport, Storage & Communication	0.31 (0.47)	0.30 (0.51)	0.29 (0.52)	0.38 (0.52)	0.35 (0.52)	0.39 (0.53)
Health & Social Work	0.59 (0.54)	0.64 (0.57)	0.85 (0.57)	0.75 (0.57)	0.65 (0.57)	0.94 (0.57)
Other Community, Social & Personal Service Activities	−0.27 (0.40)	0.03 (0.42)	0.03 (0.43)	0.17 (0.42)	0.02 (0.42)	0.15 (0.43)
London or the South East	−0.17 (0.27)	−0.15 (0.28)	−0.19 (0.28)	−0.24 (0.28)	−0.14 (0.28)	−0.27 (0.29)
General human capital						
Female-Led Business	—	**−0.54 (0.29)**[c]	**−0.56 (0.30)**[c]	**−0.55 (0.29)**[c]	**−0.53 (0.29)**[c]	**−0.57 (0.30)**[c]
Age	—	0.12 (0.09)	0.12 (0.09)	0.13 (0.09)	0.12 (0.09)	0.13 (0.09)
Age²	—	−0.00 (0.00)	−0.00 (0.00)	−0.00 (0.00)	−0.00 (0.00)	−0.00 (0.00)
Degree/Postgraduate Degree	—	0.32 (0.28)	0.32 (0.28)	0.32 (0.28)	0.32 (0.28)	0.32 (0.28)
Financial Qualifications or Training	—	**0.99 (0.28)**[a]	**1.07 (0.28)**[a]	**0.99 (0.28)**[a]	**0.98 (0.28)**[a]	**1.06 (0.29)**[a]

Table 9.3 (continued)

	Model 1	Model 2	Model 3	Model 4	Model 5	Model 6
Specific human capital						
Habitual	–	–	**1.13 (0.28)**[a]	–	–	**1.09 (0.28)**[a]
Exporter	–	–	–	**1.23 (0.46)**[a]	–	**1.11 (0.46)**[b]
Innovator	–	–	–	–	0.20 (0.34)	0.05 (0.35)
Cut1	0.03 (0.26)	3.28 (1.81)	3.40 (1.83)	3.57 (1.81)	3.28 (1.81)	3.65 (1.83)
Cut2	0.84 (0.27)	4.17 (1.82)	4.34 (1.84)	4.47 (1.82)	4.17 (1.81)	4.60 (1.84)
Cut3	2.79 (0.34)	6.24 (1.84)	6.53 (1.87)	6.59 (1.85)	6.24 (1.84)	6.84 (1.88)
LR chi^2	$\chi^2(10) = 94.06$[a]	$\chi^2(15) = 119.02$[a]	$\chi^2(16) = 135.93$[a]	$\chi^2(16) = 126.51$[a]	$\chi^2(15) = 119.46$[a]	$\chi^2(17) = 142.12$[a]
Log likelihood	−284.12	−271.64	−263.18	−267.89	−271.46	−260.09
Nagelkerke R^2	0.142	0.180	0.205	0.191	0.180	0.215
Change in Nagelkerke R^2	–	0.038	0.063	0.049	0.038	0.073

Notes:
[a] $p < 0.01$; [b] $p < 0.05$; [c] $p < 0.10$.
Excluded comparison variables: *Sector, Real Estate, Renting & Business Activities*. The ordered logit regression model estimates a score, S, as a linear function of the explanatory variables included in the model. The cut points are included to allow the reader to calculate the predicted probabilities of the models.

Source: Authors' own calculations based on the UK Survey of SME Finances 2007 (Cosh et al., 2008).

our cross-tabulations, there is no evidence that location in the munificent markets of London and the South East of England influence start-up size.

Model 2 augments the control variables with the general human capital variables. The Nagelkerke R^2 improves to 0.18. The log likelihood of model 2 is -271.64. The control variables continue to act much as they did in model 1. Of our general human capital variables, the estimations provide tentative evidence that female-led businesses were less likely to begin with larger amounts of start-up finance. Those entrepreneurs who had financial qualifications or training were more likely to have larger amounts of start-up finance; significantly so at the 1 per cent level. Those entrepreneurs with a post-secondary education were not more likely to have larger amounts of start-up finance.

In models 3–5 we add the specific human capital variables of habitual entrepreneurship, exporter and innovator, one at a time to those variables already included in model 2. The Nagelkerke R^2 improved to 0.205 in model 3, with a log likelihood of -263.18. Here, habitual entrepreneurs are shown to be significantly more likely than novice entrepreneurs to have larger amounts of start-up finance. This result is statistically significant at the 1 per cent level. Comparing model 3 to model 2 we see that the inclusion of the habitual variable has not influenced the other relationships found in model 2. In model 4, the Nagelkerke R^2 improves (relative to model 2) to 0.191, with a likelihood ratio of -267.89. The model indicates that early exporters were more likely to have larger amounts of start-up finance compared to non-exporters. Again, this is statistically significant at the 1 per cent level and does not alter relationships identified earlier. Adding our innovation variable to model 2 does not improve the Nagelkerke R^2. Novel innovation does not seem to require greater initial capital in the same way that exporting does.

Finally, model 6 incorporates all three specific human capital variables. Inclusion of all three variables improves the Nagelkerke R^2 to 0.215, relative to model 2, with a log likelihood of -260.09. In model 6 we see that the results are consistent with models 2–5: female-led businesses, financial qualifications or training, habitual entrepreneurs and early exporting are all statistically significantly associated with higher initial funding. The control variables of size, size squared, and sector dummies of manufacturing, wholesale/retail, and hotels and transport have remained statistically significant at the 5 per cent level, or better, throughout the models.

DISCUSSION AND CONCLUSIONS

Despite a voluminous literature on access to finance, there remains limited understanding of how the character of the entrepreneur and the strategies they choose at start-up may bear upon the extent of initial financing. Government agencies and authorities at the local and national level continue to devote considerable resources to promoting and assisting the start-up of businesses in the UK (Cosh et al., 2009; Braidford and Stone, 2010) and beyond (Rowland, 2009; Harding, 2009). To the extent that undercapitalisation is associated with poorer survival prospects, appreciating the non-financial factors influencing capitalisation ought to better inform interventions.

This, then, is what we attempt here. Drawing on data from a large-scale survey of UK SMEs, which was specifically concerned with their financing, we employ ordered logit regression techniques to explore the relationship between the entrepreneurs' human capital and their firms' initial financial capital. Our results suggest that the human capital profiles of the entrepreneurs are strongly related to the amount of start-up finance they use. More precisely, our multivariate analysis reveals support for four of our stated hypotheses. In the first instance, after controlling for structural influences on initial financing, female-led businesses in our sample are still marked by lower capitalisation relative to their male-led counterparts. That the lower capitalisation of female-led businesses persists while controlling for sector is revealing. In a given sector, it would seem that women are likely to start smaller businesses. Given observations on initial size and survival and growth, this may be cause for concern, and better understanding what drives this relationship ought to be a priority.

Beyond gender, it is more specific forms of human capital which seem to matter. Both entrepreneurs who had financial qualifications or training and those who had prior owner-management were more likely to have larger amounts of start-up finance. The former finding is reassuring and may suggest relatively easy avenues for intervention to support start-ups. Prior owner-management experience is also positively associated with larger amounts of start-up finance. It would appear that habitual entrepreneurs are either able to leverage their greater amount of experience, compared to novice entrepreneurs, to obtain larger amounts of start-up finance, or that their prior experience has generated a larger pool of personal funds from which to draw. Despite this, there is little evidence in the literature of superior performance on the part of habitual entrepreneurs (Ucbasaran et al., 2008). The finding that early exporters started with more funds than purely domestically oriented firms talks to the greater resource requirements attendant upon competing in international markets. Encouraging new firms to export must recognise the capital implications of this strategy.

We found that several of the control variables were statistically significant, although there were some differences in the levels of significance across the models. In particular, larger-sized firms in terms of the number of employees were found to have a larger probability of having larger sums of start-up finance, and this result was predicted.

Our results lead to several policy implications. Arguably, the results suggest that if governments want to increase the amount of start-up capital that businesses use, they should consider encouraging entrepreneurs – or would-be entrepreneurs – to undertake some form of financial training, which may or may not be associated with a paper qualification at the end of the training. Indeed, they may even seek means to encourage and support such training at the regional level, consistent with varying regional financial exigencies.

The results also suggest that women-led businesses tend to have smaller amounts of start-up finance compared to male-led businesses. Thus, our results suggest that providers of finance, and particularly banks, need to carefully monitor applications and outcomes for finance and the magnitude of finance provided by male and female applicants. Our findings also add weight to Carter's (2009) call for small business support agencies to develop women's enterprise information pertaining to the theme of start-up capitalisation.

Lastly, the results show that habituals are important. Habituals are clearly better placed to access finance at start-up compared to non-habituals. This raises a dilemma of whether policy-makers ought to identify and support habitual entrepreneurs who are already successful and may become even more prosperous, or alternatively, whether they should provide more enterprise information to non-habituals to attempt to balance the advantage of habituals. In regions with a disproportionate share of unemployment, a lack of wealth generation and limited innovation, identifying the small numbers of habitual entrepreneurs may be particularly attractive.

Limitations and Avenues for Additional Research

As with the vast majority of empirically undertaken studies, they are a compromise between the ideal and most desired set of dependent and independent variables, mitigated against the reality that questionnaires do not contain a set of variables which matches the former goals. Thus, there are limitations in our data, and these throw up avenues for future research. This chapter used the UK Survey of SME Finances 2007 which was undertaken by Cambridge researchers (Cosh et al., 2008). Our dependent variable, the amount of start-up finance, was represented by a category variable. In future research it would be interesting to try to obtain a variable which was continuous in nature. Our independent human capital variables included exporting as a dummy variable, but it would be important to see whether exporting as a percentage of sales turnover also showed a positive relationship with start-up finance. Similarly, also within specific human capital we included a habitual dummy variable, but it would be important to develop further dimensions of habitual entrepreneurship. In other words, it would be desirable to include some questions which would allow the derivation of serial and portfolio entrepreneurs to recognise that habitual entrepreneurs can encompass a wide set of entrepreneurs. Lastly, whilst our measure of innovation was whether or not the firms had introduced a new product or service, there are a wide range of other facets or types of innovation, and these could be included in future research to see whether or not innovation does have a relationship with start-up finance.

Conclusions

In this chapter we have argued that start-up finance remains an under-researched topic, especially in relation to access to finance, and we have used human capital theory as a theoretical construct to build models to better understand start-up finance in the UK using a reputable data set. Specifically, we used the data created by Cosh et al. (2008) to test seven hypotheses. Four of the hypotheses – two relating to general human capital and two relating to specific capital – were supported and were consistent with the data, and these were: female-led businesses, financial qualifications or training, habitual entrepreneurs, and exporting firms. Thus, our results have shown that gender is an important factor in relation to start-up finance. More specifically, in our models which control for size, sector, location, and general and human capital, female-led businesses continue to have smaller amounts of start-up finance compared to male-led businesses. The other general human capital variable which was found to be important was whether or not the entrepreneur had financial qualifications or training. With regard to the specific human capital variables, habitual entrepreneurs compared to novice entrepreneurs, and exporters compared to non-exporters, were found to have larger amounts of start-up finance. Taken together the results suggest four areas where policy-makers can contemplate developing and spending resources.

More broadly, we believe that regional economic development authorities may wish to reflect upon their approach to the financing of entrepreneurial ventures going forward. In an era of cheap money, we suggest that policy-makers should be increasingly focused on developing human capital, or entrepreneurial characteristics, rather than attempting to push more money into markets through such measures as small business loan guarantee schemes.

NOTES

1. Smith understood fixed capital as that which 'affords a revenue or profit without circulating or changing masters'. In this way it is a little different from the modern use of the term 'fixed capital'.
2. The survey also asked about family experience with business ownership or entrepreneurship. However, only four (of 276) respondents indicated that this was the case. For practical reasons we are unable to include this in our analyses.
3. The idea that female-owned businesses are smaller as a result of the disproportionate tendency for women to start in sectors with low initial capital requirements, such as personal services.
4. Alsos et al. (2006) calculated capital finance by adding the total debt and deposited equity of the newly registered businesses. They grouped this as follows: (1) no financial capital; (2) 1–10 000 NOK; (3) 10 001–50 000 NOK; (4) 50 001–100 000 NOK; (5) 100 001–200 000 NOK; (6) 200 001–1 000 000 NOK; and (7) 1000 001 NOK or more.
5. Novice and habitual entrepreneurs were derived by looking at the age of the business, and the number of years of business experience of the entrepreneurs. Those entrepreneurs for whom their number of years of business experience was greater than the age of the business were classified as habituals.
6. Matrix available from the authors on request.

REFERENCES

Alsos, G.A., L. Kolvereid and E.J. Isaksen (2006), 'New business early performance: differences between firms started by novice, serial and portfolio entrepreneurs', in P.R. Christensen and F. Poulfeldt (eds), *Managing Complexity and Change in SMEs: Frontiers in European Research*, Cheltenham, UK and Northampton, MA, USA: Edward Elgar Publishing, pp. 35–49.
Åstebro, T.B. and I. Bernhardt (2005), 'The winner's curse of human capital', *Small Business Economics*, **24** (1), 63–78.
Bates, T. (2005), 'Analysis of young, small firms that have closed: delineating successful from unsuccessful closures', *Journal of Business Venturing*, **20** (3), 343–58.
Beck, T., A. Demirgüç-Kunt and R. Levine (2003), 'Law, endowments and finance', *Journal of Financial Economics*, **70** (2), 137–81.
Becker, G.S. (1962), 'Investment in human capital: a theoretical analysis', *Journal of Political Economy*, **70** (5), 9–49.
Becker, G.S. (1964), *Human Capital*, New York: National Bureau of Economic Research.
Becker, G.S. (1975), 'Investment in human capital: effects on earnings', in Gary S. Becker (ed.), *Human Capital: A Theoretical and Empirical Analysis, with Special Reference to Education*, 2nd edn, New York: National Bureau of Economic Research, pp. 13–44.
Braidford, P. and I. Stone (2010), 'Solutions for business cross-product monitoring survey', report prepared for Department of Business, Innovation and Skills of the Government of the United Kingdom, Durham Business School/Policy Research Group, St Chad's College, Durham.
Carter, S. (2009), 'Access to finance', National Policy Centre for Women's Enterprise, Evidence Paper.

Carter, S. and P. Rosa (1998), 'The financing of male- and female-owned businesses', *Entrepreneurship and Regional Development*, **10** (3), 225–41.

Colombo, M.G., M. Delmastro and L. Grilli (2004), 'Entrepreneurs' human capital and the start-up size of new technology-based firms', *International Journal of Industrial Organization*, **22** (8–9), 1183–1211.

Cooper, A.C., F.J. Gimeno-Gascon and C.Y. Woo (1994), 'Initial human and financial capital predictors of new venture performance', *Journal of Business Venturing*, **9** (5), 371–95.

Cosh, A., A. Hughes, A. Bullock and I. Milner (2009), 'SME finance and innovation in the current economic crisis', Centre for Business Research, University of Cambridge, available at http://www.cbr.cam.ac.uk/pdf/CrCr_EconCrisis.pdf (accessed 20 April 2011).

Cosh, A., A. Hughes and I. Milner (2008), 'Financing UK small and medium-sized enterprises, the 2007 Survey', Centre for Business Research, University of Cambridge.

Cressy, R. (1996), 'Are business startups debt-rationed?', *Economic Journal*, **106** (438), 1253–70.

Cressy, R. (1999), 'The Evans and Jovanovic equivalence theorem and credit rationing another look', *Small Business Economics*, **12** (4), 295–97.

Cressy, R. (2008), 'The determinants of small firms survival and growth', in M. Casson, B. Yeung, A. Basu and N.Wadeson (eds), *The Oxford Handbook of Entrepreneurship*, Oxford: Oxford University Press, pp. 161–93.

Davidsson, P. and B. Honig (2003), 'The role of social and human capital among nascent entrepreneurs', *Journal of Business Venturing*, **18** (3), 301–31.

Fraser, S. (2005), 'Finance for small and medium-sized enterprises: a report on the 2004 UK survey of SME finances, Centre for SMEs', Warwick Business School, University of Warwick.

Freel, M.S. (2007), 'Are small innovators credit rationed?', *Small Business Economics*, **28** (1), 23–35.

Fritsch, M. and M. Meschede (2001), 'Product innovation, process innovation and size', *Review of Industrial Organization*, **19** (3), 335–50.

Gibbons, R. and M. Waldman (2004), 'Task-specific human capital', *American Economic Review*, **94** (2), 203–20.

Harding, R. (2009), 'Overview of existing evidence', in Women's Enterprise Task Force (ed.), *Myths and Realities of Women's Access to Finance*, available at: http://www.womensenterprisetaskforce.co.uk/ (accessed 20 April 2011).

Holtz-Eakin, D., D. Joulfaian and H.S. Rosen (1994), 'Sticking it out: entrepreneurial survival and liquidity constraints', *Journal of Political Economy*, **102** (1), 53–76.

Kalantaridis, C. (2004), *Understanding the Entrepreneur: An Institutional Perspective*, Aldershot: Ashgate Publishing Limited.

Lazear, E.P. (2003), 'Firm-specific human capital: a skill-weights approach', National Bureau of Economic Research, NBER Working Paper No. 9679 (June).

Levenson, A. and K. Willard (2000), 'Do firms get the finance they want? Measuring credit rationing experienced by small business in the US', *Small Business Economics*, **14** (2), 83–94.

Mata, J. (1996), 'Market, entrepreneurs and the size of new firms', *Economics Letters*, **52** (1), 89–94.

Mincer, J. (1958), 'Investment in human capital and the personal income distribution', *Journal of Political Economy*, **66** (4), 281–302.

Orser, B.J., A.L. Riding and K. Manley (2006), 'Women entrepreneurs and financial capital', *Entrepreneurship Theory and Practice*, **30** (5), 643–65.

Parker, S.C. (2004), *The Economics of Self-Employment and Entrepreneurship*, Cambridge: Cambridge University Press.

Parsons, D. (1972), 'Specific human capital: an application to quit rates and layoff rates', *Journal of Political Economy*, **80** (6), 1120–43.

Rowland, C. (2009), *The Provision of Growth Capital to UK Small and Medium-Sized Enterprises*, London: The Stationary Office (TSO).

Scott, M. and P. Rosa (1996), 'Opinion: has firm level analysis reached its limits? Time for a rethink?', *International Small Business Journal*, **14** (4), 81–9.

Smith, A. ([1776] 1998), *An Inquiry into the Nature and Causes of the Wealth of Nations*, Oxford: Oxford University Press.

Storey, D.J. (1994), *Understanding the Small Business Sector*, London: Routledge.

Ucbasaran, D., P. Westhead and M. Wright (2006), *Habitual Entrepreneurs*, Cheltenham, UK and Northampton, MA, USA: Edward Elgar Publishing.

Verheul, I. and R. Thurik (2001), 'Start-up capital: "does gender matter?"', *Small Business Economics*, **16** (4), 329–45.

Wagner, J. (2007), 'What a difference a Y makes – female and male nascent entrepreneurs in Germany', *Small Business Economics*, **28** (1), 1–21.

Westhead, P., D. Ucbasaran and M. Wright (2003), 'Differences between private firms owned by novice, serial and portfolio entrepreneurs: implications for policy-makers and practitioners', *Regional Studies*, **37** (2), 187–200.

Westhead, P. and M. Wright (1998), 'Novice, portfolio, and serial founders: are they different?', *Journal of Business Venturing*, **13**–204.

Westhead, P., M. Wright and D. Ucbasaran (2001), 'The internationalization of new and small firms: a resource-based review', *Journal of Business Venturing*, **16** (4), 333–58.

10. Conclusions

David Smallbone, Markku Virtanen and Arnis Sauka

In this final chapter the editors seek to draw out the main conclusions from the chapters in the volume and, where appropriate, to draw some implications for policy, some of which are specific to individual chapters, but those of wider significance are highlighted.

Well-conducted empirical investigations of entrepreneurship and innovation in former Soviet republics are welcome. Part I opens with Chapter 2 by Kalantaridis and colleagues, which shows that to be innovative businesses in Ukraine, irrespective of the nature of the innovation that is introduced, need to cope with the adverse institutional setting both at a national and a regional level, in order to tap into external knowledge sources. It is the institutional development and change related to the broader processes of market reform that are emphasised. But at the same time the researchers found significant differences in the strategies adopted by enterprises involved in different levels of innovation.

At one end of the spectrum the radical innovators were accessing external knowledge through long-established horizontal relationships with partners located abroad. At the other end of the spectrum the incremental innovators adopted a challenging strategy in relation to accessing external knowledge for innovation, coming from horizontal relationships that are not particularly durable.

Taking a broader perspective, the findings suggest that these institutional conditions influence not only the incidence of innovation but also the types of innovation that firms are engaged in. Kalantaridis et al. conclude that in considering the role of institutional change it is the wider processes of market reform that are the most important influence on radical innovation, rather than regional knowledge and infrastructure. Since this is quite different from what is found in mature market economies, these findings emphasise the need to contextualise research results.

The rate of new business start-up in Ukraine is pitifully low, even in comparison with other former Soviet republics (Smallbone and Welter, 2009). What Kalantaridis et al. are suggesting is that the most effective way of raising the level of innovative performance is to raise start-up rates. At the same time, post-socialist institutions provide a very different setting to that found in mature market economies, and that which has been reported in previous research on open innovation. Poorly defined intellectual property rights (IPR) and difficulties in the enforcement of contracts can have negative impacts on the influence of open innovation, as the Kalantaridis et al. chapter suggests. The role of institutions in the innovation process includes: firstly, defining incentive structures which can direct entrepreneurs to either more or less economically productive activities; secondly, determining how well markets operate through the effect of existing regulations and norms; and thirdly, seeking to influence the allocation of resources including labour capital and knowledge.

It is widely accepted within the rural development literature and practice that the promotion and support for innovation and the development of innovation systems, in small and medium-sized enterprises (SMEs) in particular, is much more difficult to achieve in predominantly rural regions than in their urban counterparts. In this context, Chapter 3 by Rogut and Piasecki on Eastern Poland is a valuable contribution to the literature in describing a model of open innovation, which they suggest is appropriate to the economic and social development of this part of Central Europe.

The chapter raises a number of issues of wider interest. In the context of a country that has developed rapidly within the context of its relatively recent European Union (EU) membership, Eastern Poland represents a region in need of development; a region where social exclusion is an important issue. This type of rural development issue is not confined to new member states of the EU, but it is an issue that affects most of them. The authors focus on an important area of EU policy, since increasing social inclusion alongside economic development and competitiveness are the main rationales for interventions with respect to entrepreneurship and SME development.

The chapter is a thought-provoking piece in its attempt to find potential direction and intelligent specialisation in Eastern Poland, and to characterise the conditions under which this may become a development opportunity for the region. The authors themselves conclude that smart specialisation may provide a stimulus for the development of the region by following a realistic development paradigm and combining a series of turning points with the creation and formation of a new development path. Their policy recommendation to achieve these objectives – that is, to foster the smart specialisation development scenario in Eastern Poland – is that attention is paid to the development of markets for innovation together with the development of financial engineering and technological entrepreneurship to increase the commercial application of innovation.

In Part II, Chapter 4 by O'Gorman and Curran is essentially an evaluation of entrepreneurship and SME policy in Ireland, set within the context of industrial policy. One of the conclusions from this chapter is the importance of public policy being the subject of critical public debate. Back in the 1980s industrial policy in Ireland was almost solely focused on the attraction of foreign direct investment (FDI), with very little attention paid to the nurturing and support of domestic enterprise. That situation has existed for several decades, not least because the two main political parties in Ireland supported the FDI emphasis. At the same time, the development of ideas and experience within the economic development field led to a recognition that the narrow focus on FDI as a development strategy was insufficient, and this was capsulated in the report produced by the Telesis Consultancy Group (National Economic and Social Council, 1982).

This chapter provides a very useful function, particularly with regards to new member states. Ireland is a small country with a modest population of around 4 million. It has relied on active industrial policy for many years, not least because growth-oriented companies really need to look to international markets from day one. This is a rather different context to that experienced by SMEs in the United Kingdom (UK), for example. In this context, there are many learning points that other more recent EU members might benefit from. The evolution of what originally was the Irish Linkage Programme is a case in point, because in more recent years the initial focus on helping to develop backward linkages within an Irish context has been widened considerably so that now there are quite a number of Irish suppliers to multinational companies that have continued to serve their international customers by relocating to other parts of the world, that is, outside of Ireland.

More fundamentally the chapter demonstrates the importance for new member countries to recognise that different approaches can be used to stimulate economic development within the context of a market-based approach; in other words, there is no single market-based system. An important point to emphasise in relation to the new member countries is that they need to make assessments for what is most appropriate for them in their context, rather than blindly following the advice of consultants from whatever European country won the technical advice contract.

The case of Ireland with regards to entrepreneurship and industrial policy is of potential interest and relevance to policy development in the new member states of the EU. For example, one important conclusion made by the authors of the chapter is that entrepreneurship policies do not necessarily address the challenges of industrial and economic development on their own. Instead the authors emphasise the importance of coordinated policy approaches bringing together different elements of policy. In the Irish case, a key element of industrial development policy since 1960 has been the opening up of the Irish economy to increase internationalisation forces. Another recommendation of the authors of this chapter is that policy-makers should measure the success of the entrepreneurship policies in terms of the impact on entrepreneurship in the medium and longer term, rather than looking for quick fixes and immediate effects.

O'Gorman and Curran draw a number of conclusions with regards to targeting, where their emphasis is on businesses that demonstrate a potential to grow, since the economic impact of these is greater. They describe the Irish approach as being highly selective; targeted particularly at supporting the creation of new enterprises rather than supporting existing ones.

Turning to Chapter 5 by Roper and Richter, these authors examine the success of the SME Charter and SME Policy Index in achieving policy upgrading within the Western Balkans region. The authors conclude that the Charter does seem to have been effective in its broad objective of stimulating and upgrading SME policy development across the region. Significantly, however, the coming together of these countries to cooperate with regards to SME policy development has not really worked so well, because they have doubts about the cost-effectiveness of supporting established businesses.

At the same time, the fundamental issues underlying the chapter relate to policy transfer and whether or not one can take the products created within a developing context and compare them directly with their counterparts from an EU background. An important conclusion that the authors identify is the difficulty of assessing the broad impact of the SME Charter process: partly because of the breadth of the initiative in terms of skills, legislation and targeted policy initiatives and actions, but also because of the lack of any clear or measurable objectives. It is a fundamental principle of evaluation that its prerequisite is the specification of the objectives of policy. Unfortunately it appears to be a characteristic of governments in all developed countries to be, at best, opaque about the objectives of small business policy (Storey, 2002).

Finally, the authors present the SME Policy Index in a positive light, pointing to its ability to monitor change in the development and application of SME policies across the region. Other commentators may be less enthusiastic about this prospect on the basis of doubts about the reduction of policy approaches to simple numeric values. At the same time, it may be argued that such an approach may be useful in flagging up medium-term trends in policy development.

The last chapter in Part II is Chapter 6 by Mets, who considers the question of whether Estonia is becoming a better hub over time for 'born global' companies. Mets's findings, based on the study of growth trajectories of three born global companies, is that the environment for entrepreneurship, and the acceptance of rapidly growing companies as a mechanism for wealth generation, is changing in Estonia, where the population at large appears to be increasingly recognising the importance of entrepreneurship to economic development.

Global Entrepreneurship Monitor (GEM) data are presented to show that public opinion has become more positive towards entrepreneurs in Estonia over time, and that the public media has become more supportive of changes in public opinion as well as propagating entrepreneurial behaviour among young people. In this sense, the environment for entrepreneurship has become more positive; making it somewhat surprising perhaps that some of the latest GEM data do not seem too encouraging about the level of total entrepreneurial activity in the country.

Mets also points to poor knowledge of the entrepreneurial process and poor business models as barriers for creating better policy, particularly to drive a smart specialisation economy. The author concludes that these aspects may point to the need for better long-term entrepreneurship education policy based on more comprehensive understanding than can be produced from a few simple GEM surveys. By analysing the growth trajectory of three born global companies the author identifies issues internal to these businesses as well as external conditions. One of these disadvantages of a born global approach to venture creation is that they are not exposed to the entrepreneurial process, which takes place before and during the internationalisation; in other words, they jump straight into international markets. This means that they do not have certain experience which other SMEs with more modest performance are likely to have.

Analysis undertaken by Mets raises questions that need to be considered in relation to many of the emerging market economies of Central Europe. The need is for the entrepreneurial ecosystem to become more global; for it to mature in order to provide the support for businesses with much shorter start-up periods than perhaps more traditional businesses have had; and for an ability to support the growing number of entrepreneur success stories. The main policy implication from this would seem to be the importance of continuing to promote the benefits as well as the pitfalls of entrepreneurship as a career option among young people, but across the Estonian population.

We now turn to Part III which contains three chapters, the first of which, Chapter 7 by Chepurenko and colleagues, is concerned with regional variations in entrepreneurial activity in Russia. The explanation is usually some combination of supply- and demand-side factors. For example, spatial variations in income levels across a country will tend to create more business opportunities. On the other hand, the kind of structural conditions that influence the orientation of a population towards entrepreneurship will also often vary between core regions on the one hand, and peripheral regions on the other. These factors can include attitudes towards entrepreneurship, which in the case of a country like Russia or other former Soviet republics essentially means that the pace of transformation is itself regionally variant, and this contributes to the regional variations in entrepreneurship that is discussed in this chapter.

The method used by Chepurenko and colleagues involves the use of GEM Russia data, from which their analysis leads to a number of conclusions, some of which are worth highlighting. First of all they emphasise that as far as Russia is concerned higher business densities in a region does not necessarily mean better-quality entrepreneurship. In this regard they draw particular attention to the fact that in some of Russia's more developed regions the niches left for necessity-driven entrepreneurs are few and far between. This may be the case, but equally the situation may be more dynamic than this suggestion implies. One of the core arguments for the chapter is that the overall economic impact of SMEs on the economic performance of Russia is moderate, which the authors explain in terms of a weak institutional environment which is typically associated with a lack of effective and sustainable policies to promote entrepreneurship in the regions.

One of the features that comes through in the chapter is that the majority of employees within Russian regions are working for the state or for large private sector companies, rather than choosing entrepreneurship as a career option. At the same time, the authors emphasise that the task they have taken on is not a straightforward one, because the levels of entrepreneurship are not simply a result of a narrow group of influences but rather a combination of economic, social and psychological characteristics which need to be considered in combination.

Nevertheless, at the heart of the chapter is an important policy point. The chapter describes a high level of regional diversity and heterogeneity in Russian entrepreneurship. That being the case, clearly the important policy conclusion to be drawn from this is that an overemphasis on national policies and national interventions may well exacerbate regional differences rather than reduce them. The alternative, of course, can be found in a number of European countries, particularly those with regional structures of governance. As far as SME development is concerned the regional level is arguably much more appropriate for the development of support policies than a national-level emphasis; not least because it is at the regional level that entrepreneurs are most likely to come in contact

with government institutions. In addition to this, if regions differ in levels
of entrepreneurship, in their strengths and weaknesses for entrepreneurship development, and in their support needs, then the most logical policy
approach will focus on intervention and policy programmes at a regional
level.

Chapter 8, by Venesaar and Küttim, is also concerned with regional differences in entrepreneurship, focusing on entrepreneurial perceptions and
activities in core and periphery regions in Estonia. The chapter focuses
on the contrasts of environmental influences within core and periphery
regions and how this affects entrepreneurial activity at different stages of
development. Not surprisingly, given that Estonia is a small Baltic state,
entrepreneurial activity is higher in the core regions than in the periphery,
regardless of whether the criterion is potential or early-stage entrepreneurs.
The authors also identify some differences between core and peripheral
regions in terms of the motives for starting new businesses; essentially with
a higher percentage of necessity-driven entrepreneurs within the peripheral
regions. These characteristics, of course, may be more pronounced in transition and developing countries, but nevertheless are consistently found in
more mature market economies as well.

One of the distinctive contributions of this chapter involves an exami-
nation of the perceptions of entrepreneurs towards various internal and
external conditions that a priori might have some influence on the entrepreneurial process. In this regard the authors conclude that perceptions
are indeed different in core and peripheral regions. Entrepreneurs in core
regions tend to feel more growth-oriented and more confident when it
comes to having the necessary knowledge skills and experience to start
a business, whereas entrepreneurs in the periphery seem to be more risk-
averse and yet, for some reason, positive towards entering entrepreneurship. The authors interpret this finding in terms of external stimuli.

Without doubt the existence of regional differences in entrepreneurial
activity is a phenomenon that justifies some policy response. It implies that
those parts of the country where start-up rates and SME performance are
below average have the potential for making a more substantial contribution to national economic development than they are currently doing. In
this context it is relevant to try to establish the reasons for the individual
variations over and above those mentioned previously. In other words, to
what extent is the transition context contributing different influences on
regional variations in comparison with more mature market economies?

Finally, Chapter 9 by Robson and colleagues is concerned with the
financing of new firms and the influence of entrepreneurial characteristics on start-up finance. The topic is not just on start-up finance, but on
the effects of the initial capitalisation of new ventures on the survival and

growth of these new businesses. The usual interpretation that is placed upon this in the literature is that a well-established business allows the entrepreneur time to learn how to run their business and deal with unexpected challenges. In contrast, undercapitalised firms lack this buffer and may be forced to close because of liquidity problems. In this context, the value added from the Robson et al. chapter is the attempt to answer the question: why are some firms better capitalised than others?

The analysis is based on human capital theory, with the authors distinguishing between general and firm-level specific human capital. Firm-specific human capital results from training, which is of particular value to a firm, whereas general human capital is not firm-specific. Whilst the topic under investigation in the chapter is not specific to particular regions, insofar as the supply of finance and availability of human capital varies between regions, the topic is an important one in terms of contributing to an understanding of regional development.

Overall, whilst there is no shortage of access to finance for new and small businesses, there is still limited understanding of how the characteristics of the entrepreneur and the strategies they use at start-up can influence the initial financing of their venture. The results of this study suggest that if policy-makers want to increase the amount of start-up capital that firms use, they should encourage entrepreneurs and potential entrepreneurs to undertake some form of financial training. The authors suggest that in this period of 'cheap money', policy-makers should focus on developing human capital rather than pushing more money through finance initiatives such as loan guarantee schemes. One might add to this that such a strategy would be more likely to generate sustainable benefits, as well as contributing to increasing the supply of finance because of a reduction in the demand-side failures.

Finally, before bringing this book to a close, it may be useful to briefly reflect on policy implications that have emerged from the chapters. In many ways the main policy theme is the variety of circumstances in which public policy can impact on the nature and extent of entrepreneurship. Whilst entrepreneurship results from the creativity, drive, vision and resourcefulness of individuals and groups of individuals, rather than being a direct result of government actions, nevertheless public policy is an important element in the external environment in which private business operates (Klocho and Isakova, 1996). One only has to reflect on countries such as Ukraine to observe that, in many respects, the framework conditions for sustainable and productive entrepreneurship still have to be installed.

Another important theme that emerges from some of these chapters is the need for policy to have a bottom-up element to it, rather than being entirely top-down. This helps to explain why strong regional variations in entrepreneurship continue to exist, and why little has been achieved with regards to narrowing the gap between regions. A time scale also needs to be considered in relation to public policy. For example, the problem faced in some Estonian regions, and more generally in Europe's peripheral regions, is that the lack of a positive attitude on the part of the population towards business ownership and entrepreneurship cannot be solved overnight.

At a more detailed level the book contains chapters which set out constructive ideas for regional development in areas that are in strong need of development stimuli. This applies to Chapter 3 on Eastern Poland, which is in many ways an ideas piece that needs application implementation in order to assess its full validity. There are also examples of intervention designed to address areas of market failure, which are illustrated with reference to Robson et al.'s Chapter 9; although interestingly the failure may be in terms of access to finance. The solution, according to these authors, is to focus attention on improving the financial knowledge and skills of entrepreneurs in order to reduce demand-side failure. This is an interesting emphasis which is rather different to the usual one, which tends to focus on increasing the supply of finance available. As a consequence, one can see that the public policy-related impacts on entrepreneurship are multifaceted and will vary between countries and between regions.

Increasing attention should be paid to the needs of regions in the new member states of the European Union. In this context, much can be learned from the experience of more established EU members. At the same time, to achieve this requires an approach which incorporates a learning component as well as sufficient scope for the local policy-makers to investigate the needs of their organisations and their regions, and not necessarily accepting the EU's blueprint lock, stock and barrel, which may have been developed in a rather different context. Effective use of EU Structural Funds provides a one-off opportunity for the required restructuring alongside the varied experience of other EU members. The challenge is to draw on these resources and experience whilst also recognising the distinctiveness of individual regions. Policy learning is to be encouraged, but crude policy transfer can raise more problems than it solves.

REFERENCES

Klochko, Y. and N. Isakova (1996), 'Small business sector in Ukrainian transition economy: achievements to date', *Entrepreneurship and Regional Development*, **8**, 127–40.
National Economic and Social Council (1982), *Review of Industrial Policy: A*

Report Prepared by the Telesis Consultancy Group, Report No. 64, Dublin: Government Publications.

Smallbone, D. and F. Welter (2009), *Entrepreneurship and Small Business Development in Post-Socialist Economies*, Abingdon, UK and New York, USA: Routledge.

Storey, D.J. (2002), 'Methods of evaluating the impact of public policies to support small businesses: the Six Steps to Heaven', *International Journal of Entrepreneurship Education*, **1** (2), 181–202.

Index